Theodore Roethke
A Bibliography

Theodore Roethke

A Bibliography

By James Richard McLeod
North Idaho College

The Kent State University Press

The Serif Series:
Bibliographies and Checklists, Number 27
William White, General Editor

016.81154
M22T
94081
aug 1975

ISBN 0-87338-100-9
Library of Congress Catalog Card Number 72-158715
Manufactured in the United States of America
at the press of The Oberlin Printing Company
Designed by Merald E. Wrolstad

First printing

For
Ellen and James Brock

Contents

Introduction

Theodore Roethke's death on August 1, 1963, produced an
immediate and profound sense of loss. Several poets—among
them Robert Lowell, Richard Eberhart, John Berryman,
William Stafford, and John Ciardi—honored his memory
with dedicatory poems, while others—including James Dickey,
Richard Wilbur, Stanley Kunitz, and Carolyn Kizer—
wrote eulogies and commentaries. Such tributes suggest
the esteem in which Roethke was held by colleagues,
students, and friends.

Roethke's career began with the appearance of his first
volume, *Open House*, which was published on the eve of his
thirty-third birthday in 1941; perhaps Roethke had this in mind
when he referred to himself, sardonically, as the "oldest
younger poet in the U.S.A."[1] His apprehension and pride
on the eve of the book's appearance is apparent in a letter to
Katherine Anne Porter: "Well my damned book is out Monday.
Say a little prayer if that isn't blasphemous."[2] This apprehension must have been dispelled, and the pride heightened,
with the appearance of favorable reviews by Louise Bogan,
Babette Deutsch, and Elizabeth Drew. After describing Roethke

---

[1] Stanley Kunitz, "Theodore Roethke," *New York Review of Books*, I (October 17, 1963), 21.

[2] Ralph J. Mills, Jr., ed., *The Selected Letters of Theodore Roethke* (Seattle
& London: University of Washington Press, 1968), p. 90.

as being "instantly recognizable as a good poet," W. H. Auden went on to state that the book was "completely successful."

In the *New Republic*, Rolfe Humphries added his praise and described Roethke's devotion to craftsmanship as that which made him "severe in his selection" of poems for his first volume. This judgment was made on the basis of Humphries's personal knowledge of Roethke's working methods. Roethke had made it a practice to send poems to Humphries for advice and criticism during the years prior to the appearance of the first volume in an effort to weed out the "practice pieces, poems whose chief value was in the exercise."[3] Several years after Roethke's death, Humphries read many of these discarded pieces in a lecture at the University of Washington entitled "The Early Theodore Roethke: Reminiscences and Reading."

Roethke's second volume, *The Lost Son and Other Poems*, was published in 1948, shortly after he began teaching at the University of Washington. It contained the "greenhouse poems," which he had begun earlier at Bennington where he had shown them to Kenneth Burke. Burke, after reading them, exclaimed, "Boy, you've hit it," and, proclaiming it a genuine "breakthrough," called this phase of Roethke's work the "vegetal radicalism."[4]

The Lost Son was followed by *Praise to the End!* in 1951 and the Pulitzer Prize-winning volume *The Waking: Poems 1933–1953* in 1953. *Words for the Wind: The Collected Verse of Theodore Roethke* was published in England in 1957 and was the "Christmas Choice of the Poetry Book Society." It was subsequently published in the United States in 1958 with six poems which had not appeared in the English edition

---

[3] Rolfe Humphries, "Inside Story," *New Republic*, CV (July 14, 1941), 62.

[4] Allan Seager, *The Glass House: The Life of Theodore Roethke* (New York: McGraw-Hill, 1968), p. 144.

and won eight major awards including the National Book
Award, which Roethke once referred to as the "Rubber Medal
(With or Without Varnish)."

Flair published some of Roethke's verse for children (which
was later set to music) with illustrations in May 1950. In a
letter to Ridge Riley, Roethke described the poems in *Flair*:
"I'm doing some kids' things, some terrific, some good,
some just slobbery and corny."[5] Roethke's attempts to publish
these poems met continual frustration. While in England
in the summer of 1953, he wrote T. S. Eliot concerning
their publication by Faber & Faber. Eliot replied the same day:
"I was pleased that you should submit your manuscript of
children's verse with illustrations to this firm, and I am sorry
that it does not fit into our list."[6] The poems were not published
until 1961, when they appeared in *I Am! Says the Lamb*.

Roethke's last volume, *The Far Field*—which included the
earlier volume, *Sequence, Sometimes Metaphysical*, published
in 1963—appeared after his death and won the 1964 National
Book Award. It was also scheduled to be published in Ireland
by the Dolmen Press with the title, *Dance On, Dance On,
Dance On*; after his death, the title was changed, and the
plans for the Irish edition were evidently dropped. However,
a Polish edition, with most of the poems appearing in *The Far
Field*, appeared in 1971 with translations by Ludmila Marjańska.

The Collected Poems was published in 1966 and included
fifteen previously uncollected poems and one previously
unpublished poem—"Duet." An Italian edition, *Theodore
Roethke: Sequenza Nordamericana E Altre Poesie*, appeared
the same year and contained poems selected from Roethke's
previous works. Faber & Faber also published *Selected Poems*

---

[5] Unpublished letter to Ridge Riley, February 1, 1950. (UW, PSU)
[6] Seager, *The Glass House*, p. 144.

in 1969; the poems included were selected by Beatrice Roethke
from *The Collected Poems.*

Since the publication of *The Collected Poems* several
volumes have appeared which contain previously unpublished
and uncollected prose and poetry: *Selected Letters of
Theodore Roethke, On the Poet and His Craft: The Selected
Prose of Theodore Roethke,* and *Straw for the Fire: From
the Notebooks of Theodore Roethke, 1943–63,* arranged by
David Wagoner. Shortly after Roethke's death in August
of 1963, David Wagoner wrote Henry Rago of *Poetry* and
described the contents of the notebooks: ". . . he left behind
a tremendous collection of notebooks, full of the maddest
and most wonderful work of all, which only a few close
friends ever had much of a look at: not whole poems but
fragments, aphorisms, scurrilous diatribes, libelous literary
observations."[7]

These last volumes—along with the publication of Roethke's
biography, *The Glass House*—provide the materials necessary
for future Roethke scholarship. With the notable exception
of *Theodore Roethke* by Ralph J. Mills, Jr., there were no
full-scale critical treatments before Roethke's death; however,
the following critical studies and reference works have been
published since that time: *Profile of Theodore Roethke,
Theodore Roethke: An Introduction to the Poetry, The
Achievement of Theodore Roethke, Theodore Roethke: A
Manuscript Checklist,* and *A Concordance to the Poems of
Theodore Roethke.* In a recent assessment of the state of
Roethke scholarship, R. J. Gangewere foresees a boom in
Roethkean studies:

> What to make of himself, or rather how to make himself a
> reputation, was a problem that exercised Roethke throughout his
> career. He was always eager for recognition, a bit greedy for prizes,

---

[7] *See* II, C31.

businesslike about his market value as a poet. No doubt this was essential to his perpetual interest in self-definition. . . . With the biography and the selected letters now available to the general reader, there is some reason to speculate upon a potential boom in Roethkean studies. In areas of criticism I have roughly described as biographical, psychological, philosophical, and technical, Roethke is still a poet with a future. It remains for those dreary "text-creepers," the academics, to tell us more about the value of the man who described himself as "slug-nutty in the technique mines."[8]

Although no full-length textual studies have appeared, several articles have treated technical and textual matters. Louis L. Martz, David A. Lupher, and J. C. Maxwell examined the change from "into" to "until" in "Big Wind." Lupher also commented on textual errors in "The Lost Son" and "Where Knock Is Open Wide," and Maxwell examined a revision of a line from "The Dying Man" which was commented on by Karl Malkoff in *Theodore Roethke*. The metrical structure of "The Lost Son" was analyzed by Charlotte Lee in "The Line as a Rhythmic Unit in the Poetry of Theodore Roethke." Donald Bowerman and J. C. Maxwell noted specific sources for "I Need, I Need" (John Clare) and "Death Piece" (A. E. Housman). Louis L. Martz and David A. Lupher both noted the omission of "Frau Bauman, Frau Schmidt, and Frau Schwartze" in the first edition of *The Collected Poems of Theodore Roethke*. Changes in the arrangement of the poems of "The Lost Son" sequence in various editions were noted by John Lucas, David A. Lupher, and Louis L. Martz.

Roethke's reputation as a poet is nearly matched by his renown as a reader and teacher of poetry. Dylan Thomas once referred to him as the "greatest reader of poetry in America" because of his powerful style. In 1960, Roethke

---

[8] R. J. Gangewere, "Theodore Roethke: The Future of Reputation," *Carnegie Studies in English*, II (1970), 65–73.

read with Stanley Kunitz at the YM-YWHA Poetry Center
in New York City. Kunitz recalled later how Roethke
captivated the audience:

> He had a high fever, and backstage he was jittery, sweating
> copiously from every pore as he guzzled champagne by the bottle.
> On stage, for the first portion of his program he clowned and
> hammed incorrigibly, weaving, gyrating, dancing, shrugging his
> shoulders, muttering to himself intermittently, and now and then
> making curiously flipperlike or foetal gestures with his hands.
> But gradually, as the evening wore on, he settled into a straight
> dramatic style that was enormously effective and moving. When he
> came to the new "mad" sequence, particularly the poem that
> begins, "in a dark time that eye begins to see," his voice rang out
> with such an overwhelming roll of noble anguish that many of
> the audience wept.[9]

Roethke's conscience and philosophy regarding these readings
were poignantly portrayed by Robert Heilman in a
reminiscence:

> He had an equally goading conscience about readings. He wanted
> to be paid well, he had a Byronic disinclination to give anything
> away. But then he wanted to put on the best show the audience had
> ever seen and heard; he had in him none of the languid youth
> on the poetry circuit, listlessly dropping pearls before swine
> unaware of their good fortune, nor of the turtleneck-sweatered
> adolescents using unkept mien and verse and instruments of
> retaliation against an unheeding world. Roethke wanted to delight,
> move, "send," overwhelm the audience. He gave everything he had
> lavishly—of voice, variety of pace, mimetic talent, gesture, of
> energy rushing out as it were over and above its physical channels,
> as though he were forcing life into an audience, bringing them
> to a new height of vital participation and excitement. The strain was
> exhausting; he came to know that he could not accept a third of
> the invitations that kept coming to him. Weeks before a reading,
> he would begin to tense up. He told me that sometimes he vomited
> twice before a public appearance. He planned the "show"

---

[9] Kunitz, "Theodore Roethke," pp. 21–22.

carefully; he did not drift around as though he did not know what
was coming next. He wanted to be the ultimate showman, to read
as soaringly as Dylan Thomas—or better—and to combine the
reading with a vaudeville or night-club act. He strove to be a great
public entertainer, a combination of powerful, sublime reader
with comedian and humorist and even satirist. In the latter role his
judgment was unsure, and his consciously funny topical verses,
quips at the audience, topical references, and jokes about others
and himself often fell below his best level of private spontaneous
humor, not to mention his bardic performance. But whatever
faults of this kind he may have had, if faults they were, were
intimately attached to the extraordinary virtue of commitment to
the maximum excellence of the poet holding and enthralling his
audience.[10]

Fortunately, Roethke's renown as a reader will not have to
rest solely with such descriptions, since many of his readings
and lectures have been preserved. The documentary film,
In a Dark Time, permits not only the auditory experience of
his poetry, but the visual experience as well. The significance
of the "auditory imagination" in Roethke's work was
emphasized repeatedly by Roethke himself: "I think of
myself as a poet of love, a poet of praise. And I wish to read
aloud."[11] His poetry was written more for the "ear than eye,"
and in "Some Remarks on Rhythm" he stresses the reliance
of his poetry on the "natural rhythms of speech." The reading
of his poetry aloud, then, was an integral part of his idea
of what a poem should be. In *In a Dark Time*, he heightens
the auditory life of the poem not only with the rhythmic quality
of speech but by the motion of his body. "My Papa's Waltz"
is read as Roethke's whole body undulates with the illusion of
dance, and in "The Sloth" the slow, labored pace of his speech
is matched with heavy nodding and turning of his head.

---

[10] Robert B. Heilman, "Theodore Roethke: Personal Notes," *Shenandoah*,
XVI (Autumn 1964), 59–60.

[11] "Theodore Roethke Writes. . . ," in *On The Poet and His Craft*, ed. Ralph J.
Mills, Jr. (Seattle and London: University of Washington Press, 1965), p. 60.

Roethke's humor and his use of the "gag" described in
Seager's *Glass House* and by Robert Heilman came to life in
such informal readings as the one recorded on August 20,
1959, at the University of Washington. Other facets of his
personality appear in "An American Poet Introduces Himself
and His Poems" and the "James Dickey Poetry Reading."
"An American Poet Introduces Himself and His Poems"
was Roethke's first broadcast over the BBC. In this recording
he described his childhood and its relationship to his poetry.
James Dickey described Roethke's introduction to the
poetry reading as one instance of ". . . qualities that must
have astonished and confounded others besides himself.
. . . when he introduced me at the reading, he . . . talked for
eight or ten minutes about himself, occasionally mentioning
me as though by afterthought. I did not resent this, though
I found it curious. . . ."[12] Thus, the recordings and the film can
bring Roethke to life with a sense of immediacy available
by no other means.

Professor Jack B. McManis's discovery of a mass of Roethke's
forgotten papers in an old desk (43 sheets of student verse
"containing Roethke's keen jottings of criticism and praise")
created a considerable stir at Pennsylvania State University
in 1966. Later, McManis recalled Roethke's dedication as a
teacher while at Penn State: "Roethke, unlike most of us
who fight to detach ourselves from the classroom to do our work,
threw himself into teaching with the same kind of intensity
with which he wrote poetry. . . ."[13] John G. Fuller, a former
student of Roethke's at Penn State, described Roethke's
classroom presence at that time:

---

[12] James Dickey, "The Greatest American Poet," *Atlantic*, CCXXII (November
1968), 55.

[13] Anonymous, " 'And So Much I Have Missed,' " *Penn State Alumni News*,
LIII (Fall 1967), 18.

He would heave into the classroom, a large, bulky, but athletic figure, flop down at his desk with an anguished look of despair at his disciples. Often he would rub his hands across his face and stare at us with a strange form of benevolent contempt. "Boys," he would say, "I may not get through to you today. One reason is that you look just a little more stupid than usual. The other is that I feel lousy." Yet as a teacher, he was sharp, discerning, relentless. He had no patience with the superficial and little regard for convention.[14]

Although Fuller tempered Roethke's rather sardonic classroom presence, another former student described his office presence as follows: "If a student were lucky enough to find him in his office, he would still have to wait while the lumbersome instructor searched through the scattered remains of old shoes and magazines, and hopefully, salvaged the composition papers covering his desktop."[15] Apparently, those student papers found by McManis were among the unsalvaged.

There were times, as well, when he longed for detachment from the classroom. In a letter to Babette Deutsch in 1952, he contends, "I only wish I could read and work for about five years at this point, instead of having the hoorah and hullabaloo of teaching (as I try to teach, at any rate.)"[16] However, Robert B. Heilman does not see this desire for solitude as issuing out of any vanity: "He never had the vanity, common among both writers and scholars, of thinking that classroom work was only a necessity of existence, a nominal reason for rewarding his genius, but a task that properly belonged to lesser men."[17]

---

[14] John G. Fuller, "Another Poet," *Saturday Review*, XLIII (March 7, 1959), 10–11.

[15] Amanda Smith, "Theodore Roethke: The Penn State Years" (term paper, Pennsylvania State University, 1965).

[16] Mills, *The Selected Letters of Theodore Roethke*, p. 179.

[17] Heilman, "Theodore Roethke: Personal Notes," p. 56.

David Wagoner, a former student of Roethke's at Penn State and a colleague at Washington, described his teacher as a "magician" in the classroom, and Oliver Everett, a former student at Washington, described the methods that composed that magic:

> He had no desire to make his students copies of himself. He encouraged each to pursue his own natural bent. He was the advocate of originality, individuality, the hater of the cliche and the insipid, the advocate of hard work and multiple revision. A small bit of verse was to be polished thoroughly as the most finished marble statue. His emphasis was on quality, not quantity; and when Dylan Thomas spoke lightly of "fat poets with slender volumes," he snorted with revulsion. The prolific student was his despair and the tersely exacting one was his delight. Yet if a student were prolific by nature, he magnanimously made concessions while insisting on exactness of revisions and counter-revisions.[18]

This was Roethke's magic as a teacher—a magic that the students of Bennington College recognized when they declared him the "best teacher they ever had."[19] Perhaps Roethke intimated the nature of that magic in a poem entitled "Saturday Eight O'Clock," where he concludes: "I teach out of love."[20]

These three facets of Roethke—poet, reader, and teacher—fuse powerfully to leave the single impression that he is and will remain a major force in modern poetry, perhaps our "Greatest American Poet."[21]

---

[18] Oliver Everett, "Theodore Roethke: The Poet as Teacher," *West Coast Review*, III (Spring 1960), 5–11.

[19] Leo Sherman, "The Shoutings about at Bennington," *Junior Bazaar*, October 1946, p. 223.

[20] For further information regarding Roethke as a teacher *see*: I, A11, 14; C147, 212, 214, 228, 235, 239; II, B1, 12, 14, 17, 19, 22, 26, 27, 29, 70, 82–85, 121; C383; F11; G9, 16.

[21] Dickey, "The Greatest American Poet," p. 53.

Acknowledgments

In compiling this bibliography, I have had the generous
assistance of staffs of the following repositories: The American
Academy of Arts and Letters, Bennington College, Boston
Public Library, the British Museum, Columbia University,
Dartmouth College, DePauw University, Eastern Washington
State College, Gonzaga University, Harvard University,
Lafayette College, The Library of Congress, North Idaho
College, Northwestern University, Saginaw Public Library,
San Francisco Public Library, University of California
(Berkeley, Davis, Riverside), University of Connecticut,
University of Idaho, and University of Washington.

I wish also to thank Alfred A. Knopf, Arnoldo Mondadori
Editors, Chilmark Press, Crowell-Collier Press, Doubleday
& Company, Faber and Faber, Indiana University Press,
Institute Editorial Italiano, Ryerson Press, Stone Wall Press,
*Cimmarron Review, Denver Quarterly, The National Observer,
Partisan Review, Pebble, The Guardian, Voyages,* The
Academy of American Poets, The Theodore Roethke Memorial
Foundation, The YM-YHA Poetry Center of New York City,
Caedmon Records, Columbia Records, Desto Records,
Folkways/Scholastic Records, Listening Library, Spoken Arts,
British Broadcasting Corporation, Canadian Broadcasting
Corporation, KPFA of Berkeley, California, KUOW of the
University of Washington, WUOM of the University of

Michigan, WCBS-TV of New York City, and National
Education Television.

A special note of appreciation is extended to M. Gary Bettis;
Judith O. Combs; William V. Davis; Stanley Keen; John
Lehmann; Ned Rorem; William Stafford; Elfrieda Lang of
Indiana University; Martha Hubbard of Johns Hopkins University; Martha Berquist of Reed College; Charles W. Mann,
Louise K. Kelly, and A. H. Reede of Pennsylvania State
University; Estelle Rebec of the University of California,
Berkeley; Dorothee Bowie, Margery A. Kepner, Nelson Bentley,
David Wagoner, Robert Monroe, Richard C. Berner, and
Karl Winn of the University of Washington. Finally I wish
to thank Sarah Gramentine, Jean Glee Schaefer, Mrs. Dexter R.
Amend, George L. Ives, and Eastern Washington State College
for their assistance in preparing the manuscript; also,
Beatrice Roethke for her kindness in granting permission to
use the Roethke papers at the University of Washington.
For her inspiration and guidance throughout the compilation
of this manuscript, I am deeply grateful to Dr. R. Jean Taylor
of Eastern Washington State College.

J. R. M.
Coeur d'Alene
October 15, 1972

Abbreviations

Biographical Notes: *1908--1963*

1908

Born at 1725 Gratiot Avenue, Saginaw, Michigan, on May 25 (the house number was later changed to 1805).

1922

Roethke's father died of cancer, and Roethke gave speech for Junior Red Cross (*see* II, B32).

1926

Published review in the *Michigan Chimes* (*see* I, C210).

1929

Received A.B. from the University of Michigan and graduated Phi Beta Kappa.

1929–1930

Attended the University of Michigan graduate school and law school from the fall of 1929 to February 1930.

1930

Published his first poems ("Lost," "Method," and "To Darkness") in the May–June issue of *The Harp* (*see* I, C1).

1930–1931

Did graduate work at Harvard and was encouraged by Robert Hillyer to publish his poems (*see* II, C105).

1931–1935

Taught at Lafayette College.

1932–1935

Served as varsity tennis coach at Lafayette.

1933

Worked on the Hartland **Area** Project, the biography of
    J. B. Crouse, in Michigan during the summer.

1935

Taught from the end of September until mid-November at
    Michigan State University. Had his first breakdown in
    November, was hospitalized, and then moved to
    Mercywood Sanitarium.

1936

Received M.A. from the University of Michigan. Released
    from Mercywood Sanitarium at the end of January.

1936–1947

Taught at Pennsylvania State College, starting in the fall
    of 1936, as an instructor.

1938

Read "The Summons" at the "First Annual Invitation Banquet
    of the Phi Beta Kappa Society" at Pennsylvania State
    College on June 2 (*see* I, C37).

1939

Promoted to Assistant Professor at Pennsylvania State College.

1939–1943

Served as varsity tennis coach at Pennsylvania State College
    (*see* I, C57 and II, B44, 45, 47).

1940

Attended the "Writers' Conference" at Olivet College, Michigan, with Allan Seager in July.

1941

Entertained W. H. Auden at Pennsylvania State College the week of February 17–25 (*see* II, B48).
Open House was published in March.
Attended the School of Creative Writing near Middlebury College at Breadloaf, Vermont, in August.

1942

Read selections from *Open House* and other poems at Harvard at 4:30 P.M. on April 7 as part of the Morris Gray Series. He was the youngest poet to have ever read in the Widener Library Poetry Room (*see* II, B57). Read "Dedicatory Poem" for the opening of the Mineral Industries Art Gallery at Pennsylvania State College on April 11 (*see* II, B59).
Reviews: *Centre Daily Times* [State College, Pa.], April 13, 1942, p. 1 (PSC); *Mineral Industries*, II (May 1942), 3 (PSU).

1943

Began teaching at Bennington College in April, on leave of absence from Pennsylvania State. (*see* II, B65–67).

1944

Worked on the "greenhouse poems."
Left Bennington College in February.

1945

Given grant for the Yaddo Writers' Colony.
Given a John Simon Guggenheim Memorial Fellowship of $2,500 (*see* II, B68).

Received shock treatments in December at Albany General
Hospital and then was sent to the Leonard Nursing Home
in Londonville, New York.

1946

Left the Leonard Nursing Home in March.
Worked on "The Lost Son," "The Long Alley," and "The
Shape of the Fire" while on the Guggenheim Fellowship.

1947

Awarded the Eunice Tietzen Memorial Prize from *Poetry*.
Recorded his poetry at Harvard College (*see* I, E3).
Recorded his poetry at the Library of Congress on January 3
(*see* I, E2).
Returned to Pennsylvania State to teach the spring semester
in February.
Worked from July 2 to August 30 at the Yaddo Writers' Colony
at Saratoga Springs, New York, with Robert Lowell.

1947–1963

Taught at the University of Washington until his death.

1948

The Lost Son and Other Poems was published in March.
Lectured and read at Tufts College, Boston College, Yale
University, University of Michigan, University of Indiana,
and Wayne State University in March.
Made full professor at the University of Washington in April.
Review: "Roethke Acting, Poetic Reading Charm Audience,"
Detroit Collegian [Wayne State University], March 17, 1948,
p. 1. (UW)
Recorded "The Lost Son" at the Library of Congress (*see* I, E4).

1949

Awarded Music and Art Foundation of Seattle Citation.
Leave of absence taken from the University of Washington

during winter and spring quarters, 1949–1950, for illness. Was treated at Fairfax Hospital in October and then was transferred to the Pinel Foundation.

1950

Released from the Pinel Foundation in March.

Awarded his second John Simon Guggenheim Fellowship in the spring (*see* II, B76).

Worked at the Yaddo Writers' Colony at Saratoga Springs, New York, from April 4 to August 31.

1951

Awarded the Levinson Prize by *Poetry* (the highest award given for a poem or group of poems published in *Poetry*).

Praise to the End! was published in November.

1952

Honored by *Poetry* as the outstanding teacher of verse writing in the United States.

Awarded the National Institute Grant in Literature by the American Academy of Arts and Letters in February.

Introduced Dylan Thomas for a reading given in Seattle on April 10, 1952 (*see* II, B6, 13).

Given fellowships by the Ford Foundation and the Fund for the Given Advancement of Education in April and May (*see* II, B88–91).

Nominated for honorary membership in the International Mark Twain Society in July.

Read at the Massachusetts Institute of Technology on December 2.

Read at the YM-YWHA Poetry Center in New York City on December 4.

1953

Given Fulbright Award to lecture in Florence, Italy.

Married Beatrice O'Connell of Winchester, Virginia, with
W. H. Auden as best man and Louise Bogan as
matron of honor.

Read "The Sloth" and probably "The Waking" at the
Circle-in-the-Square Theatre in New York City at 2:40
P.M. on January 25 (*see* I, F7–8).
Review: *New York Times Book Review*, LVII (February 8, 1953),
8.

Read at New Hope Community Center in New Hope,
Pennsylvania, on February 4 (*see* II, B94).

Read poems from *Open House* and children's poems as part of
the Simmons Series at Pennsylvania State on February 17
(*see* I, E5 and II, B95,96).
Review: "Roethke Poems Delight Audience," *Daily Collegian*,
February 19, 1953, p. 2. (PSC)

Sailed for Naples on February 24 for honeymoon at
W. H. Auden's villa on Forio d'Ischia.

Departed from Italy for Ireland on May 25.

Recorded "An American Poet Introduces Himself and His
Poems" for the BBC in London on July 30 (*see* I, E6)
and visited Dylan Thomas.

The Waking: Poems 1933–1953 published in September.

1954

Leave of absence taken from the University of Washington
for illness during winter quarter 1953–1954.

Read "Bring the Day!," "Give Way, Ye Gates," "I Need,
I Need," "O Lull Me! Lull Me!," "Sensibility! O La!,"
and "Where Knock is Open Wide" at San Francisco
State College on February 24 (*see* II, B100).

Recorded all of the preceding poems and "The Long Alley,"
"A Field of Light," and "The Shape of the Fire" on

February 25 at station KPFA in Berkeley. Recorded
"The Lost Son" at station KPFA on February 28
(*see* I, E7).
Read at the University of British Columbia at Vancouver
on March 4.
> Review: "Poet Reads, Reels to Own Ribald Rhyme," *The Ubyssey*,
> March 5, 1954, p. 1.

Read at the Vancouver Art Museum on March 5.
Awarded the Pulitzer Prize for *The Waking: Poems 1933–1953*
in May (*see* II, B101–111 and II, D2).
Moved into Morris Graves's home in Woodway Park in
Edmonds, Washington, in the fall, where he later wrote
"The Slug," "The Small," "A Walk in Late Summer,"
and "The Happy Three." The Roethkes tried unsuccessfully
to buy this house while they were in Europe.

1955

Roethke's mother died in February.
Probably read "The Cycle," "Interlude," and "Big Wind"
on May 3 over the Canadian Broadcasting Corporation
series entitled "Anthology."
Went to Europe in early fall to be a Fulbright Lecturer in
Florence, Italy, during 1955–1956 (*see* II, B121).
Travels included Spain, France, Austria, and England.
A mimeographed typescript entitled *Selected Poems of
Theodore Roethke* used in Florence during this period
is located at the University of Washington with the
Roethke Papers and includes the following poems:
"The Heron," "Interlude," "The Adamant," "Cuttings
(*later*)," "Big Wind," "My Papa's Waltz," "I Need,
I Need," "I Cry, Love! Love!," "Four for Sir John Davies,"
"The Waking" (I wake to sleep), "The Dream," "Words
for the Wind," "The Beast," and "The Dying Man."

1956

Named member of the National Arts and Letters Intsitute
    in February (*see* II, B116–120).
Traveled to Austria in May, where he gave readings at the
    University of Innsbruck, the University of Vienna, and
    the Austro-American Institute.
Stayed at Auden's villa on Forio d'Ischia in June and July.
During July and August he was in Nice, Paris, and London.
Given the Northwest Writers' Award in August.
Recorded "Meditation of an Old Lady," "I'm Here," and
    "Third Meditation" in August for the BBC in London.
Docked in New York on August 22.
Read at William and Mary College in Virginia as the Phi Beta
    Kappa poet on December 5.

1957

Received the second prize ($1,250) for "A Walk in Late
    Summer" from the Borestone Mountain Poetry Awards.
Leave of absence taken from the University of Washington
    for illness during fall and spring quarters 1957–1958.
    Taken to Harborview Hospital in October and then
    admitted to Halycon House Sanitarium.
Beatrice became ill with tuberculosis and was in a sanitarium
    from January to May.
In the spring, Roethke purchased the house at 3802 East John
    Street which remained his residence until his death.
Read at Reed College during the first of May (*see* I, E8).
Words for the Wind published in England and made the
    "Christmas Choice of the Poetry Book Society."

1958

Given Chapelbrook Foundation Grant.
Read at the YM-YWHA Poetry Center in New York City in
    March.

The American edition of *Words for the Wind* published
in November.

1959

Leave of absence taken from the University of Washington
for illness during winter quarter 1958–1959.

Awarded the third prize for "Sequence" ("In a Dark Time,"
"In Evening Air," and "The Sequel") by the Borestone
Mountain Poetry Awards.

Awarded the Yale University Bollingen Prize ($1,000)
in January (*see* II, B126–131, 136–137).

Won the Edna St. Vincent Millay Prize ($200) of the Poetry
Society of America for *Words for the Wind* in January
(*see* II, B132–135).

Given Ford Foundation Grant in February (*see* II, B138–141).

Received the National Book Award ($1,000) for *Words for
the Wind* in March (*see* II, B143–144).

Recorded his poetry at the YM-YWHA Poetry Center in
New York City in July (*see* I, E9).

Read at the San Francisco State College Poetry Center
at 8:00 P.M. and the Little Theatre in San Francisco at
12:30 P. M. on July 9 (*see* II, B149–150).

Given the Pacific Northwest Writers' Award for *Words for
the Wind* in August (*see* II, B151–152).

Recorded his poetry at a reading given at 8:00 p.m. in the
Health Science Auditorium at the University of Washington
on August 20 (*see* I, E10).

Reviews: "Roethke Gives Warm Informal Reading," *Seattle
Times*, August 21, 1959, p. 27; "Books and Readers,"
Argus [Seattle], September 1, 1959. (UW)

Recorded his poetry at CBS in New York City on October 3
(*see* I, E11).

1960

Given the Longview Foundation Award ($300) under the
auspices of the Academy of American Poets in January
(*see* II, B153–154).

Honored by *Pageant Magazine* as one of "Ten Americans to
Watch in 1960" (*see* II, B156, 157).

Read "In a Dark Time" at the YM-YWHA Poetry Center
in New York City on March 31 with Stanley Kunitz
(*see* II, B20).

Attended the Carnegie Hall Recital of seven of his poems
("The Waking," "Root Cellar," "Orchids," "Snake,"
"Memory," "My Papa's Waltz," and "Night Crow")
on April 3 (*see* I, F9–11, 13–15).

Read at Columbia University on April 19.
Reviews: *Musical America*, LXXX (May 1960), 41; *New York Times*, April 4, 1960, p. 38; *Seattle Times*, April 4, 1960, p. 34.

Stayed with Robert Lowell and read poems from *I Am!
Says the Lamb* and *Words for the Wind* at Wellesley
College on April 25.
Review: "Roethke Gives Poetry Reading," *Wellesley College News*, April 28, 1960, p. 1.

Read at Harvard as part of the Morris Gray Series on April 27
(*see* II, B162).

Read at New York University on April 30.

Read "In A Dark Time" and "The Sequel" for the Spring
Poetry Festival at Wesleyan University at Middletown,
Connecticut, on May 12.
Review: "Poetic Greats," *The Wesleyan Argus*, May 20, 1960. (UW)

Delivered the Hopwood Lecture on "The Poetry of Louise
Bogan" at the University of Michigan on May 19
(*see* I, E21), and attended the "Writers' Conference"
at Michigan on May 20.
Review: "Poet Bogan Called Lyric by Roethke," *Michigan Daily* [Ann Arbor], May 20, 1960, p. 1. (UW)

Honored as the "Distinguished Alumnus" of Arthur Hill
High School in Saginaw on May 24 (*see* II, B163–167).

Traveled to Europe in June while Louise Bogan taught his
courses at the University of Washington.

Read poems from *I Am! Says the Lamb* to children at the
Day's Hotel in Inishbofin, Ireland, on September 5.
Richard Murphy, the Irish poet, and his daughter were
present.

Review: "Roethke Chooses Remote Irish Isle for Poetry Premiere,"
Seattle Times, September 6, 1960, p. 29. (UWSC)

Entered St. Brigid's Hospital in Ballinisloe, Ireland, for
treatment in September.

1961

Appointed to the Advisory Board of the Academy of
American Poets.

Appointed member of the National Advisory Committee of
the YM-YWHA Center in New York City.

Read at the Dulwich Community Center in London on
January 25, 1971.

Recorded "The Living Poet: Theodore Roethke" for the BBC
on February 8 (*see* I, E13).

Appeared with Peter Ustinov and Trevor Roper in London
on the live television broadcast "The Bookman"
on February 8.

Recorded "Journey to the Interior," "Journeys," "The Long
Water," and "Meditation at Oyster River" for the BBC
on February 13 (*see* I, E 14).

Read for the Oxford University Poetry Society at Oxford
on February 18 (*see* II, B170).

Returned to the United States early in March.

Read "Cuttings," "My Papa's Waltz," "I Need, I Need,"
"The Cow," "The Sloth," "The Lady and the Bear,"
"Words for the Wind," "I Knew a Woman," and

"The Waking" at Williams College in early March.
Review: "Pulitzer Poet Roethke Reads Works, Comments on Life, Love, Literature," *The Williams Record*, March 10, 1961, p. 1.

Read at the YM-YWHA Poetry Center in New York City on March 13.

Gave the Bergen Lecture at Yale University on March 15.

Read at the University of Connecticut on March 16 (*see* II, B171, 173).

Read at Trinity College on March 17–19 (*see* II, B172).

Read "Journeys" at the DePauw University Poetry Festival on May 3 (*see* II, B174).
Review: "Roethke Punctures Facade of Beatniks," *The DePauw*, May 4, 1961, p. 1.

Was the outside judge of the Carruth Poetry Contest at the University of Kansas on May 10.

I Am! Says the Lamb was published in July.

Awarded the "Golden Plate" by the Academy of Achievement of Monterey, California, in September (*see* II, B176).

1962

Attended the American Poetry Society Awards Banquet in January in New York City and received the Shelley Award (*see* II, B177–181).

Read at the San Francisco Art Festival and at San Francisco State College on May 4 (*see* II, B182–184).

Read at the University of California at Berkeley on May 7 (*see* II, B184).

Received honorary degree of Doctor of Letters at the University of Michigan on June 16 (*see* II, B185–188).

Appointed "Poet in Residence" at the University of Washington (the only honorary title in the University) late in June (*see* II, B190).

Read "Once More, the Round," "My Papa's Waltz," "Words for the Wind," "The Adamant," "Cuttings (*later*),"

"Night Journey," "Gob Music," [Occasional Poems],
"I Knew a Woman," "Elegy for Jane," "I Need, I Need,"
"Pickle Belt," and the *North American Sequence* in the
Opera House at the Seattle World's Fair on October
14 (*see* II, B192–193 and II, F33).

Reviews: "Roethke Proves Himself an Entertainer, Too," *Seattle
Times*, October 15, 1962, p. 21 (UW); Roethke's Poetry in
Mime and Song is Love Feast," *Seattle Post-Intelligencer*, October
16, 1963, p. 26 (UW); "Roethke 'Wows Em' in World's Fair
Reading," *University of Washington Daily* [Seattle], October 18,
1962, p. 1 (UW); "Roethke: Voice of Balder through Mouth
of Groucho," *The Argus* [Seattle], October 19, 1962, p. 69
Reprinted: *The Glass House*, pp. 280–282.

Read at the University of California at Davis on October 24.

Read at the Contra Costa College Art Festival in Richmond,
California, on October 26 (*see* II, B194, 197).

Read at the University of California at Riverside on October 29
(*see* II, B195, 196, 199).

Read at the Occidental College in Los Angeles on October 30
(*see* II, B198).

Review: "Noted Poet," *The Occidental*, November 2, 1962, p. 1.

1963

In a Dark Time was filmed at Roethke's home and in his
classroom at the University of Washington on January 14
(*see* I, E1 and II, B201–203).

Delivered statement "On 'Identity' " at the Northwestern
University Symposium "Spectrum of Perspectives" on
February 9 (*see* II, B205, 206, 208).

The Steuben Glass Exhibition with Roethke's poem "The
Victorians" opened in New York City in April
(*see* I, B16).

Party at the Zoo was published on June 27.

Died suddenly of a heart attack on Bainbridge Island near
Seattle on August 1 (*see* II, B213–233 and II, D1).

Memorial services held in Seattle; ashes then taken to Saginaw
for interment.

On September 11 Allan Seager read "The Rose" during the
service in Saginaw at the Oakwood Cemetery.

Sequence, Sometimes Metaphysical was published on
December 1.

Awards, Memorials, Reminiscences, Tributes: *1963--1972*

1963

A memorial broadcast was given twice in the fall over the western and national network of the Canadian Broadcasting Corporation by A. J. M. Smith. It opened with music from Bach ("Sleepers awake . . ."), and Roethke reading "The Waking," "The Flight" (from "The Lost Son"), and "I Knew a Woman." Smith also read "The Exulting."

In the fall issue, *Poetry Northwest* announced the establishment of the Theodore Roethke Prize of $50 to be awarded annually. Carol Hall was the first recipient of that prize.

"I Knew a Woman" was read as a tribute over the Monitor Programme of the BBC on September 29.

A memorial program and panel discussion of Roethke's poetry by Arnold Stein, David Wagoner, and Nelson Bentley was held at the University of Washington on October 15.

"A Tribute to Ted" with Stanley Kunitz and Robert Lowell was broadcasted and filmed by CBS as part of the Camera Three Series on October 27 (*see* II, E2).
Reference: "Problems, Aid and the Poets," *Centre Daily Times,* CLXXII (October 22, 1963), 2.
Review: "C.B.S. Offers Warm Tribute to Roethke," *Seattle Times,* October 28, 1963. (UWE, UWSC)

Stanley Kunitz spoke on Roethke at the Northwest Premiere of *In a Dark Time* at the University of Washington in December (*see* I, E1).

xxxviii

References: "Kunitz to Speak on Poet Roethke," *University of Washington Daily* [Seattle], November 22, 1963 (UWSC); "Theodore Roethke," *University of Washington Daily*, December 4, 1963 (UWSC); "*In a Dark Time* to Open Roethke Tribute Program," *University of Washington Daily*, December 6, 1963 (UWSC).

1964

Richard Hugo and Kenneth D. Hanson received the second Theodore Roethke Prize awarded by *Poetry Northwest*.

Richard Wilbur was the host for the first Theodore Roethke Memorial and the premiere of *In a Dark Time* at the YM-YWHA Poetry Center on March 16 at 8:30 p.m.
Reference: *New York Times*, March 15, 1964, p. 5x.

"The First Theodore Roethke Memorial Reading" was given by John Crowe Ransom on May 25 at the University of Washington (*see* II, E11 and II, F44).
Reference: "Noted Poet to Present First Roethke Reading," *Seattle Times*, May 21, 1964, p. 31. (UW)

Roethke's papers and books were displayed by the Suzzalo Library of the University of Washington May 28–June 14.
References: "University of Washington Display Honors Roethke," *Seattle Times*, May 28, 1964, p. 23 (UWSC); "Library Exhibit in Honor of Poet," *University of Washington Daily*, May 28, 1964, p. 1.

The Far Field was published in July.

Richard Eberhart delivered a memorial lecture at San Francisco State College on October 27 and read "Root Cellar," "Night Crow," "The Waking," "I Knew a Woman," "The Sky Man," and a dedicatory poem, "The Birth of the Spirit" (*see* II, F31). *In a Dark Time* was shown after the reading (*see* II, C40).
Reprinted: *Southern Review*, n.s. I (July 1965), 612–620.

Beatrice Roethke reminisced about her life with Roethke and discussed future plans and memorials in the *Seattle Times*, November 11, 1964, p. 18.

1965

Kenneth O. Hanson received the third Theodore Roethke
Prize awarded by *Poetry Northwest.*

John Ciardi lectured on Roethke and read his dedicatory poem
for Roethke, "Was a Man," in the Saginaw area during
the winter of 1964–1965 (*see* II, F15).

Nelson Bentley lectured on Roethke at the University of
Washington on February 9.
Reference: "Poet Lectures on Roethke," *University of Washington
Daily* [Seattle], February 9, 1965, p. 1. (UWR)

The Far Field won the National Book Award, and Stanley
Kunitz made the acceptance speech on March 9 in
New York City (*see* II, B20–21).
References: "Late Theodore Roethke: Saginaw Native Wins Book
Award," *Saginaw News*, March 10, 1965; "Posthumously
Published Roethke Poems Win Award," *Seattle Times*, March 10,
1965, p. 51 (UWSC); "Roethke Book 'The Far Field' Wins
Award," *University of Washington*, March 10, 1965; "National
Book Award Given to Roethke," *Centre Daily Times*, March 13,
1965, p. 7 (PSC); "Roethke Honored," *Faculty Bulletin*
[Pennsylvania State University], LII (March 19, 1965), 4 (PSC);
"National Book Awards: That Was the Week that Was,"
Publisher's Weekly, March 22, 1965, p. 34 (UWE).

Poems from *I Am! Says the Lamb* were performed at the
Olympic Hotel Ballroom in Seattle. "Improvisations
on 'The Nonsense Poems' of Theodore Roethke" was
originated and produced by Stanley Keen, and the poems
were read and mimed to music (*see* I, F22).
Reference: "Roethke Poems Inspire 'Jazz Fantasy,'" *Seattle Times*,
March 25, 1965, p. 36. (UWR, UWSC)
Review: "Theodore Roethke's Poems Unify Music and Dance,"
Seattle Times, April 2, 1965. (UWR)

"Tribute to Theodore Roethke" with A.J.M. Smith, Allan
Seager, Nelson Bentley, and Donald Hall was broadcasted
and recorded by WUOM at the University of Michigan

in May. This broadcast included Roethke reading "The Lost Son" (*see* I, E17 and II, E4). *The Far Field* was selected as one of the "Notable Books of 1964" by the American Library Association in May.

Reference: "A New Honor for Roethke," *Seattle Times*, May 16, 1965, p. 19. (UWR)

"The Second Theodore Roethke Memorial Reading" was given by Robert Lowell on May 25 at the University of Washington (*see* II, E9).

Review: "Pulitzer Prize Poet Lauds Roethke," *University of Washington Daily* [Seattle], May 26, 1965, p. 1. (UWR)

On the Poet and His Craft was published in June.

Reference: "Theodore Roethke: A Great Poet and His Craft," *Northwest Today* (*Seattle Post Intelligencer*), September 19, 1965, p. 1.

1966

William Stafford was the winner of the fourth Theodore Roethke prize awarded by *Poetry Northwest*.

Stanley Kunitz hosted the Second Memorial Program, "Homage to Theodore Roethke," at the YM-YWHA Poetry Center in New York City on January 17. *In a Dark Time* was shown during the program; it was released by National Education Television in February with the title: *U.S.A. Poetry: Theodore Roethke*.

Rolfe Humphries gave a lecture and reading, "The Early Theodore Roethke: Reminiscences and Reading," at the University of Washington in the spring (*see* I, E29 and II, E6).

On the Poet and His Craft was honored as the American Library Association "Notable Book of 1965" in April.

References: "Roethke Book Wins Award," *University of Washington Daily* [Seattle], April 8, 1966, p. 14 (UW); "Library Group Honors Roethke, Kayira Books," *Seattle Times*, April 17, 1966, p. 19.

Four of Roethke's poems were read by actors at the Seattle
Repertory Playhouse. This reading included "I Knew a
Woman" and "In a Dark Time."
Review: "Actors Read Northwest Poets," *Seattle Times*, April
18, 1966, p. 21. (UWSC)

"The Third Theodore Roethke Memorial Reading" was given
by Rolfe Humphries on May 25 at the University of
Washington (*see* I, E29 and II, E7).

The Collected Poems of Theodore Roethke was published
in July. Fourteen poems ("Terrible is death: young wombs
filled with rotteness and shadows," "Pickle Belt,"
"Thirty-Five an Hour," "Growth," "Summer School
Marms," "The Adamant," "The Signals," "The Warning,"
"The Gossips," "Elegy," "Rant," "To Be Said Slowly,"
"Saturday Eight O'Clock," and "Artist") were discovered
in an old desk at Pennsylvania State University in
September.
References: *The Pennsylvania State University Department of
Public Information Bulletin*, September 11, 1966, p. 3 (PSC);
"Noted Poet, Former Professor: Scribblings Recall Roethke,"
Daily Collegian, September 25, 1966, p. 3. (USC)

Roethke's papers, including the complete manuscript of
Open House and recently discovered poems, were on
display at the Pattee Library of Pennsylvania State Uni-
versity in November (*see* II, B67).
Reference: Roethke Material on Display," *Centre Daily Times*
[State College, Pa.], LXIX (November 15, 1966), 6. (PSC)

1967

Carolyn Stoloff was the winner of the fifth Theodore Roethke
Prize awarded by *Poetry Northwest*.

The establishment of the Theodore Roethke Memorial
Foundation was announced in Saginaw in March. A prize
of $6,000 is awarded every three years.

References: "Roethke Foundation Planning Award," *Publisher's
Weekly*, CXCI (March 20, 1967), 40 (UWR); "Award in Memory
of Roethke," *New York Times*, March 23, 1967, p. 32; "$6,000
Prize Due to Honor Roethke," *Seattle Post-Intelligencer*, March 24,
1967, p. 3 (UWSC); "Roethke Poetry Prize," *Christian Science
Monitor*, LIX (April 27, 1967), 11; "Ex-Penn State Professor:
Saginaw Plans Recognition for Famed Poet Roethke," *Centre
Daily Times*, June 7, 1967, p. 10 (PSC).

"An Evening with Ted Roethke" with Stanley Kunitz, Allan
Seager, and John Ciardi inaugurated the Theodore
Roethke Memorial Foundation at the Arthur High School
in Saginaw on May 24 (*see* I, E27, 31, 37 and II, E5).
References: "Hometown to Honor," *The Saginaw News*, May 7,
1967; "Evening with Roethke," *The Saginaw News*, May 18, 1967;
"Theodore Roethke Memorial Poetry Prize Inaugurated," *The
Saginaw News*, May 21, 1967 (PSC).

"The Fourth Theodore Roethke Memorial Reading" was
given by Archibald MacLeish on May 25 at the University
of Washington (*see* I, E32, 34 and II, E10).
Review: "Fitting Tribute to Theodore Roethke," *University of
Washington Daily* [Seattle], May 26, 1967, p. 12. (UW)

1968

John Woods was the winner of the sixth Theodore Roethke
Prize awarded by *Poetry Northwest*.

Selected Letters of Theodore Roethke was published in May.
"The first Theodore Roethke Poetry Award" was given to
Howard Nemerov at the Douglas MacArthur High School
in Saginaw on May 21 (*see* II, E8).
Reference: "Nemerov Named Winner of First Roethke Award,"
New York Times, May 21, 1967, p. 44.

"The Fifth Theodore Roethke Memorial Reading" was given by
Robert Penn Warren on May 25 at the University of
Washington (*see* II, E3).

The Glass House: The Life of Theodore Roethke by Allan
Seager was published in October.

1969

Theodore Roethke: Selected Poems, selected by Beatrice Roethke, was published in London.

Thomas James was winner of the seventh Theodore Roethke Prize awarded by *Poetry Northwest*.

"The Sixth Theodore Roethke Memorial Reading" was given by John Berryman on May 27 at the University of Washington.

1970

Philip Booth was winner of the eighth Theodore Roethke Prize awarded by *Poetry Northwest*.

The University of Washington regents announced the naming of an auditorium in memory of Roethke.

Reference: "Regents Do Their Thing (Again) . . . Building Named," *University of Washington Daily*, February 17, 1970, p. 4.

"The Seventh Theodore Roethke Memorial Reading" was given by Howard Nemerov on May 25 at the University of Washington.

1971

Dave Etter was winner of the ninth Theodore Roethke Prize awarded by *Poetry Northwest*.

"The Eighth Theodore Roethke Memorial Reading" was given by Richard Wilber on May 26 at the University of Washington.

1972

Albert Goldbarth was winner of the tenth Theodore Roethke Prize awarded by *Poetry Northwest*.

Straw for the Fire was published in March.

"The Ninth Theodore Roethke Memorial Reading" was given by James Wright on May 25 at the formal dedication of the Roethke Auditorium at the University of Washington.

I Works and Materials by Theodore Roethke

A Books

A1 *Open House*

First and only edition:

OPEN HOUSE / [ornament] / THEODORE ROETHKE / [publisher's device] / ALFRED [dot] A [dot] KNOPF / *NEW YORK* / 1941

21 x 14½. Published on March 10, 1941, at $2.00. This edition consisted of 1,000 copies. Issued in blue cloth with design stamped on the front cover and stamped in gold along the backstrip. Backstrip, reading down: *Open House* [ornament] THEODORE ROETHKE [ornament] / Knopf [last line reads across the backstrip]. Back cover: publisher's device and name is stamped in the lower right corner. Top edges stained red; top and bottom edges trimmed and fore edges untrimmed; dust jacket.

Collation: [i]–[xviii] + [1]–[73], as follows: [i]–[iii] blank; [iv] colophon; [v] blank; [vi] other poetry titles by Knopf; [vii] half title; [viii] blank; [ix] title page as above; [x] notice of copyright, note of origin, and reservation of rights; [xi] dedication: *TO / MY MOTHER*; [xii] blank; [xiii]–[xv] Contents; [xvi] blank; [xvii] acknowledgment; [xviii] blank;

2

[1] I; [2] blank; 3–70 text; [71] blank; [72] note on the type; [73] blank.

Contents: I "Open House," "Feud," "Death Piece," "Prognosis," "To My Sister," "The Premonition," "Interlude," "Orders for the Day," "Prayer," "The Signals," "The Adamant," II "The Light Comes Brighter," "Slow Season," "Mid-Country Blow," "In Praise of Prairie," "The Coming of the Cold": (1 The late peach yields a subtle musk, 2 The ribs of leaves lie in the dust, 3 The small brook dies within its bed), "The Heron," "The Bat," III "No Bird," "The Unextinguished," " 'Long Live the Weeds,' " "Genesis," "Epidermal Macabre," "Against Disaster," "Reply to Censure," "The Auction," "Silence," "On the Road to Woodlawn," IV "Academic," "For an Amorous Lady," "Poetaster," "Vernal Sentiment," "Prayer before Study," "My Dim-Wit Cousin," "Verse with Allusions," V "Ballad of the Clairvoyant Widow," "The Favorite," "The Reminder," "The Gentle," "The Reckoning," "Lull," "Sale," "Highway: Michigan," "Idyll," "Night Journey"

Colophon: "THE FIRST EDITION / OF / OPEN HOUSE / CONSISTS OF ONE THOUSAND COPIES / OF WHICH THIS IS NUMBER"

Note on the Type: "This book was set on the Linotype in Janson, a / recutting made direct from the type cast from / matrices (now in possession of the Stempel / Foundry, Frankfurt am Main) made by Anton / Janson some time between 1660 and 1687. / Of Janson's origin nothing is known. He may / have been a relative of Justress Janson, a printer of Danish birth who practiced in Leipzig from 1614 / to 1635. Some time between 1657 and 1668 Anton / Janson, a punch-cutter and type-founder, bought / from the Leipzig Johann Erich Hahn the / type-foundry which had formerly been a part of / the printing house of M. Friedrich Lankisch. / Janson's types were first shown in a specimen / sheet issued at Leipzig about 1657. Janson's successor and perhaps his son-in-law, Johann Karl / Edling, issued a specimen sheet of Janson types / in 1689. His heirs sold the Janson matrices in / Holland to Wolfgang Dietrich Erhardt. / Composed and printed by / The Golden Eagle Press, Mount Vernon, New York. / *Bound* by H. Wolff, New York. / Paper made by / S.D. Warren Company, Boston. / The binding is after designs by / W.A. Dwiggins."

"The Premonition," "Mid-Century Blow," "On the Road to Woodlawn," "My Dim-Wit Cousin," "The Favorite," "The Reminder," and "The Gentle" appeared first in *Open House*. "The Coming of the Cold" went through a title change and textual revisions before appearing in *Open House* (*see* I, C11, 24, 35; for a possible source for "Death Piece," *see* II, C20).

John Holmes advised Roethke on the arrangement and sequence of the poems for his first volume, and Stanley Kunitz suggested the title *Open House*. The poem "Strange Distortion" (*see* I, C16) was retitled "Open House" and was placed first in the volume.

Roethke submitted an early manuscript of this book to the Oxford University Press in 1939, but it was returned in a letter dated July 19, 1939 (*see* II, A7, p. 224). The Ryerson Press of Toronto distributed the book for Alfred A. Knopf in Canada, and the book may carry their imprint.

A presentation copy of *Open House* presented to Fred Lewis Pattee is located at the Rare Book and Special Collections Division of Pennsylvania State University. The Rare Book and Special Collections Division at the University of Washington has two copies of the book. The dust jacket has a letter press and ornament in blue on a pale brown background. The front inside flap carries an appreciation with remarks by John Holmes. A biographical note appears on the black flap, and a list of recent Borzoi books by Knopf appears on the back cover.

A2 *The Lost Son and Other Poems*

First and only American edition:

THE LOST SON / *and* / OTHER POEMS / *by* / THEODORE ROETHKE / [publisher's device in green] / *Garden City, New York* / Doubleday & Company, Inc. / 1948 [the whole enclosed by a triple rule of black, green and black] 21¼ × 14½. Published March 11, 1948, at $2.50. Issued in black cloth and stamped in gold along the backstrip. Backstrip, reading down: *The Lost Son and Other Poems* [dash] THEODORE ROETHKE [dash] Doubleday. All edges trimmed; dust jacket.

Collation: [1]–[64], as follows: [1] half title; [2] blank; [3] title page as above; [4] notice of copyright, note of origin, and reservation of rights; [5] acknowledgment; [6] blank; [7]–[8] Contents; 9–62 text; [63]–[64] blank.

Contents: I "Cuttings," "Cuttings (*later*)," "Root Cellar," "Forcing House," "Weed Puller," "Orchids," "Moss-Gathering," "Big Wind," "Old Florist," "Transplanting," "Child on Top of a Greenhouse," "Flower-Dump," "Carnations," II "My Papa's Waltz," "Pickle Belt," "Dolor," "Double Feature," "The Return," "Last Words," "Judge Not," III "Night Crow," "River Incident," "The Minimal," "The Cycle," "The Waking," IV "The Lost Son," "The Long Alley," "A Field of Light," "The Shape of the Fire"

"First Edition" appears on page [4] but not in the later impressions. This edition was first printed on January 16, 1948, and consisted of 1,000 copies. The second impression of 1,000 copies was completed on March 18, 1948. The edition went out of print on October 18, 1949.

"Cuttings," "Orchids," "Transplanting," "The Waking," and "A Field of Light" (which appeared in *The Tiger's Eye* at approximately the same time) appeared first in *The Lost Son and Other Poems* (*see* I, C85). An early version of "The Shape of the Fire" appears on page 100 of "The Vegetal Radicalism of Theodore Roethke" (*see* II, C24). "Cuttings (*later*)" appeared in *Harper's Bazaar* as "Cuttings" (*see* I, C84). The first line and title of "Double Feature" were changed after its appearance in *Commonweal* (*see* I, C63). "Last Words" was originally section III of an unpublished sequence entitled "Enough! or Too Much (Suburban Frenzies)" (*see* II, A7, p. 68).

"Frau Bauman, Frau Schmidt, and Frau Schwartze" was added to *The Lost Son* sequence in *The Waking* in 1953. No note of this appears in *Words for the Wind* or *The Collected Poems of Theodore Roethke* (*see* II, C128, p. 27). "Frau Bauman, Frau Schmidt, and Frau Schwartz" was inadvertently omitted from the first impression of *The Collected Poems of Theodore Roethke* (*see* II, C78). For commentary on textual variations of "Big Wind," *see* II, C128, pp. 25–26; *see also* I, A7, and II, C335. Four poems were removed from this volume in subsequent editions; they included "Double Feature," "Judge Not," "River Incident," and "The Waking" (I strolled across). For further comment on this deletion, *see* C128, p. 40.

"The Lost Son," "The Long Alley," "A Field of Light,' and "The Shape of the Fire" appeared in part 2 of *Praise to the End*! and are thus arranged as part of the *Praise to the End*! sequence in *The Waking* and *Words for the Wind*; they appeared again as part of *The Lost Son* sequence in *The Collected Poems of Theodore Roethke* (for further comment on this arrangement *see* I, A3 and II, C76, 77). Only the English edition (I, A10) of *The Collected Poems* notes the return of these poems to their original sequential position. For additional information, *see* II, A6.

Two presentation copies of *The Lost Son and Other Poems* are located at the Rare Book Department of Washington University. They are described (in the catalog of the exhibit at Washington University, item 46, March 15–May 30, 1969) as follows: "(1) A presentation copy 'for Waldon & Ann Kess' with five corrections in Roethke's hand, three of them textually important; (2) a presentation copy 'for Malcolm Cowley' of a later impression probably March 18, 1948. In this later impression (not marked 'First Edition' on the verse of the title-page) two of the three textual errors noted above were corrected by the printer, e.g. 'A dish for fat [rather than "flat"] lips' in the first line of 'The Shape of the Fire.' " The University of Washington Rare Book and Special Collections also possesses a "First Edition" of *The Lost Son*.

Page 151 of *The Selected Letters of Theodore Roethke* reads as follows: " 'By the way, there were some mistakes in the text of the first edition; corrected in the second: In "The Lost Son": p. 45 "Toads brooding *in* wells" ("in" is omitted, wrongly); in "The Shape of the Fire": page 63 "When the *herons* floated" etc. *not* "waterbirds"; also page 63: "When the sun for me glinted the sides of a sandgrain" ("a" is omitted wrongly); also page 60: "A dish for fat lips," not flat. And "stir from *your* cave of sorrow." ' "

The dust jacket is dark to pale green with letter press in white and off-white. Jacket drawings are by Charles Seide and are described as "Pastel on Gesso Ground" on the inside flap (*see* II, C128, p. 23). An appreciation appears on both the front and back inside flap. The back cover is lettered in pale green and black on a white background and carries a biographical note and comments by W. H. Auden, Louise Bogan, Yvor Winters, and William Carlos Williams (*see* II, B3).

English edition:

THE LOST SON / *and other poems by* / THEODORE ROETHKE / [publisher's device] LONDON / *John Lehmann*

19¾ × 13. Published in 1949, at 6s. Issued in orange cloth and lettered in gold with 3 black lines edged with a single gold rule on the backstrip. Backstrip, reading down: [volute tooled in gold] THE LOST SON [title stamped on a rectangular, black block with the edge tooled in gold] THEODORE ROETHKE [stamped on a rectangular, black block with the edge tooled in gold] / [across the foot in gold] JOHN LEHMANN [volute tooled in gold]. All edges are trimmed; dust jacket.

Collation: [1]–[64], as follows: [1] half title; [2] blank; [3] title page as above; [4] notice of copyright and

printer's note: Made and printed in Great Britain By /
PURNELL AND SONS LTD / PAUTON (SOMERSET) AND
LONDON / SET IN 12 POINT PERPETUA 1 POINT LEADED;
[5] Contents; [6] blank; [7] I; [8] blank;
9–[62] text; [63–64] blank.

Contents: Identical to the revised American edition with
the exception of the pagination and the spelling of "Dolor"
as "Dolour." The titles appear all in small caps.

John Lehmann stated in a recent letter that the book did not enjoy
a large sale; after several months, it had only sold 200 copies.
Information regarding the number of copies issued was not
available, but it is likely that this edition consisted of 1,000 copies.
Karl Malkoff failed to note the appearance of this edition in
England. See II, C82, 335.

   The dust jacket has a green scroll border over a sepia background
and is lettered in green. A photo of Roethke by Frank Murphy
appears with a biographical note inside the back flap. Excerpts from
reviews by W. H. Auden (see II, C143), the New York Herald
Tribune (see II, C175), and the New York Times Book Review
(see II, C181) appear on the front inside flap.

A3 *Praise to the End!*

First and only edition:

PRAISE TO THE END! / By *THEODORE ROETHKE* /
Doubleday & Company, Inc., *Garden City,
New York*, 1951

21 × 14. Published November 8, 1951, at $3.00. Half
bound in black cloth with tan cloth over the fore section
and stamped in gold on the black backstrip. Backstrip,
reading down: PRAISE TO THE END! By THEODORE
ROETHKE / DOUBLEDAY. All edges trimmed; dust jacket.

Collation: [1] half title; [2] blank; [3] title page as
above; [4] notice of copyright, note of origin, and reservation of rights; [5] dedication: FOR K. B. AND W. C. W.;

[6] blank; [7] acknowledgment; [8] blank; [9] Contents; [10] blank; [11] PART ONE; [12] blank; [13] WHERE KNOCK IS OPEN WIDE; [14] blank; 15–89 text; [90]–[94] blank.

Contents: Part One "Where Knock Is Open Wide," "I Need, I Need," "Bring the Day!," "Give Way, Ye Gates," "Sensibility! O La!," "O Lull Me, Lull Me," Part Two "The Lost Son" ("The Flight," "The Pit," "The Gibber," "The Return"), "A Field of Light," "The Shape of the Fire," "Praise to the End!," "Unfold! Unfold!," "I Cry, Love! Love!"

This edition of 750 copies was printed September 4, 1951, and went out of print on March 12, 1952. "First Edition" appears on page [4].

The title is from Wordsworth's *The Prelude*, Book I, line 350. For Roethke's remarks regarding the sources for the titles of the poems appearing in this volume, *see* I, A12, p. 252

The initials in the dedication refer to Kenneth Burke and William Carlos Williams.

"O Lull Me, Lull Me" and "Sensibility! O La!" appear for the first time in *Praise to the End*!; They also appeared in *Poetry* approximately the same time (*see* I, C99). "Praise to the End!," "Bring the Day!" "Give Way, Ye Gates," and "I Need, I Need" appeared first in Italy in *Botteghe Oscure* (*see* I, D14, 15). "I Cry Love! Love!" appeared in the *Hudson Review* with "Hedge-Wren's" hyphenated; compare to section 2. For a comment on the use of the word "roundy" in "I Need, I Need," *see* II, C335.

"O, Thou Opening, O" was added to this sequence in *The Waking* (*see* I, A4) in 1953. No note of this appeared in *Words for the Wind* or *The Collected Poems of Theodore Roethke*. John Lucas in *The Oxford Review* (*see* II, C77) notes the following: "When *The Lost Son* was originally published, the poems appeared in the order in which I have discussed them as in *The Collected Poems of Theodore Roethke*. However, when he brought out *Praise to the End*, Roethke began the second part with

'The Lost Son,' 'The Long Alley,' 'A Field of Light,' and 'The Shape of the Fire,' and the order was retained in the volume *Words for the Wind,* also *The Waking,* where the fifth section of 'The Lost Son' first received a title. And the sequence then ended with 'O, Thou Opening, O' which had first been published in *The Waking.* In *The Collected Poems of Theodore Roethke,* Doubleday, the poems are returned to their original position." *See also* II, 6 and II, C78.

The University of Washington Rare Book and Special Collections has a copy of the first edition.

The dust jacket is orange-brown with letter press in cream-white and pale-orange. Jacket photograph is by Lotte Jacobi. An appreciation appears inside the front flap along with the following announcement: THEODORE ROETHKE IS WINNER / OF THE LEVINSON PRIZE FOR 1951, / POETRY MAGAZINE'S HIGHEST AWARD. A biographical note with a photograph is lettered in orange and black on a cream background and carries excerpts about *Open House* by W. H. Auden and Elizabeth Drew (*see* II, C143, 151) and about *The Lost Son and Other Poems* by Louise Bogan (*see* II, C172).

A4 *The Waking Poems: 1933–1953*

First and only edition:

THEODORE ROETHKE / THE WAKING / POEMS: 1933–1953 / 1953 [rule] / DOUBLEDAY & COMPANY, INC. / GARDEN CITY, NEW YORK

21 × 14. Published September 10, 1953, at $3.00 ($3.35 in Toronto]. Issued in dark blue cloth and stamped in silver on the backstrip. Backstrip, reading down: Theodore Roethke [dot] THE WAKING [dot] Doubleday. All edges trimmed; dust jacket.

Collation: [i]–[ii] blank; [1] half title; [2] other titles by Roethke; [3] title page as above; [4] notice of copyright, note of origin and reservation of rights; [5] acknowledgment; [6] blank; 7–9 Contents; [10] blank;

[11] From OPEN HOUSE (1941); [12] blank; 13–120 text; [121–124] blank.

Contents: From *Open House* (1941), "Open House," "Death Piece," "To My Sister," "Interlude," "Prayer," "The Adamant," "Mid-Country Blow," "The Heron," "The Bat," "No Bird," " 'Long Live the Weeds,' " "Epidermal Macabre," "On the Road to Woodlawn," "Academic," "Vernal Sentiment," "Sale," "Night Journey"

From *The Lost Son and Other Poems* (1948), I "Cuttings," "Cuttings (*later*)," "Root Cellar," "Forcing House," "Weed Puller," "Orchids," "Moss-Gathering," "Big Wind," "Old Florist," "Frau Bauman, Frau Schmidt, and Frau Schwartze," "Transplanting," "Child on Top of a Greenhouse," "Flower-Dump," "Carnations," II "My Papa's Waltz," "Pickle Belt," "Dolor," "The Return," "Last Words," "Night Crow," "The Minimal," "The Cycle"

From *Praise to the End!* (1951), I "Where Knock is Open Wide," "I Need, I Need," "Bring the Day!," "Give Way, Ye Gates," "Sensibility! O La!," "O Lull Me, Lull Me," II "The Lost Son," "The Long Alley," "A Field of Light," "The Shape of the Fire," "Praise to the End!," "Unfold! Unfold!," "I Cry, Love! Love!," "O, Thou Opening, O"

NEW POEMS: "The Visitant," "A Light Breather," "Elegy for Jane," "Old Lady's Winter Words," "Four for Sir John Davies" (I "The Dance," II "The Partner," III "The Wraith," IV "The Vigil"), "The Waking"

This edition of 1,500 copies was first printed on July 8, 1953. The second impression of 1,000 copies was completed on May 6, 1954. The edition went out of print on June 1, 1957. The first impression has "First Edition" on page [4].

"The Wraith" (from "Four for Sir John Davies") appeared first in *The Waking*. For a comment on an ambiguous line in "The

Waking," *see* II, C335. "O, Thou Opening, O" appeared in italics in *The Waking* and *Words for the Wind*, but the italics were omitted in *The Collected Poems of Theodore Roethke*. "Frau Bauman, Frau Schmidt, and Frau Schwartze" and "O, Thou Opening, O" were added to *The Lost Son* and *Praise to the End!* sequence in *The Waking*. No note of this addition appears here or in *Words for the Wind* and *The Collected Poems of Theodore Roethke*.

For comments regarding the arrangement of "The Lost Son," "The Long Alley," and "The Shape of the Fire," *see* the notes in I, A2, 3, 10 and II, A6.

The University of British Columbia has the galley proofs for this edition (for further information regarding this collection, *see* II, A7). The University of Washington Rare Book and Special Collections Division has a first edition.

The book received the Pulitzer Prize in May 1954 (*see* II, B101–111).

The dust jacket is dark to light blue with letter press in white and pale blue. Jacket photograph is by Lotte Jacobi. An appreciation appears inside the front flap with a comment by W. H. Auden. A biographical note and comments by William Arrowsmith and Hayden Carruth appear inside the back flap. A sketch by Robert W. White (1953) in black and white appears on the back cover. The back cover is lettered in black. For Roethke's comment on this jacket, *see The Selected Letters of Theodore Roethke*, page 193.

A5 *Words for the Wind*

First English edition:

THEODORE ROETHKE / *Words for the Wind* / *London*: SECKER & WARBURG: 1957

20½ × 13¾. Published in the fall (probably November) of 1957, at 15s. Issued in green cloth and stamped in silver on the backstrip. Backstrip, reading down: ROETHKE [dot] *Words for the Wind* [dot] S&W. All edges trimmed; dust jacket.

Collation: [i]–[201], as follows: [i] blank; [1] title page as above; [2] notice of copyright and printer's note:

Printed in England by / Burler & Tanner Ltd London & Frome.; [3] acknowledgment; [4] blank; [5] half title: Selected Poems; [6] blank; 7–11 Contents; [12] blank; [13] PART ONE / THE WAKING; [14] blank; [15] From / OPEN HOUSE / 1941; [16] blank; 17–200 text; [201] blank.

Contents: PART ONE / THE WAKING / From OPEN HOUSE (1941), "Open House," "Death Piece," "To My Sister," "Interlude," "Prayer," "The Adamant," "Mid-Country Blow," "The Heron," "The Bat," "No Bird," " 'Long Live the Weeds,' " "Epidermal Macabre," "On the Road to Woodlawn," "Academic," "Vernal Sentiment," "Sale," "Night Journey"

From THE LOST SON AND OTHER POEMS (1948), I "Cuttings," "Cuttings (*later*)," "Root Cellar," "Forcing House," "Weed Puller," "Orchids," "Moss-Gathering," "Big Wind," "Old Florist," "Frau Bauman, Frau Schmidt, and Frau Schwartze," "Transplanting," "Child on Top of a Greenhouse," "Flower Dump," "Carnations," II "My Papa's Waltz," "Pickle Belt," "Dolour," "The Return," "Last Words," "Night Crow," "The Minimal," "The Cycle"

From PRAISE TO THE END! (1951), I "Where Knock Is Open Wide," "I Need, I Need," "Bring the Day!," "Give Way, Ye Gates," "Sensibility! O La!," "O Lull Me, Lull Me," II "The Lost Son," "The Long Alley," "A Field of Light," "The Shape of the Fire," "Praise to the End!," "Unfold! Unfold!," "I Cry, Love! Love!," "O, Thou Opening, O"

SHORTER POEMS (1951–1953) "The Visitant," "A Light Breather," "Elegy for Jane," "Old Lady's Winter Words," "Four for Sir John Davies": (I "The Dance,"

II "The Partner," III "The Wraith," IV "The Vigil"),
"The Waking"

PART TWO / NEW POEMS / I / LIGHTER PIECES
AND POEMS FOR CHILDREN / (*an interlude*)
"Song for the Squeeze-Box," "Reply to a Lady Editor,"
"Dinky," "The Cow," "The Serpent," "The Sloth," "The
Lady and the Bear" II / LOVE POEMS "The Dream,"
"All the Earth, All the Air," "Words for the Wind,"
"I Knew a Woman," "The Voice," "She," "The Other,"
"The Sententious Man," "The Sensualists," "Love's
Progress," "The Surly One," "Memory"

III / VOICES AND CREATURES " 'The Shimmer of
Evil,' " "Elegy," "The Beast," "The Song," "The Small,"
"A Walk in Late Summer," "Snake," "Slug," "The Siskins"

IV / THE DYING MAN, *In Memoriam*: *W. B. Yeats*
I "His Words," II "What Now?," III "The Wall,"
IV "The Exulting," V "They Sing, They Sing"

MEDITATIONS OF AN OLD WOMAN: ("First Meditation,"
"I'm Here," "Third Meditation," "What Can I Tell
My Bones?")

"I Knew a Woman" appeared first in *The Times Literary
Supplement* (*see* I, C110) as "Poem"; "The Siskins" appeared
first in the *Nation* (*see* I, C107) as "Pastorale"; "The Surly One"
appeared first in the *New Yorker* (*see* I. C137) as "The
Cantankerous One"; "They Sing, They Sing" appeared first in the
New Yorker (*see* I, C128) as "They Sing (A Dying Man
Speaks)"; "First Meditation" appeared first in *Partisan Review*
(*see* I, C120) as "Old Woman's Meditation"; "I'm Here"
appeared first in the *New Yorker* (*see* I, C132) as "I'm Here
(Old Lady on the Way to Sleep)"; "Third Meditation" appeared
first in *Harper's Bazaar* (*see* I, C135) as "An Old Lady Muses"
and later as "Fourth Meditation" in the American edition of
Words for the Wind in 1958; "What Can I Tell My Bones?"

appeared first in *Partisan Review* (*see* I, C134) as "What Can I Tell My Bones? (An Old Lady Musing)."

"O, Thou Opening, O" appeared in italics in *The Waking* and *Words for the Wind*, but the italics were omitted in *The Collected Poems of Theodore Roethke*. For a comment on a revision in "The Dying Man," *see* II, C335. *Words for the Wind* included only seventeen poems from *Open House* (*see* II, C356).

An early set of galley proofs of the English edition of the title page and four poems was sent to Eddie [Nichols] (*see* II, A7, p. 28) in the summer of 1957. The title page reads as follows: THEODORE ROETHKE / *SELECTED POEMS* / London: SECKER & WARBURG: *1957*. The title was later changed to *Words for the Wind*. The "Weed Puller," "Forcing House," "Root Cellar," and "Cuttings" galleys all have notes with biographical significance in Roethke's hand. These galleys are on microfilm at the University of Washington Manuscript Division.

This edition was the Poetry Book Society "Christmas Choice" for 1957. "A Walk in Late Summer," which appeared first in the *New Yorker* and was collected first in this edition, also received the Borestone Mountain Poetry Award for second prize as the "Best Poem of 1957."

The dust jacket is light green with letter press in dark green and black. The announcement of the volume as the "Choice of the Poetry Book Society" appears on the front cover. The front flap carries a biographical note and comment by W. H. Auden. The back flap is black, The back cover lists other poetry titles by Secker & Warburg.

First American edition:

[verso page] *The Collected Verse of* / THEODORE ROETHKE / 1958 / [recto page] WORDS / FOR / THE WIND / DOUBLEDAY & COMPANY, INC. / GARDEN CITY, N. Y.

20¾ × 14. Published November 5, 1958, at $4.00 ($4.50 in Toronto). Issued in black cloth and stamped in gold in two lines on the backstrip. Backstrip, reading down: The Collected Verse of Theodore Roethke DOUBLEDAY /

WORDS FOR THE WIND. Top edges stained green; all edges trimmed; dust jacket.

Collation: [1] half title; [2] verse of title page as above; [3] recto title page as above; [4] notice of copyright, note of origin, and reservation of rights; [5] acknowledgment; [6] blank; 7–11 Contents; [12] PART ONE; [13] *THE WAKING*; [14] blank; [15] *from* OPEN HOUSE / 1941; [16] blank; 17–212 text; [213–[216] blank.

Contents: PART ONE, THE WAKING, *From Open House*, 1941 "Open House," "Death Piece," "To My Sister," "Interlude," "Prayer," "The Adamant," "Mid-Country Blow," "The Heron," "The Bat," " 'Long Live the Weeds,' " "Epidermal Macabre," "On the Road to Woodlawn," "Academic," "Vernal Sentiment," "Sale," "Night Journey"

From The Lost Son and Other Poems, 1948 1 "Cuttings," "Cuttings (*later*)" "Root Cellar," "Forcing House," "Weed Puller," "Orchids," "Moss-Gathering," "Big Wind," "Old Florist," "Frau Bauman, Frau Schmidt, and Frau Schwartz," "Transplanting," "Child on Top of a Greenhouse," "Flower Dump," "Carnations," 2 "My Papa's Waltz," "Pickle Belt," "Dolor," "The Return," "Last Words," "Night Crow," "The Minimal," "The Cycle"

From Praise to the End, 1951 1 "Where Knock Is Open Wide," "I Need, I Need," "Bring the Day!," "Give Way, Ye Gates," "Sensibility! O La!," "O Lull Me, Lull Me," 2 "The Lost Son," 1 "*The Flight*," 2 "*The Pit*, 3 "*The Gibber*," 4 "*The Return*," 5 "(*It was beginning winter*)" "The Long Alley," "A Field of Light," "The Shape of the Fire," "Praise to the End!" "Unfold! Unfold!," "I Cry, Love! Love!," "O, Thou Opening, O"

Shorter Poems, 1951–1953 "The Visitant," "A Light
Breather," "Elegy for Jane," "Old Lady's Winter Words,"
"Four for Sir John Davies" (1 *"The Dance,"* 2 *"The
Partner,"* 3 *"The Wraith,"* 4 *"The Vigil"*), "The Waking"

PART TWO, NEW POEMS, *Lighter Pieces and Poems
for Children, AN INTERLUDE* "Song for the Squeeze-
Box," "Reply to a Lady Editor," "Dinky," "The Cow,"
"The Serpent," "The Sloth," "The Lady and the Bear"

Love Poems "The Dream," "All the Earth, All the Air,"
"Words for the Wind," "I Knew a Woman," "The Voice,"
"She," "The Other," "The Sententious Man," "The Pure
Fury," "The Renewal," "The Sensualists," "Love's
Progress," "The Surly One," "Plaint," "The Swan,"
"Memory"

Voices and Creatures " 'The Shimmer of Evil,' " "Elegy,"
"The Beast," "The Song," "The Exorcism," "The Small,"
"A Walk in Late Summer," "The Snake," "Slug,"
"The Siskins"

The Dying Man, IN MEMORIAM: W. B. YEATS
"The Dying Man," (1 *"His Words,"* 2 *"What Now?,"*
3 *"The Wall,"* 4 *"The Exulting,"* 5 *"They Sing,
They Sing"*)

Meditations of an Old Woman, "First Meditation,"
"I'm Here," "Her Becoming," "Fourth Meditation,"
"What Can I Tell My Bones?"

This edition was first printed on September 2, 1958, and consisted
2,500 copies. Subsequent impressions were completed on March
3, 1959 (500 copies), April 10, 1959 (1,000 copies), July 11,
1960 (1,000 copies), February 5, 1964 (2,000 copies), August 1,
1966 (2,000 copies). The edition went out of print on January
1, 1964 but was reissued as *Words for the Wind.* The verso of the
title page of this impression reads: *THEODORE ROETHKE.*

The backstrip reads in two lines: *Theodore Roethke* DOUBLEDAY / *WORDS FOR THE WIND*. The following note appears on page [4]: "This book was formerly published as *Words for the Wind: The Collected Verse of Theodore Roethke*." The impressions are identical other than the changes listed above and the dust jacket. The first impression has "First Edition" on page [4].

"The Renewal," "The Swan," and "Her Becoming" appeared first in the American edition of *Words for the Wind*. All of the preceding poems, with "The Exorcism," "Plant," and "The Pure Fury" appeared only in the American edition. "Her Becoming" was added to the sequence *Meditations of an Old Woman* as the third section, and "Third Meditation" became "Fourth Meditation." "The Swan" was especially written for *Poets and the Past* (*see* I, B13) but actually appeared first in *Words for the Wind* by permission of Dore Ashton. For comment on the arrangement of "The Lost Son," "The Long Alley," and "The Shape of the Fire," *see* the notes for I, A2, 3, 10, and II, A6. "Part One" is a reprint of *The Waking*. Part 5 of "The Lost Son," "(*It was beginning winter*)," received a title for the first time in *Words for the Wind*.

Louis L. Martz, in his essay "A Greenhouse Eden" (*see* II, C84, pp. 25–26), notes a textual change in "Big Wind" in the American edition of *Words for the Wind*: " 'into the calm morning' is the original reading: 'into' has become 'until' in the 1958 printing of this poem. . . ." J. C. Maxwell (*see* II, C86, p. 265) comments that in the London edition of *Words for the Wind*, 1957, (*see* I, A5 [first English edition] above) it is "into," rather than "until," that appears. Maxwell goes on to explain, however, that "until" appears as early as 1953 in *An American Poet Introduces Himself and His Poem* (*see* I, A11, p. 10). During a reading at Reed College in May, 1957, Roethke read "Big Wind" using "into." He then commented: "I did that last line wrong, didn't I?"; then he read: "She sailed into the calm morning,/ Carrying her full cargo of roses" (exactly the way he had read it previously) and commented: "Ahh! Still wrong" (*see* I, E8). The evidence, as Maxwell points out, for the revision of "into" to "until" does seem to be considerable.

"They Sing, They Sing" [the last section of "The Dying Man" which appeared in the *New Yorker* (*see* I, C128) as "They Sing (A Dying Man Speaks)"] was revised before its appearance in *Words for the Wind* (as Karl Malkoff notes: *see* II, C82, p. 158). The last line of the poem originally appeared as: "Against the wide abyss, the gray waste nothingness of things" but was changed in *Words for the Wind* to: "Against the immense immeasureable emptiness of things." For further comments regarding this change and its possible source, *see* II, C86, p. 266.

This edition, or poems within it, were honored by the following awards and prizes: the Borestone Mountain Poetry Award ($1,250) awarded for the poem "A Walk in Late Summer" which appeared first in the *New Yorker* (*see* I, C136); the Edna St. Vincent Millay Award ($200); the Yale Bollingen Prize ($1,000); the Longview Award ($300); the Pacific Northwest Writer's Award; National Book Award ($1,000). For announcements regarding these prizes and awards, *see* II, B126–145.

The dust jacket is light-green and the letter press is white. Jacket photograph is by Lotte Jacobi, and the jacket design is by Remy Charlip. An appreciation appears on the front flap. A biographical note and a sketch by Robert W. White (1953) appear on the back flap. The back cover is white with letter press in black and carries comments by Babette Deutsch, Edith Sitwell, Louise Bogan, and W. H. Auden. Those impressions made after 1959 may carry the National Book Award emblem on the front cover. The dust jacket of the reissued volume (March 1, 1964) is gold with a red and black collage. The letter press is black and gold. The National Book Award emblem in black, white, and gold appears in the lower left corner of the front cover. The jacket collage was designed by Alex Gotfryd. The appreciation on the front flap is identical with the earlier jacket; the back flap and the back cover are also identical.

American paperback edition:

[verso] *The Collected Verse of* / THEODORE ROETHKE [recto] *WORDS* / *FOR* / *THE WIND* / INDIANA UNIVERSITY PRESS [slash] BLOOMINGTON

20 × 13. Published in 1961, at $1.75. Issued in stiff white paper and lettered in white, green, and black. The collage

design on the front cover is in green and black with the title appearing in white on the black background. This is an exact reprint of the Doubleday 1958 edition with the following exceptions: "1958" does not appear on the verso title page and the following note appears on page [4]: FIRST POETRY PAPERBACK EDITION PUBLISHED 1961 / BY ARRANGEMENT WITH DOUBLEDAY & COMPANY, INC.

This edition was into its fourth impression in 1965.

A6 *I Am! Says the Lamb*

First and only edition:

THEODORE ROETHKE / *I Am! Says the Lamb* / DRAWINGS BY ROBERT LEYDENFROST / DOUBLEDAY & COMPANY, INC. / GARDEN CITY, NEW YORK

20¾ × 14. Published July 28, 1961, at $2.50 ($2.75 in Toronto). Quarter bound in yellow cloth with tan cloth over the fore edge. An illustration of a lamb is stamped in blue on a yellow background. Backstrip, reading down: *I AM! SAYS THE LAMB* THEODORE ROETHKE Doubleday. All edges are trimmed; dust jacket.

Collation: [1]–[72], as follows: [1] half title; [2] blank; [3] other titles by Roethke; [4] an illustration by Leydenfrost; [5] title page as above; [6] acknowledgment, notice of copyright, note of origin, and reservation of rights; [7]–[8] Contents; [9] *PART ONE / THE NONSENSE POEMS*; [10]–[71] text and illustrations; [72] blank.

Contents: *Nonsense Poems*: "The Kitty-Cat Bird," "The Whale," "The Yak," "Dinky," "The Donkey," "The Ceiling," "The Chair," "Myrtle," "Myrtle's Cousin," "Goo-Girl," "The Cow," "The Gnu," "The Sloth,"

"The Monotony Song," "Philander," "The Hippo,"
"The Boy and the Bush," "The Lady and the Bear,"
"The Serpent," "The Lamb," "The Lizard," "The Wagtail"

The Greenhouse Poems: "The Shape of a Rat?," "The
Heron," "The Bat," "Vernal Sentiment," "My Papa's
Waltz," "Snake," "Cuttings," "Cuttings (*later*)," "Root
Cellar," "Forcing House," "Weed Puller," "Orchids,"
"Moss-Gathering," "Big Wind," "Old Florist," "Frau
Bauman, Frau Schmidt, and Frau Schwartze," "Transplant-
ing," "Child on Top of a Greenhouse," "Flower Dump,"
"Carnations"

This edition was first printed on May 10, 1961, and consisted of
3,000 copies. Subsequent impressions appeared on August 29, 1961
(1,000 copies) and on November 11, 1964 (15,000 copies).
The edition went out of print on April 1, 1968.

"The Whale," "The Donkey," "The Gnu," "The Hippo,"
"The Lizard, "The Wagtail (For J.S. His Son)," and "Philander"
appeared first in *I Am! Says the Lamb*; however, "The Donkey,"
"The Lizard," and "The Whale" made their first public
appearance on February 18, 1953 (*see* I, E5). For an early
version of "Philander," *see* I, C208. "The Shape of a Rat?" is an
excerpt from section 1 of "The Lost Son"; although the "Note" to
The Collected Poems of Theodore Roethke indicates that the
"volume contains all the poems from previous books by Theodore
Roethke, except *Party at the Zoo* . . . ," the poem does not appear
except as part of section 1 of "The Lost Son." For further
background notes, *see* the introduction to this section, Biographical
Notes 1960, and I, C208.

This edition was submitted to Faber & Faber in 1961 but was
apparently rejected by T. S. Eliot (*see* I, A12, p. 250).

The dust jacket is blue with letter press in white with an
illustration of a lamb in white, yellow, and green. A photo of
Roethke by Imogen Cunningham appears on the back flap. An
illustration of a sloth appears on the back cover.

A7 *Party at the Zoo*

First and only American edition:

THEODORE / ROETHKE / *PARTY* / *AT THE* / *ZOO* / Illustrated by / *Al Swiller* [lettering down left half of the page, and an illustration of a rabbit in a hat by Swiller on the right half of the page]

28½ × 19½. Published June 27, 1963, at $1.95. Issued in purple paper over boards with an illustration by Swiller on the front cover in various colors. Lettered in white, green, and blue on the front cover and white on the backstrip. Front cover: [white] THEODORE ROETHKE / [green] *PARTY* / *AT* / *THE* / *ZOO* [blue] Illustrated by AL SWILLER / [white] Modern Masters Book for Children. Backstrip, reading down: *PARTY AT THE ZOO* THEODORE ROETHKE THE CROWELL-COLLIER PRESS. All edges trimmed.

Collation: [1]–[65], as follows: [1] half title; [2] note of origin; [3] title page as above; [4] dedication: For Lillian Hellman and Meggie Walkinshaw; notice of copyright and reservation of rights; [5]–[61] text and illustrations; [62] other titles by Modern Master Books; [63]–[65] blank.

Contents: "Party at the Zoo"

This edition consisted of 20,000 copies and was also published simultaneously by Collier-Macmillan in London (*see* below). Louis Untermeyer was the general editor for this series. Meggie (Margaret Valerie) Walkinshaw was Roethke's godchild (*see* II, C278).

First and only English edition:

THEODORE / ROETHKE / [green] *PARTY* / *AT THE* / *ZOO* [blue] Illustrated by / *AL SWILLER* [lettering

down left half of the page and an illustration of a rabbit
in a hat by Swiller on the right half of the page].

28½ × 19½. Published June 27, 1963, at 15s. This edition
is identical to the American edition and was published
by Collier-Macmillan in London.

A8 *Sequence, Sometimes Metaphysical*
Special edition:
SEQUENCE / Poems by Theodore Roethke / *SOMETIMES
/ METAPHYSICAL* / With Wood Engravings / By
John Roy / The Stonewall Press, Iowa City

26½ × 17. Published December 1, 1963, at $30.00.
Quarter bound in red Oasis Goatskin with paper sides
over boards bearing a black and white engraving by Roy
on the front and back cover. Stamped in gold along
the backstrip. Backstrip, reading down: SEQUENCE
SOMETIMES METAPHYSICAL / ROETHKE / ROY.
Top edges trimmed; bottom and fore edges untrimmed and
vary in size; black slipcase.

Collation: 103 unnumbered pages, [i]–[iv] + [1]–[99],
as follows: [i]–[iv] blank; [1] half title; [2] blank;
[3] black and white engraving; [4]–[6] blank; [7] title
page as above; [8] notice of copyright and acknowledgment; [9] contents and colophon; [10] blank;
[11] black and white engraving; [12]–[14] blank;
[15]–[83] text and engravings; [84] blank; [85] black
and white engraving; [86]–[88] blank; [89] printer's
note: Printed on Washington press from / hand-set
Romanic type and original blocks. / The papers are Rives
Heavy and Mullbery [the engravings appear on the
Mullbery]; [90]–[99] blank.

Contents: I "In a Dark Time," II "In Evening Air,"
III "The Sequel," IV "The Motion," V "Infirmity,"
VI "The Decision," VII "The Marrow," VIII "I Waited,"
IX "The Tree, the Bird," X "The Restored," XI "The
Right Thing," XII "Once More, the Round"

Colophon: "This is ———— of an edition limited to 330
copies." I through LX have been signed by / the author and
the engraver [the signatures of Roethke and Roy appear
above the colophon].

The text of this volume is reprinted in *The Far Field* (I, A9) and
The Collected Poems of Theodore Roethke (I, A10). In an
early plan for *The Far Field*, the sequence is entitled *Metaphysical
Sequence*.

This edition was issued in a black slipcase.

Trade edition:

SEQUENCE / Poems by Theodore Roethke / *SOMETIMES*
/ *METAPHYSICAL* / With Wood Engravings / By
John Roy / The Stonewall Press, Iowa City

26½ × 17. Published December 1, 1963, at $15.00.
Issued in red Fabriano paper over boards with gold lettering
stamped along the backstrip. Backstrip, reading down:
SEQUENCE, SOMETIMES METAPHYSICAL /
ROETHKE / ROY. Top edges trimmed; bottom and
fore edges untrimmed, and the pages vary in size; black
slipcase on numbers LX–CCLXX.

Collation and Contents: Identical to the specially bound
edition above.

"In a Dark Time," "In Evening Air," and "The Sequel" appeared
in the *New Yorker* (*see* I, C149–151) with the title "Sequence"
and were awarded third prize for the "Best Poems of 1960" by the
Broestone Mountain Poetry Awards.

A9 *The Far Field*

American edition:

The Far Field / [rule] / Theodore Roethke / [rule] /
DOUBLEDAY & COMPANY, INC. / GARDEN CITY, NEW YORK

21 × 14. Published July 3, 1964, at $3.50. Quarter
bound in reddish brown cloth with black cloth over the
fore edge. Stamped in gold and black along the backstrip.
Backstrip, reading down: Theodore Roethke [slash]
The Far Field [slash] DOUBLEDAY. All edges trimmed;
dust jacket.

Collation: [1]–[96], as follows: [1] blank; [2] other
titles by Roethke: [3] half title; [4] blank; [5] title page
as above; [6] legal disclaimer, notice of copyright, and
acknowledgments; [7] dedication: To Marguerite Caetani;
[8] blank; 9–10 Contents; [11] North American
Sequence; [12] blank; 13–95 text; [96] blank.

Contents: *North American Sequence*: "The Longing,"
"Meditation at Oyster River," "Journey to the Interior,"
"The Long Waters," "The Far Field," "The Rose"

Love Poems: "The Young Girl," "Her Words," "The
Apparition," "Her Reticence," "Her Longing," "Her
Time," "Song," "Light Listened," "The Happy Three,"
"His Foreboding," "The Shy Man," "Her Wrath,"
"Wish for a Young Wife"

Mixed Sequence: "The Abyss," "Elegy," "Otto," "The
Chums," "The Lizard," "The Meadow Mouse," "Heard
in a Violent Ward," "The Geranium," "On the Quay,"
"The Storm (Forio d'Lschia)," "The Thing," "The Pike,"
"All Morning," "The Manifestation," "Song," "The
Tranced," "The Moment" *Sequence, Sometimes Meta-
physical*: "In a Dark Time," "In Evening Air," "The

Sequel," "The Motion," "Infirmity," "The Decision," "The
Marrow," "I Waited," "The Tree, the Bird," "The
Restored," "The Right Thing," "Once More, the Round"

This edition was first printed on December 30, 1963, and
consisted of 2,500 copies. Subsequent impressions appeared on
June 4, 1964 (15,000 copies), July 29, 1964 (2,000 copies),
October 2, 1964 (2,500 copies), January 12, 1965 (3,000 copies),
March 16, 1965 (3,500 copies), September 10, 1965 (3,500
copies) and March 16, 1967 (3,500 copies).

   J. C. Maxwell comments in *Notes and Queries* (*see* II, C86,
pp. 265–66) on the erroneous listing of first appearances in
The Far Field by Ursula Genung Walker in her *Notes on Theodore
Roethke* (*see* II, A10). There were no first appearances in *The
Far Field*. "On the Quay" appeared in the *New York Times*
(*see* I, C180) as "On the Quay (Inishbofin, Ireland)"; "The
Manifestation" appeared in the *New Yorker* (*see* I, C146) as
"Many Arrivals" and in *The Listener* (*see* I, C157) as "Poem";
"Song" appeared in the *Yale Review* (*see* I, C172) as "From
Whence?"; "The Right Thing" appeared in *The Observer* (*see* I,
C182) as "Villanelle."

   The last stanza of "The Longing" has undergone several
revisions since its first appearance in *The Times Literary
Supplement*. It has appeared twice in the *Saturday Review* (*see* I,
C148) with the last section added in the second appearance.
The last stanza appearing in *The Far Field* omits the word
"Ogalala"; whereas, *The Collected Poems of Theodore Roethke*
includes it. Note the spelling variations of the words "Ogalala"
and "Iroquois" in the first appearance of "The Longing" in *The
Times Literary Supplement* (I, C148) and *The Collected Poems*
(the paperback edition below also omits "Ogalala").

   In an early plan of *The Far Field*, the *Sequence, Sometimes
Metaphysical* poems are arranged under the title: *Metaphysical
Sequence*. In Beatrice Roethke's "Note" appearing in *The
Collected Poems of Theodore Roethke*, she states: "In *The Far
Field*, the sections entitled 'North American Sequence' and
'Sequence, Sometimes Metaphysical' are, in content and order, as
arranged by Theodore Roethke in the original manuscript. The
other sections in that book were altered slightly to withhold for

later publication two of the pub songs, 'The Saginaw Song' and 'Gob Music'—pieces that did not seem appropriate in a last book of poems—and to add 'Wish for a Young Wife' and 'The Tranced,' one of the last poems Theodore Roethke wrote." For further comments on Roethke's plan of composition, *see* II, C82, p. 172.

"In a Dark Time," "In Evening Air," and "The Sequel" appeared in the *New Yorker* (*see* I, C149–151) with the title "Sequence" and were awarded third prize for the "Best Poems of 1960" by the Borestone Mountain Poetry Awards. *The Far Field* won the National Book Award in 1965 and was selected as one of the "54 Notable Books of 1964" by the American Library Association (*see* Biographical Notes 1965).

The dust jacket is burnt orange with letter press in white and black. The jacket design is by Ursula Suess, and a photograph of Roethke by Mary Randlett appears on the back cover. An appreciation and biographical note appear inside the front and back flaps. The jackets for later editions bear the emblem of the National Book Award in the lower left corner.

English edition:

The Far Field / [rule] / Theodore Roethke / [rule] / FABER AND FABER / 24 RUSSELL SQUARE / LONDON

21½ × 13½. Published September 30, 1965, at 18s. Issued in green cloth and stamped in gold along the backstrip. Backstrip, reading down: THE FAR FIELD [the whole enclosed by a broad gold rule] Theodore Roethke Faber. All edges trimmed; dust jacket

Collation: [1]–[96], as follows: [1]–[2] blank; [3] half title; [4] blank; [5] title page as above; [6] notice of copyright, legal disclaimer, and acknowledgment; [7] dedication: To Marguerite Caetani; [8] blank; 9–10 contents; [11] North American Sequence; [12] blank; 13–95 text; [96] blank.

Contents: Identical with the American edition.

1,500 copies were printed on September 30, 1965.

The dust jacket is green with letter press in black and white. A list of other titles by Faber & Faber appears on the back cover.

Irish edition:

An Irish edition, *Dance On, Dance On, Dance On,* was to be published by the Dolmen Press of Dublin, but Roethke's sudden death in August 1963 may have interfered with this plan (*see* I, A12, p. 262).

American paperback edition:

Theodore Roethke / *The Far Field* / ANCHOR BOOKS / DOUBLEDAY & COMPANY, INC. / GARDEN CITY, NEW YORK

21 × 13. Published February 5, 1971, at $2.25. Issued in stiff white paper and lettered in black. The cover design is blue, green, and yellow. This is a reprint of the Doubleday 1964 edition with the exception of the lettering of the front cover, which reads: The Far Field / Last Poems / Theodore Roethke.

Excerpts from reviews by James Schevill, X. J. Kennedy (*see* II, C299), Alan Pryce-Jones (*see* II, C307), and John Willingham (*see* II, C319) appear on the back cover.

"Ogalala," which appears in the last stanza of "The Longing" in *The Collected Poems of Theodore Roethke,* has been omitted in this reprint.

A10 *The Collected Poems of Theodore Roethke*

First American edition:

The Collected Poems / of / Theodore Roethke / [ornament] / *Doubleday & Company, Inc., Garden City, New York*

23½ × 15½. Published on July 1, 1966, at $5.95 ($6.95 in Toronto). Issued in black cloth with blue section at the top of backstrip upon which the title is stamped in gold. Backstrip, reading across: *The / Collected / Poems / of / Theodore / Roethke /* [on black] DOUBLEDAY. All edges trimmed; dust jacket.

Collation: [i]–[xiv] + [1]–[282], as follows: [i] half title; [ii] *by Theodore Roethke*; [iii] title page as above; [iv] notice of copyright and acknowledgments; [v–xi] Contents; [xii] blank; [xiii] *Note*; [xiv] blank; [1] OPEN HOUSE [rule] 1941; [2] blank; 3–224 text; 275–279 *Index of First Lines*; [280–282] blank.

Contents: *1941*: I "Open House," "Feud," "Death Piece," "Prognosis," "To My Sister," "The Premonition," "Interlude," II "The Light Comes Brighter," "Slow Season," "Mid-Country Blow," "In Praise of Prairie," "The Coming of the Cold," "The Heron," "The Bat," III "No Bird," "The Unextinguished," " 'Long Live the Weeds,' " "Genesis," "Epidermal Macabre," "Against Disaster," "Reply to Censure," "The Auction," "Silence," "On the Road to Woodlawn," IV "Academic," "For an Amorous Lady," "Poetaster," "Vernal Sentiment," "Prayer before Study," "My Dim-Wit Cousin," "Verse with Allusions," V "Ballad of the Clairvoyant Widow," "The Favorite," "The Reminder," "The Gentle," "The Reckoning," "Lull," "Sale," "Highway: Michigan," "Idyll," "Night Journey"

1948: I "Cuttings," "Cuttings (*later*)," "Root Cellar," "Forcing House," "Weed Puller," "Orchids," "Moss-Gathering," "Big Wind," "Old Florist," "Transplanting," "Child on Top of a Greenhouse," "Flower Dump," "Carnations," "Frau Bauman, Frau Schmidt, and Frau Schwartze," II "My Papa's Waltz," "Pickle Belt," "Dolor," "Double Feature," "The Return," "Last Words," "Judge Not," III "Night Crow," "River Incident," "The Minimal," "The Cycle," "The Waking," IV "The Lost Son," "The ʻLong Alley," "A Field of Light," "The Shape of the Fire"

From *1951*: I "Where Knock Is Open Wide," "I Need,
I Need," "Bring the Day!," "Give Way, Ye Gates,"
"Sensibility! O La!," "Lull Me, Lull Me," II "Praise to
the End!," "Unfold! Unfold!," "I Cry, Love! Love!"

From *1953*: "O, Thou Opening, O," "The Visitant,"
"A Light Breather," "Elegy for Jane," "Old Lady's
Winter Words," "Four for Sir John Davies,"
"The Waking"

From *1958*: I "Song for the Squeeze-Box," "Reply to a Lady
Editor," Dinky," "The Cow," "The Serpent," "The Sloth,"
"The Lady and the Bear," II "The Dream," "All the Earth,
All the Air," "Words for the Wind," "I Knew a Woman,"
"The Voice," "She," "The Other," "The Sententious
Man," "The Pure Fury," "The Renewal," "The Sensual-
ists," "Love's Progress," "The Surly One," "Plaint,"
"The Swan," "Memory," III "The Shimmer of Evil,"
"Elegy," "The Beast," "The Song," "The Exorcism,"
"The Small," "A Walk in Late Summer," "Snake," "Slug,"
"The Siskins," IV "The Dying Man," V "First Medita-
tion," "I'm Here," "Her Becoming," "Fourth Meditation,"
"What Can I Tell My Bones?"

From *1961*: "The Kitty-Cat Bird," "The Whale," "The
Yak," "The Donkey," "The Ceiling," "The Chair,"
"Myrtle," "Myrtle's Cousin," "Goo-Girl," "The Gnu,"
"The Monotony Song," "Philander," "The Hippo,"
"The Boy and the Bush," "The Lamb," "The Lizard,"
"The Wagtail"

1964: I "The Longing," "Meditation at Oyster River,"
"Journey to the Interior," "The Long Waters,"
"The Far Field," "The Rose," II "The Young Girl,"
"Her Words," "The Apparition," "Her Reticence,"
"Her Longing," "Her Time," "Song," "Light Listened,"

"The Happy Three," "His Foreboding," "The Shy Man,"
"Her Wrath," "Wish for a Young Wife," III "The
Abyss," "Elegy," "Otto," "The Chums," "The Lizard,"
"The Meadow Mouse," "Heard in a Violent Ward,"
"The Geranium," "On the Quay," "The Storm [Forio
d'Ischia]," "The Thing," "The Pike," "All Morning,"
"The Manifestation Song," "The Tranced," "The
Moment," IV "In a Dark Time," "In Evening Air,"
"The Sequel," "The Motion," V "Infirmity," "The
Decision," "The Marrow," "I Waited," "The Tree, the
Bird," "The Restored," "The Right Thing," "Once More,
the Round"

Previously Uncollected Poems: "Light Poem," "Medita-
tion in Hydrotherapy," "Lines upon Leaving a Sanitarium,"
"Song," "The Changeling," "The Follies of Adam,"
"Three Epigrams," 1 Pipling, 2 The Mistake, 3 The
Centaur, "The Harsh Country," "A Rouse for Stevens,"
"The Saginaw Song," "Gob Music," "The Reply," "Duet,"
"Supper with Lindsay"

This edition of 8,500 copies was first printed on September 1,
1965. Subsequent impressions appeared on July 10, 1966 (5,000
copies), January 24, 1967 (7,500 copies), and September 6, 1968
(3,000 copies),
    "Duet" appeared first in this edition. The last stanza of "The
Longing" has been revised since its appearance in "The Far
Field" (see I, A9). "Praise," "Song," "A Wheeze for Wystan,"
and "Wind over the City" were considered for inclusion but
did not appear.
    There has been no indication that "Frau Bauman, Frau Schmidt,
and Frau Schwartze" was added to The Lost Son sequence and
"O, Thou Opening, O" was added to the Praise to the End!
sequence in The Waking. "O, Thou Opening, O," which was added
to "The Lost Son" sequence in The Waking, did not appear in
italics as it did in The Waking and Words for the Wind in this
edition. For comments regarding the arrangement of "The Lost

Son," "The Long Alley," "A Field of Light," and "The Shape of the Fire," *see* the notes for I, A3–5 and II, A6.

The publication date for *Words for the Wind* is listed as 1958 in the table of contents; however, *Words for the Wind* appeared first in England in 1957.

The galley proofs for this edition are located at Washington University (*see* II, A7).

The dust jacket is blue with letter press in white. A photograph of Roethke by John Deakin appears on the front cover and backstrip. The jacket design is by Robert Laydenfrost, who did the illustrations for *I Am! Says the Lamb*. A biographical note appears on the back cover.

English edition:

The Collected Poems / of / Theodore Roethke / [ornament] */ Faber and Faber / 24 Russell Square / London*

21½ × 14. Published in 1968, at 42s. Issued in burnt orange cloth and stamped in gold on the backstrip. Backstrip: THE / COLLECTED / POEMS / OF / THEODORE / ROETHKE / FABER. All edges trimmed.

Collation: [i]–[282], as follows: [i] half title; [ii] *by Theodore Roethke*; [iii] title page as above; [iv] acknowledgment and copyright; v–xi Contents; [xii] blank, [xiii] Note; [xiv] blank; [1] OPEN HOUSE / [rule] / 1941; [2] blank; 3–274 text; 275–279 *Index of First Lines*; [280–282] blank.

Contents: Identical with the American edition.

2,500 copies were printed and published on May 6, 1968. The following note appears on page 67 but not in the American edition: "This sequence ('The Lost Son,' 'The Long Alley,' 'A Field of Light,' and 'The Shape of the Fire') is continued in *Praise to the End!*, Part II, and concluded with 'O, Thou Opening, O' in *The Waking*."

Dust jacket is green and white with letter press in white and blue. A biographical note appears inside the back flap.

A11 *On the Poet and His Craft*

First American edition:

ON THE POET / AND HIS CRAFT / Selected Prose of Theodore Roethke / [ornament] Edited with an / Introduction by Ralph J. Mills, Jr. / University of Washington Press / Seattle and London, 1965

21½ × 13. Published in June 1965, at $4.95. Issued in black cloth and stamped in gold along the backstrip. Backstrip, reading across and down: [across] MILLS / [along the backstrip in two lines] *On the Poet and His Craft* / SELECTED PROSE OF THEODORE ROETHKE / *Washington*. All edges trimmed; dust jacket.

Collation: [i]–[xvi] + [1]–[160], as follows: [i] half title; [ii] blank; [iii] title page as above; [iv] notice of copyright; v–vii acknowledgments; [viii] blank; ix–x contents; xi–xvi introduction; [1] PART ONE; [2] blank; 3–254 text; [255]–[260] blank.

Contents: PART ONE: "Some Self-Analysis," "An American Poet Introduces Himself and His Poems," "Theodore Roethke," "On 'Identity,' " PART TWO: "Verse in Rehearsal," "Open Letter," "The Teaching Poet," "A Word to the Instructor," "Theodore Roethke Writes . . . ," "How to Write Like Somebody Else," "Some Remarks on Rhythm," PART THREE: "One Ring-Tailed Roarer to Another," "Dylan Thomas: Elegy," "Richard Selig," "Last Class," PART FOUR: *Reviews*, "Five American Poets," "The Poetry of Louise Bogan," EPILOGUE: "A Tirade Turning"   o

The first impression consisted of 6,000 copies.

"A word to the Instructor" (originally written for inclusion in the anthology *Twelve Poets*, edited by Glenn Leggett) appeared first in this volume.

The *Reviews* included: *The Last Look and Other Poems*, by Mark Van Doren; *And Spain Sings: Fifty Loyalist Ballads*, adapted by American poets, edited by M. J. Bernadete and Rolfe Humphries; *The Five-Fold Mesh*, by Ben Belitt; *Concerning the Young*, by Willard Mass; *The Alert*, by Wilfred Gibson; *A Lost Season*, by Roy Fuller; *The Earth Bound*, by Janet Lewis (*see* I, C248, 250, 251, 252, 254, 256, 257).

"Big Wind," "The Buds Now Stretch," "The Dance," "Dolor," "Elegy for Jane," "The Heron," "I Need, I Need," "A Light Breather," and "This Light" are reprinted in this volume; an early version of "Genesis" appears on page 32.

On the Poet and His Craft was selected as the "Notable Book of 1965" by the American Library Association in April 1966 (*see* Biographical Notes 1966).

The dust jacket is green, black, and white with lettering in green and black. A photograph of Roethke by Imogen Cunningham appears on the front cover. Jacket design is by Dianne Weiss. An appreciation appears inside the front and back flap.

American paperback edition:

ON THE POET / AND HIS CRAFT / *Selected Prose of Theodore Roethke* / [ornament] / *Edited with an Introduction by Ralph J. Mills, Jr.* / *University of Washington Press* / *Seattle and London, 1965*

21½ × 13. Published in February 1966 (1965 appears on the title page), at $1.95. Issued in stiff white paper and printed in green and black. A photo of Roethke by Imogen Cunningham appears on the front cover.

Collation and Contents: Identical with the first edition.

The first printing consisted of 4,000 copies; the second printing consisted of 2,000 copies; the third printing consisted of 2,000 copies.

English edition:

This impression appeared in England in 1967, at 37s. It is identical to the American edition and was distributed by the Book Centre Ltd. for the University of Washington Press.

A12 *Selected Letters of Theodore Roethke*
First American edition
[double rule] SELECTED / LETTERS OF / THEODORE ROETHKE [double rule] / EDITED WITH AN INTRODUCTION BY / *Ralph J. Mills, Jr.* / UNIVERSITY OF WASHINGTON PRESS / *Seattle & London*

23½ × 15½. Published in April 1968, at $6.95. Quarter bound in black cloth with green paper over the fore edge and stamped in gold along the backstrip. Front cover: The initials "*TR*" have been stamped in the lower right corner. Backstrip, reading down: [Stamped along the backstrip in two lines] SELECTED LETTERS OF THEODORE ROETHKE / EDITED BY RALPH J. MILLS, JR. UNIVERSITY OF WASHINGTON PRESS [the whole enclosed by a broad gold rule].

Collation: [i]–[xxii] + [1]–[274], as follows: [i] half title; [ii] blank; [iii] title page as above; [iv] notice of copyright; [v] excerpt from "The Waking;" [vi] blank; vii–[viii] Acknowledgments; ix contents; x illustrations; xi–xviii introduction; xix–xxii *A Note on the Edition*; xxi–xxii *Brief Roethke Chronology*; [1] half title; [2] blank; 3–263 text; [264] blank; 265–273 *Index*; [274] blank.

Contents: *The Letters*: 1931–37, 1938–39, 1940–47, 1948–49, 1950–53, 1954–59, 1960–63.

The first impression consisted of 5,000 copies.
    The following collected poems appear in this volume: "To My Sister," "No Bird," "Hurray for Weeds," "Reply to Censure" (2 versions), "On the Road to Woodlawn," "Mid-Country Blow," "Double Feature," "Slow Season," "Judge Not," "The

Lamb," "The Stumbling," and "The Moment." All of the
preceding are early versions except "Judge Not," "The Lamb,"
and "The Moment."

The following uncollected poems appear in this volume (the
titles of untitled poems appear in brackets) : ["The Conqueror"],
"This Curious Light," ["Change"], ["Unessential Truth"],
"More Pure Than Flight," "Exhortation," "The Knowing Heart,"
"Fugitive," "Hay-Fever Lament," "The Bringer of Tidings,"
"The Summons," "Elegy," "Statement," "Coward's Song," "Windy
Weather," "The Victims," "Suburban Lament," "City Limits,"
["Second Shadow"], "Germinal," "Dirge," "The Dancing Man,"
and "The Knowing." "Coward's Song" is listed as unpublished
but appeared in *Opinions on War* (*see* I, B4); "Dirge" ("O What
I say, and without end") is also listed as unpublished but appeared
in the *Hudson Review* (*see* I, C152); "The Knowing" is also
listed as unpublished but appeared in the *New Yorker* (*see* I,
C162).

The following unpublished poems (*see* II, A7) appear first in
this volume (the titles of untitled poems appear in brackets) :
"Evening Eye," "The Tribute," "Difficult Grief," "Song for
Hemingway," ["Words for the Hesitant"] (2 versions),
"Conscience," "The Cure," "Three Poems on F. Prokosch,"
"Agrarian," "The Curious People," ["For the Sake of These"],
"Side-Line Comment," "Suburbia: Michigan," "The Specialist,"
"Pastoral," ["The Desperate"], "Poem," "Rune," ["The
Purgation"], ["Chrysanthemums"], "Gooses," and The Old
Florist's Lament."

The dust jacket is black and white with lettering in white. A
photograph of Roethke appears on the front cover. An appreciation
appears inside the front and back flaps.

English edition:

[double rule] / SELECTED / LETTERS OF / THEO-
DORE ROETHKE / [double rule] / EDITED WITH AN
INTRODUCTION BY / *Ralph J. Mills, Jr.* / FABER
AND FABER / London

21½ × 13½. Published on June 1, 1970, at 60s. Issued
in black cloth over boards and stamped in gold along

the backstrip. Backstrip, reading down: [along the backstrip in two lines] SELECTED LETTERS OF THEODORE ROETHKE / EDITED BY RALPH J. MILLS, JR. / FABER AND FABER [the whole enclosed by a broad gold rule].

Collation: Identical to the American edition.

Contents: This is a reprint of the American edition with the exception of the inclusion of photographs of Roethke by Imogen Cunningham.

This edition consisted of 1,500 copies.

The dust jacket is sepia with letter press in red and black. Biographical and critical notes appear inside the front flap.

A13 *Theodore Roethke: Selected Poems*

THEODORE ROETHKE / SELECTED POEMS / Selected by / BEATRICE ROETHKE / FABER AND FABER / 24 Russell Square / London

18½ × 12½. Published in 1969, at 10s. Issued in stiff white paper and lettered in orchid and black. The cover design is orchid and black. This is a reprint of poems selected from the English edition of *Collected Poems* (*see* I, A10) by Beatrice Roethke. Backstrip, reading down: Theodore Roethke [black] Selected Poems [orchid] FABER [white on a black background]. All edges trimmed.

Collation: [1]–[72], as follows: [1–2] blank; [3] THEO-DORE ROETHKE / *Selected Poems*; [4] other titles by Roethke; [5] title page as above; [6] legal disclaimer, notice of copyright, conditions of sale; 7–8 Contents; 9–71 text; [72] blank.

Contents: "Cuttings," "Cuttings (*later*)," "Child on Top of a Greenhouse," "Weed Puller," "Moss-Gathering," "Big Wind," "Frau Bauman, Frau Schmidt, and Frau

Schwartze," "My Papa's Waltz," "The Lost Son,"
1 *The Flight*," 2 "The Pit," 3 "The Gibber," 4 "The
Return," 5 " 'It was beginning winter,' " "Praise to
the End!," "Elegy for Jane," "Four for Sir John Davies,"
1 *The Dance*," 2 *The Partner*," 3 "The Wraith,"
4 "The Vigil," "The Waking," "The Dream," "All the
Earth, All the Air," "Words for the Wind," "I Knew
a Woman," "The Voice," "She," "The Renewal,"
"Her Becoming," "Fourth Meditation," "The Far Field,"
"The Rose," "The Young Girl," "Her Longing,"
"Light Listened," "The Happy Three," "His Forboding,"
"Wish for a Young Wife," "The Abyss," "Otto," "All
Morning," "Song," "In a Dark Time," "In Evening
Air," "The Sequel," "The Motion," "Infirmity," "The
Decision," "The Marrow," "Once More, the Round"

A14 *Straw for the Fire*

Special edition:

STRAW FOR / THE FIRE / From the Notebooks of /
Theodore Roethke / 1943–63 / [rule] / SELECTED
AND ARRANGED BY DAVID WAGONER / 1972 /
Doubleday & Company, Inc. / GARDEN CITY,
NEW YORK

20½ × 13½. Published in March 1972, at $25.00.
Issued in wine-red cloth and stamped in gold on the cover
and along the backstrip. Front cover: STRAW /
FOR / THE FIRE / [rule] / FROM THE / NOTE-
BOOKS / OF / THEODORE / ROETHKE / 1943–63 /
[rule] / Edited by / David Wagoner. Backstrip, reading
down: [stamped along the backstrip in two lines] STRAW
FOR THE FIRE Edited by / THEODORE ROETHKE
David Wagoner [across the base of the spine] Doubleday.

Collation: [1]–[264], as follows: [1] colophon; [2]
other titles by Roethke; [3] half title; [4] blank; [5] title
page as above; [6] acknowledgment, copyright and
legal disclaimer; [7]–[8] Contents; [9]–14 introduction;
[15] dedication: "To the Memory of Theodore Roethke";
[16] blank; [17] excerpt from a notebook; [18] blank;
[19]–262 text; [263]–[264] blank

Colophon: "This is copy number ——— of a limited
edition of 250 copies."

Contents: Introduction; Straw for the Fire (1953–62);
Poetry: "In the Lap of a Dream [1948–49]," "A Nest
of Light (1948–49)," "The Loveless Provinces (1948–49),"
"All the Semblance," "All the Loss (1948–49)," "The
Stony Garden (1949–50)," "The Wrath of Other Winds
(1949–50)," "In the Bush of Her Bones (1949–50),"
"The Dark Angel (1950–53)," "Love Has Me Haunted
(1950–53)," "The Dance of the One-Legged Man
(1951–53)," "Father-Stem and Mother-Root (1951–53),"
"The Root of the Wind (1951–53)," "Heart, You Have
No House (1951–53)," "The Middle of a Roaring
World (1954–58)," "I Sing Other Wonders (1954–58),"
"Recall This Heaven's Light (1954–58)," "She Took
My Eyes (1954–58)," "The Plain Speech of a Crow
(1954–62)," "In The Large Mind of Love (1954–62),"
"The Things I Steal from Sleep (1954–62)," "Between
the Soul and Flesh (1957)," "The Mire's My Home
(1959–63)," "The Desolation (1959–63)," "My Flesh
Learned to Die (1959–63)," "And Time Slows Down
(1960–63)," "The Thin Cries of the Spirit (1959–63),"
"My Instant of Forever (1959–63)"; Prose: "All My
Lights Go Dark (1943–47)," "The Cat in the Classroom
(1943–47)," "The Turn of the Wheel (1943–47),"

"The Poet's Business (1943–47)," "Words for Young Writers (1948–49)," "The Proverbs of Purgatory (1948–49)," "I Teach Out of Love (1949–53)," "First Class (1950–53)," "The Right to Say Maybe (1948–53)," "The Hammer's Knowledge (1954–58)," "From Roethke to Goethe (1954–58)," "The Teaching of Poetry (1954–58)," "These Exasperations (1954–58)," "A Psychic Janitor (1959–63)," "The Beautiful Disorder (1954–63)"

The following excerpts from the notebooks appeared first in *Straw for the Fire*: "Love Has Me Haunted (1950–53)," "The Middle of a Roaring World (1954–58)," "I Sing Other Wonders (1954–58)," "Recall This Heaven's Light (1954–58)," "She Took My Eyes (1954–58)," "Between the Soul and Flesh (1957)," "The Mire's My Home (1959–63)," "The Desolation (1959–63)," "My Flesh Learned to Die (1959–63)," "And Time Slows Down (1960–63)," "The Thin Cries of the Spirit (1959–63)," "My Instant of Forever (1959–63)," "All My Lights Go Dark (1943–47)," "The Cat in the Classroom (1943–57)," "The Turn of the Wheel (1943–47)," "The Hammer's Knowledge (1954–58)," "From Roethke to Goethe (1954–58)," "The Teaching of Poetry (1954–58)," "These Exasperations (1954–58)," "A Psychic Janitor (1959–63)." For further information, *see* 1, C223–244 and II, A1, 7.

This edition was issued in a sepia slipcase with letter press in gray, black and red.

Trade edition:

STRAW FOR / THE FIRE / From the Notebooks of / Theodore Roethke / 1943–63 / [rule] */ SELECTED AND ARRANGED BY / DAVID WAGONER /* 1972 */ Doubleday & Company, Inc. / Garden City, New York*

20½ × 13½. Published in March 1972, at $7.95. Issued in wine-red cloth and stamped in gold on the cover and along the backstrip. Front cover: STRAW / FOR / THE

FIRE / [rule] FROM THE / NOTEBOOKS / OF / THEODORE / ROETHKE / 1943–63 / [rule] / Edited by / David Wagoner. Backstrip, reading down: [stamped along the backstrip in two lines] STRAW FOR THE FIRE Edited by / THEODORE ROETHKE David Wagoner [across the base of the spine] Doubleday.

Collation: [1]–[264], as follows: [1] blank; [2] other titles by Roethke; [3] half title; [4] blank; [5] title page as above; [6] acknowledgment, copyright and legal disclaimer; 7–8 Contents; [9]–14 introduction; [15] dedication: "To the Memory of Theodore Roethke"; [16] blank; [17] excerpt from a notebook; [18] blank; [19]–262 text; [263]–[264] blank.

Contents: Identical to the special edition.

B Contributions to Books, Broadsides, and Pamphlets

This section lists in books, broadsides, and pamphlets the first appearances of Roethke's poetry and prose. In those instances where a poem is listed which is not a first appearance, the criteria for inclusion in this section are dependent on the unique or special nature of the item.

A comprehensive list of anthology appearances of Roethke's poetry appears in John William Matheson's "Theodore Roethke: A Bibliography," which was completed in 1958 (*see* II, G4). The University of Washington Reference Department has also maintained a bibliography listing anthology appearances since 1958.

Poetry

B1 *The Heron*

THE HERON / BY / THEODORE ROETHKE / ILLUSTRATED AND PRINTED / BY / PETAH CULLINGHAM

24½ × 16½. [1]–[12]. No date of publication or price. Issued in gray paper and lettered in black on the front cover. Front cover: THE HERON / [ornament] / THEODORE ROETHKE. Top and fore edges trimmed; bottom edge untrimmed. This is apparently a limited printing (perhaps less than ten copies) of Roethke's poem "The Heron" with three block prints in white, green, and brown.

Two copies of this pamphlet (one inscribed: "To Mr. Roethke from Petah Cullingham") are located at the University of Washington Manuscripts Division.

B2 *Trial Balances*

[a double rule and a long single rule below] *TRIAL BALANCES* / *Edited by* / Ann Winslow / NEW YORK / THE MACMILLAN COMPANY / 1935 [a long single rule and a double rule below]

21½ × 14¾. [i]–[xvi] + [1]–[225]. Published in October 1935, at $2.00 [8s 6d in England, $3.00 in Toronto]. Issued in blue cloth and stamped in silver on the front cover and backstrip. Backstrip, reading across: [double rule] / TRIAL BALANCES / [double rule]/ EDITED BY / ANN WINSLOW / MACMILLAN / [ornament]. Front cover: AN ANTHOLOGY OF NEW POETRY / TRIAL BALANCES [title enclosed in double, rectangular rule]. Top and bottom pages trimmed; fore edges untrimmed; dust jacket.

Contents: "Epidermal Macabre," "Silence," "Genius," "Prayer," "Death-piece," "Fugitive," "Essay"

"Fugitive (Her flesh is quick; a furious vein)" appeared first in *Trial Balances*, pages 134–137. Roethke's poetry appears with the title "Stitched on Bone" with critical remarks by Louise Bogan. There is biographical note on page 216. This is the first appearance of Roethke's poetry in any book. For his comment on this volume, *see* the *Selected Letters of Theodore Roethke*, p. 31.
The dust jacket is silver with blue lettering.

B3 *New Michigan Verse*

NEW / *MICHIGAN VERSE* / *Edited by* / CARL EDWIN BURKLUND / With *a foreword by* LOUIS UNTERMEYER / ANN ARBOR / UNIVERSITY OF MICHIGAN PRESS / 1940

23 × 15¼. [i]–[xv] + [1]–[114]. Published in 1940, at $2.00. Quarter bound in green cloth and brown

paper over the fore edge. The cover and green backstrip are stamped in gold. Backstrip, reading across: *NEW* / *MICHIGAN* / *VERSE* / UNIVERSITY / OF MICHIGAN / PRESS. Front cover: [on green] *NEW* / [on brown] *MICHIGAN* / *VERSE*. All edges trimmed; dust jacket.

Contents: "The Light Comes Brighter," "Highway: Michigan," "The Heron," "Feud," " 'Long Live the Weeds'—(Hopkins)," "Autumnal" ("The ribs of leaves lie in the dust"), "No Bird," "To My Sister," "Interlude," "Slow Season"

"Autumnal" is an early version of section II of "The Coming of the Cold," which appeared in *Open House*. Two boxed copies of this volume in mint condition are located with Roethke's library in storage in Seattle.
The dust jacket is green with black lettering.

B4 *Opinions on War*

OPINIONS [dot] *ON* [dot] *WAR*— / ROCKWELL KENT — / PROF. THEODORE ROETHKE — / DICK O'DONNEL — / PROF. A. H. REEDE — / PROF. WM. WERNER — / [with an illustration by R. B. Hurme of a policeman holding a scroll with the words: "summons for American youth" and two graves with headstones engraved with: "Joe Q. Sucker Killed in action 1917" and "Joe Q. Sucker Jr. Killed in action 1941"]

11 × 8. 1–6. Published in April 1941 at Pennsylvania State College. The issue consisted of a large number of mimeographed sheets. The cover, as shown above, serves as the title page.

Contents: "Coward's Song (For Lady ——— Endorser of Cold Cream)"

This is the first appearance of this poem; it was reprinted in the *Selected Letters of Theodore Roethke* on pages 62–63 (the poem is erroneously labeled "Unpublished").

A copy of this circular is located at Pennsylvania State University in the Penn State Collection (*see* II, A7, p. 64).

Professor A. H. Reede of Pennsylvania State University notes the following in his Diary on April 5, 1941: "B. W. William Werner, who was head of the American literature at Penn State and a close friend of Roethke's, asked if the text of Social Problems Club address could be used in a mimeographed circular which also includes a poem by Ted Roethke and an article of his own. Bill Werner was the moving spirit."

B5 *New World Writings II*

NEW / WORLD / WRITING / SECOND MENTOR SELECTION / PUBLISHED BY [Publisher's device] / THE NEW AMERICAN LIBRARY

18 × 10½. [1]–[352]. Published in 1952, at 50¢. Issued in stiff paper in black, orange, white, and blue; printed in red, blue, white, and black on the front cover and backstrip. The front cover carries essentially the same information as the title page above except it lists some of the contributors. All edges trimmed.

Contents: "The Yak," "The Boy and the Bush," "Myrtle," "Myrtle's Cousin," "Goo-Girl"

Roethke's poems appear with the collective title "Poems for Children." There is a biographical note on page 223. This is the first appearance of these poems.

A typescript of poems for this volume is located at the University of Washington Manuscripts Division.

B6 *New Poems by American Poets*

NEW / POEMS / By American Poets / [rule] / Edited by ROLFE HUMPHRIES / BALLANTINE BOOKS [dot] NEW YORK [dot] 1953

19½ × 13. [i]–[xx] + 1–[180]. Published in 1953, at $2.00. Issued in green cloth and lettered in yellow along

the front cover and backstrip. Front Cover: NEW POEMS /
[rule] / By American Poets. Backstrip, reading down:
NEW POEMS [slash] Bq American Poets [publisher's
device]. All edges trimmed; dust jacket.

Contents: "Song for the Squeeze-Box," "Frau Schwartze
(Scene: A Greenhouse in my Childhood)," "The Dance,"
"The Partner," "The Sloth"

"Song for the Squeeze-Box" appeared first in this volume. There is
a biographical note on page 127. A minor textual error appears in
the last line of "The Sloth."
    This edition also appeared in paperback at 35¢. The stiff paper
cover is gold, black, blue, and white and carries the following
note: "This magnificent collection represents the best poetry being
written in American today. Most of these poems have never been
published anywhere before."
    The dust jacket is yellow, blue, and black with lettering in black
and white.

B7 *New World Writing IV*
    NEW / WORLD WRITING / FOURTH MENTOR
    SELECTION / PUBLISHED BY [publisher's device] / THE
    NEW AMERICAN LIBRARY

18 × 10½. [1]–[320]. Published in 1953, at 50¢. Issued
in stiff paper of orange, white, gold, purple, and black,
and lettered in black, white, and red. The front cover
carries essentially the same information as the title page
above except it lists some of the contributors. The
backstrip is orange and is lettered in white and black.
Backstrip, reading down and across: [in black and across]
Ms 96 / [in white and down] NEW WORLD WRITING
[dash] FOURTH MENTOR SELECTION [in black].
All edges trimmed.

Contents: "The Vigil" and "The Waking" appear for the
first time in this volume.

Roethke comments on a textual error in "The Vigil" on page 196 of the *Selected Letters of Theodore Roethke*. "The Waking" was reprinted from this volume in the *New York Times Book Review*, LVI (September 27, 1953), 2 (*see* I. B18).

B8 *The Pocket Book of Modern Verse*

THE POCKET BOOK OF / *Modern Verse* / [a series of dots] / ENGLISH AND AMERICAN POETRY OF / THE LAST HUNDRED YEARS FROM / WALT WHITMAN TO DYLAN THOMAS / REVISED EDITION / EDITED BY / *Oscar Williams* / [publisher's device] / WASHINGTON SQUARE PRESS, INC. [dot] NEW YORK

16½ × 10½. [1]–[640]. Published in 1958 (first edition printed in February 1954), at 60¢. Issued in green stiff paper. The front cover is in green and tan and is lettered in white and black. Photos of Whitman, Yeats, Frost, Hardy, Millay, and Thomas appear below the title. The front cover carries essentially the same information as the title page above except those items already noted above. The backstrip is green and is lettered in black and white. Backstrip, reading down: [in black and across] 60¢ / [in white and down] A POCKET BOOK OF MODERN VERSE [ornament in tan and white] / [in black and across] EDITED BY / [in white and across] *Oscar Williams* / [in black and across] W [dot] 554 / [publisher's device]. All edges trimmed.

Contents: "Elegy for Jane (My student, thrown by a horse)," "Epidermal Macabre," "Pipling"

"Pipling" appeared first in the first edition of this volume. The following note regarding the first edition appears on page 1: "*The Pocket Book of Modern Verse* was published in 1954 in a Cardinal Giant edition and sold nearly 250,000 copies. It has now be revised to include an even more generous representation of contemporary poetry and will hereafter be published in a Washington Square Press edition."

B9 *7 Arts*

7 ARTS / NUMBER 3 / edited by / FERNANDO PUMA / [left half of page] DANCE / MUSIC / THEATRE / PAINTING / SCULPTURE / LITERATURE / ARCHITECTURE / [publisher's device] THE FALCON'S WING PRESS / INDIAN HILLS COLORADO

18½ × 12½. [i]–[xvi] + [1]–[238]. Published in the spring of 1955, at 95¢. Issued in stiff paper cover in light blue and lettered in black, blue, and maroon. The front cover carries essentially the same information as the title page, a partial list of contributors, and a photograph of one of the art objects. Backstrip, reading across: [publisher's device] / 95¢ / 7 /ARTS / No. 3 / [in two lines reading down] edited by Fernando Puma / [publisher's device] / FALCON'S / WING PRESS. All edges trimmed.

Contents: "A Rouse for Stevens (To be Sung in a Young Poet's Saloon)"

"A Rouse for Stevens" appeared first in this volume on page 117. The edition includes forty-eight reproductions of fine art. A biographical note appears on page 115. For Roethke's comment on the poem and *7 Arts, see* I, A12, p. 228.

A copy is located at the University of Washington Manuscript Division.

B10 *Poems in Folio*

POEMS IN FOLIO [ornament] / *THE EXORCISM by* THEODORE ROETHKE / [a comment on the poem by Roethke] / [a biographical note] / [colophon as below] / VOL. 1 NO. 9 COPYRIGHT 1957, POEMS IN FOLIO BOX 448, SAN FRANCISCO [the above appears on a 19½ × 27½ broadside, preceding the text of "The Exorcism," which constitutes a title page].

31 × 45½. Unpaginated by No. 9 in the series. Published in 1957. Issued as part of a broadside series that includes several authors. All pages trimmed unevenly.

Colophon: "*1150 copies have been printed and decorated with a woodcut initial / by Mallette Dean at Fairfax, California. The Type is Goudy 30 / and American Uncial initials. 150 copies on mould made Arches paper, are signed and numbered by the poet.*"

Contents: "The Exorcism"

The broadside includes the following introduction by Roethke [The "T" is a woodcut in gray and black extending down the page]: "THE EXORCISM is one of several poems, short and longish. / I have written on the general theme of flight and the dissociation of / personality that can occur in states of terror. I make no apologies for / this. In these times, some of us have to run more than once; and what / happens is by no means always the same. What *is* the same, I suppose, / is the urgency, the sense of obsessiveness which should mark any hon- / est record or imaginative creation based on such experience. Frankly, / it astonishes me that editors have chosen to print, and, presumably, / some readers to read, poems of this sort. I take this, not as a preverse / or maschoistic delight on the part of a limited body of readers, but rather as a sign of spiritual health: A willingness to take at least a look—if not Hardy's 'full look'—at the worst."
    Copies are located at the University of Washington (UWSC) and Ohio State University.

B11 *New Poems by American Poets* ♯2
    NEW / POEMS / BY AMERICAN POETS */ ♯2 / Edited by Rolfe Humphries /* BALLANTINE BOOKS [dot] New York [dot] 1957

18½ × 11½. [1]–[179]. Published in 1957. Issued in orange, blue, and white stiff paper; lettered in black, blue on white, and white on blue on front cover and backstrip.

Backstrip, reading down: NEW POEMS [slash] By
American Poets #2 [publisher's device]. All edges trimmed.

Contents: "I Knew a Woman," "The Mistake," "The
Sensualists," " 'The Shimmer of Evil' "

"The Mistake" appeared first in this volume.

B12 *Landmarks and Voyages*

*LANDMARKS / AND/ VOYAGES / Poetry Supplement
/ edited by / Vernon Watkins / for the Poetry Book
Society / Christmas 1957 / Poetry Book Society Ltd /* 4 St
James' Square / London SW I

19¾ × 13½. Unpaginated, [1]–[12]. Published during
Christmas 1957. Front cover appears as above. All
pages trimmed.

Contents: "Plaint"

"Plaint" appears first in this pamphlet; it also appeared in the
Northwestern University Tri-Quarterly Review, I (Fall 1958), 24.
The following appears on the back cover: *John Roberts Press,
Limited / London.*

B13 *Poets and the Past*

*POETS AND THE PAST / An Anthology of Poems, and
objects of art of / the pre-Columbian past /* EDITED
BY DORE ASHTON / PHOTOGRAPHS BY LEE BOLTIN /
[initials of gallery] / *André Emmerich Gallery
/ New York*

24¼ × 17½. [1]–[63]. Published in 1959, at $5.00 for
copies LI–1500 and $50.00 for copies I–L. Quarter bound in
black cloth with white textured cover. Stamped in white
along the back backstrip. Backstrip, reading down: POETS
AND THE PAST [publisher's device]. All edges
trimmed; dust jacket.

Colophon: "Of this volume fifteen hundred copies have been made. The first fifty / copies, containing autographs of contributing poets, have been espe- / cially bound and are numbered I through L. The engravings are by Publicity Engravers of Baltimore: The Com- / position, in English Monotype Wallbaum, and the press work are / by Clarke and Way at The Thistle Press in New York; format by / Bert Clarke."

Contents: "The Swan"

The poem appears opposite an engraving of the "Mammalion Bowl," Chupicuaro 1000–500 B.C. "The Swan" was especially written for inclusion in this volume but appeared first in *Words for the Wind* (*see* I, A5); it also appeared in the *New Statesman* [London], LVIII (July 4, 1959), 20.

The dust jacket is black, white, and gray and includes an engraving and list of contributors on the front cover. The following note appears on the inside back flap: "Autographs of each of the contributing poets / are included in the first fifty copies of this book. These copies, specially bound and containing the autographs of each poet on indi- / vidual pages, are numbered from I to L. / They are priced at fifty dollars."

B14 *Journeys*

JOURNEYS / A NEW POEM / by / Theodore Roethke / Presented at the 1961 ART FESTIVAL/ DEPAUW UNIVERSITY

$21\frac{1}{4}$ × 14. Unpaginated, [1]–[8]. Published May 3, 1961. No price given. Issued in stiff white paper with end flaps and lettered in black on the front cover. Front cover: *Journeys* / [long vertical rule] / THEODORE / ROETHKE. All edges trimmed.

Contents: "Journeys"

"Journeys" appeared first in this program; it was later retitled "The Far Field" and appeared in the *Sewanee Review* (*see* I,

C184). "Journeys" was also recorded for the BBC on February 13, 1961.

A biographical note and presentation information appear on page 8. Presentation information: " 'Journeys' is the third commissioned poem / in the DePauw Arts Festival series. Poets who / previously have presented commissioned poems / to the University are W. H. Auden (1958) and Richard Wilbur (1959)." *See also* II, B174.

Copies are located at the University of Washington Manuscripts Division and DePauw University.

B15 *Ten Poets*

TEN POETS / [black rule under the title] / [yellow ornament] / Seattle: 1962

30 × 15½. Unpaginated, [1]–[28]. Published in 1962, at $5.00 for copies 38–537 and $25.00 for copies 1–37. Issued in tweedweave and lettered in black on the front cover: [gold ornament] / *TEN POETS* / [rule] / SEATTLE: 1962 / [orange ornament]. All edges trimmed.

Colophon: This is of a limited edition of 537 copies, designed by Diana Bower and handset in Goudy's / Italian old style type by Paul Hayden Duensign, and / printed on Curtis Tweedweaver text. / Copies 1 to 37 have been specially bound and decorated, and / signed by the poet, / the designer and the printer. The edition / is sold for the benefit of the / Seattle Peace Information Center Fund.

Contents: "Once More, the Round"

"Once More, the Round" appeared first in this volume on page [23]; it also appeared in *Harper's Bazaar*, CCXXV (January 1963), 117.

The special editions are not specially bound, but they do have a circular pattern of ten colored ornaments enclosing the title (as

above) on the front cover. Roethke's signature appears with others on page [27].
Copies of both editions are located at the University of Washington Manuscripts Division and Special Collections Division.

B16 *Poetry in Crystal*

[red ornament] / [in black] POETRY IN CRYSTAL / [in red] BY STEUBEN GLASS / [black ornament]

26¾ × 17½. [1]–[86]. Published in 1963, at $5.00. Issued in red-brown cloth and stamped in gold on the front cover and backstrip. Front Cover: *POETRY / IN / CRYSTAL*. Backstrip, reading down: POETRY IN CRYSTAL. All edges trimmed; dust jacket.

Contents: "The Victorians"

"The Victorians" was especially written for this volume and appears on page 50; a glass design by George Thompson, with engravings by Don Wier, appears on page 51. A biographical note appears on page 80 and includes the following comment: "One of his great interests is in the oral presentation of poetry." The volume was printed by the Spiral Press with plates by the Meriden Gravure Co.
"The Victorians" was reprinted in the *Saturday Review*, XLVI (April 27, 1963), 15 (in an ad announcing the Steuben Collection Exhibition in New York) and in *The Angus* [Seattle], LXXI (March 20, 1964), 6. *See also*: "Roethke Work in Steuben Collection," *Seattle Post-Intelligencer*, March 1, 1964 (UWSC); "Crystal Forms on Display," *Centre Daily Times*, LXIX (July 28, 1967), 11 (PSC).

Prose

B17 *Mid-Century American Poets*

EDITED *by* JOHN CIARDI / *Mid-century / American / Poets* / [dot] / [rule] / *Twayne Publishers, Inc. New York* 4 [the whole surrounded by a double black rule]

19½ × 13½. [i]–[xxxvi] + [1]–300. Published in December 1949 [copyright 1950], at $4.00. Issued in blue

cloth and stamped in green on the front cover and backstrip.
Front cover. MID-CENTURY / AMERICAN / POETS.
Backstrip, reading down: MID-CENTURY / AMERICAN
POETS. All edges trimmed; dust jacket.

Contents: "Open Letter"

"Open Letter" appeared first in this volume on pages 67–72.
"The Lost Son," "The Shape of the Fire," "Child on Top of a
Greenhouse," "Vernal Sentiment," "Academic," and "My Papa's
Waltz" also appeared in this volume; there is a biographical note
on page 67. See the *Selected Letters of Theodore Roethke*,
pp. 139, 150–151, 153–154, 156–160.

A manuscript of "Open Letter" and the poems is located at
Wayne State University; two galleys are located at the University
of Washington Manuscripts Division.

The dust jacket is blue and white with white and blue lettering.

B18 *New World Writing IV*

NEW / WORLD / WRITING / FOURTH MENTOR SELEC-
TION / PUBLISHED BY [publisher's device] / THE AMERICAN
LIBRARY

18 × 10½. [1]–[320]. Published in 1953, at 50¢. Issued
in orange, white, gold, purple, and black stiff paper and
lettered in black, white, and red. The front cover carries
essentially the same information as the title page above
except it lists some of the contributors. The orange
backstrip is lettered in white and black. Backstrip, reading
down and across: [in black and across] MS 96 / [in white
and down] NEW WORLD WRITING [dash] fourth
mentor selection [in black].

Contents: "Five American Poets"

"Five American Poets" appeared first in this volume (*see* I, 87).

B19 *Twentieth Century Authors*

TWENTIETH CENTURY / AUTHORS / FIRST SUP-
PLEMENT / A Biographical Dictionary of Modern

Literature / *Edited by* / Stanley J. Kunitz / *Assistant Editor*
VINETA COLBY / [publisher's device] / NEW YORK / THE
N. W. WILSON COMPANY / NINETEEN HUNDRED FIFTY-FIVE

25 × 17¼. [1]–vii + 1–1142. Published in 1955, at $8.00.
Issued in black cloth and stamped in gold on the backstrip.
Backstrip, reading across: TWENTIETH / CENTURY /
AUTHORS / [gold rule] / A BIOGRAPHICAL DICTIONARY /
[gold rule] / *First Supplement* / KUNITZ / THE H. W.
WILSON / COMPANY. All edges trimmed; dust jacket.

Contents: "Theodore Roethke"

"Theodore Roethke" appeared first in this volume on pages
837–838. A biographical note appears on page 838.

B20 *Poems in Folio*
See B10.

B21 *New World Writing #19*
19 / NEW WORLD WRITING / [publisher's device] / J.
B. LIPPINCOTT COMPANY / *Philadelphia & New York*

21¼ × 13½. 1–224. Published in 1961 at $1.65. Issued in
red and tan stiff paper and lettered in black and white on
the front cover and backstrip. The front cover carries
essentially the same information as the title page as well as
a list of contributors. Backstrip, reading down: [in black]
KB33 / [in white] New World Writing. 19 / [in black]
Keystone / Books / [publisher's device] / LIPPINCOTT.
All edges trimmed.

Contents: "Theodore Roethke Comment"

"Theodore Roethke Comment" appeared first in this volume on
pages 214–219. "In a Dark Time" also appeared in this volume on
pages 190–191. (*See* II, C72, 103, 109.)

B22 *Poet's Choice*

POET'S / CHOICE / [ornament] / EDITED BY / Paul Engle
and Joseph Langland / [publisher's device] / THE DIAL
PRESS NEW YORK 1962

23 × 15½. 1–303. Published in 1962, at $6.95. Issued in
red cloth and stamped in gold on the backstrip. Backstrip,
reading down; [ornament] / POET'S CHOICE /
[ornament] / EDITED BY / ENGLE / AND /
LANGLAND / [ornament] / [publisher's device] /
DIAL. All edges trimmed; dust jacket.

Contents: Untitled introduction to "Words for the Wind"

This introduction appeared first in this volume on pages 99–100.
"Words for the Wind" also appeared on pages 96–99.
   The dust jacket is off-white and lettered in red and black. A
facsimile of Roethke's signature appears on the back of the dust
jacket. The following comment appears on the front cover:
"103 of the Greatest Living Poets Choose / Their Favorite Poem
from Their Own Work / and Give the Reason for Their Choice."

B23 *Grooves in the Wind*

GROOVES IN THE WIND / C. A. TRYPANIS / CHILMARK
PRESS [publisher's device] NEW YORK

22 × 14. [i]–[xii] + 1–62. Published in 1964, at $3.50.
Quarter bound in gray cloth with gray and white paper over
the fore edge and stamped in gold along the backstrip.
Backstrip, reading down: C. A. TRYPANIS *GROOVES IN
THE WIND* [publisher's device] CHILMARK PRESS. All
edges trimmed; dust jacket.

An introduction by Roethke for *Grooves in the Wind* was intended
for this edition but did not appear because of Roethke's sudden
death in 1963; however, an excerpt from the introduction does
appear near the bottom of the front of the jacket and on the inside
of the front flap as follows: "He [Trypanis] is a poet close to

greatness at times . . . the master of what I call the plain style in the English language. He writes poems which are cut down to the bare bones of language. The American young should read, cherish, and imitate Mr. Trypanis; I know I have done just this. He is not merely a linear poet; he is capable—miraculous as it may seem—of song." Allan Seager, *The Glass House*, page 285, incorrectly states that the introduction had been published. For further information concerning the text of the introduction, *see* II, A7, p. 108.

The dust jacket is gray and white with letter press in black.

B24 *The Glass House*

THE GLASS HOUSE / The Life of Theodore Roethke / BY ALLAN SEAGER / MCGRAW-HILL BOOK COMPNY / New York Toronto London Sydney

22½ X 15. [i]–[xiv] + 1–[306]. Published in the fall of 1968, at $7.95. Issued in green cloth and stamped in gold along the backstrip. Backstrip, reading across and down: [across] ALLAN / SEAGER / [top line down] THE GLASS *HOUSE* / [bottom line down] *The Life of Theodore Roethke* / [accross] MCGRAW-HILL. All edges trimmed; dust jacket.

Contents: "Fish Tail," "Papa," "Pilot Material"

"Fish Tail," "Papa," and "Pilot Material" first appeared in this volume on pages 23–24, 24–26, and 40–41, respectively. "Method," "The Premonition," "The Question," "Side-Line Comment," "Difficult Grief," "To Darkness," and "Words in a Violent Ward" also appeared in this volume on pages 66, 129, 122, 121, 164, 166, and 181, respectively. 'The Question," "Side-Line Comment," and "Difficult Grief" appeared in the *Selected Letters of Theodore Roethke*, which was published in the spring of 1968.

The Allan Seager Papers in The Bancroft Library, University of California, Berkeley, have photocopies of various drafts, printer's copy, galleys, and corrected galleys of *The Glass House*.

The dust jacket is black, with a photo of Roethke by Mary Randlett on the front cover, and is lettered in white and green.

Notebook Excerpts

B25 *The Wild Cascades*

The / *Wild Cascades* / *By* HARVEY MANNING /
Photographs by ANSEL ADAMS, PHILIP HYDE / DAVID
SIMONS, BOB AND IRA SPRING, / CLYDE THOMAS, JOHN
WARTH, AND OTHERS / WITH LINES FROM THEODORE
ROETHKE / FOREWORD BY WILLIAM O. DOUGLAS / EDITED
BY DAVID BROWER / SIERRA CLUB [dot] SAN FRANCISCO

23¾ X 16½. 1–160. Published in 1965, at $3.95. Issued in
stiff white paper with a color photograph by Philip Hyde
of Lake Ann on the front cover: [publisher's device]
A SIERRA CLUB [slash] BALLANTINE BOOK 0161 $3.95 /
color photograph of Lake Ann / *The Wild Cascades* /
FORGOTTEN PARKLAND. Blackstrip, reading down:
[publisher's device] THE WILD 01620 $3.95 / CASCADES.
All edges trimmed.

Contents: Excerpts from "The Things I Steal from Sleep,"
"The Plain Speech of a Crow," "Straw for the Fire"

This is the first appearance of the notebook excerpts. Excerpts from
the following poems appear in this volume: "Dolor," "The Far
Field," "The Longing," "A Walk in Late Summer," "The Abyss,"
"A Field of Light," "The Sequel," "Shape of the Fire," "I Cry,
Love! Love!," "Words for the Wind," "The Long Waters,"
"Carnations," "What Can I Tell My Bones?," "The Rose," "The
Pike," and "The Pure Fury." "The Harsh Country," "The Cycle,"
"Once More, the Round," "The Right Thing," "The
Manifestation," "A Light Breather," "Moss-Gathering," "Cuttings
(*later*)," and "The Visitant" are complete. Excerpts from the
following prose pieces also appear in this volume: "Some
Self-Analysis" and "On 'Identity.'" An acknowledgment regarding
the use of Roethke's works appears on page 14.

C Contributions to Periodicals

This section lists chronologically the first appearances of Roethke's poetry, as well as certain prose pieces, in periodicals; however, some early appearances in England may yet remain undiscovered. Roethke sent many poems to Dorothy Gordon, who attempted to market them to various periodicals in England during 1933 and 1934. According to Constantine FitzGibbon, one or more of these poems (possibly "Difficult Grief") appeared in "Poets' Corner" in the *Sunday Referee* in 1934 or 1935 (*see* II, B13). Efforts on the behalf of this researcher to identify definitely the poem and poems were not fruitful.

Subsequent publication of variant versions is noted in this listing whenever identifiable. Reprints (in periodicals and books) are included when the poem was published in both the United States and England (a few items from Canadian and Irish periodicals also appear) and when they have special significance. Generally, the poems appeared first in the United States, but when that pattern is interrupted the English appearance is cited first.

Poetry

1930
C1 "Lost" (so close were we), "Method, To Darkness"
   The Harp, VI (May–June 1930), 8.

1931
C2 "The Conqueror"
   Commonweal, XIV (October 7, 1931), 544.

1932

C3 "Silence"
New Republic, LXIX (January 20, 1932), 263.

C4 "Second Version"
Sewanee Review, XL (January–March 1932), 88.

C5 "Epidermal Macabre"
Saturday Review of Literature, VIII (May 7, 1932), 709.
Reprinted: *The Exile's Anthology*, ed. H. Neville and Harry
Roskolenko. Prairie City, Illinois: Exile's Press, 1940, pp. 64–66.

C6 "Bound," "Fugitive" (The supple virtue of her mind)
Poetry, XL (September 1932), 316–317.

1933

C7 "The Buds Now Stretch"
The Adelphi [London], n.s. VI (April 1933), 9.
Untitled in this appearance.
New York Times, LXXXVIII (November 9, 1938), 22.

1934

C8 "Genius"
Atlantic, CLII (May 1934), 550.

C9 "Death Piece"
Nation, CXXXVIII (May 2, 1934), 511.

C10 "To My Sister"
The Adelphi [London], n.s. VIII (August 1934), 300.

C11 "Autumnal" (The old brook dies within its bed)
The Adelphi [London], n.s. VIII (September 1934), 409.

C12 "Essay," "Exhortation," "I Sought a Measure," "The
Knowing Heart," "Now We the Two," "Prepare Thyself
for Change," "Some Day I'll Step," "This Light" (This
light the very flush of spring; it is innocent and warm)
American Poetry Journal, XVII (November 1934), 3–6.
"This Light" was reprinted in *The Poet's Work*, ed. John Holmes.
New York: Oxford University Press, 1939.

C13 "No Bird"
Atlantic, CLIV (November 1934), 543.

1935
C14 "Prayer"
New Republic, LXXXIII (July 10, 1935), 242.
C15 "Feud"
New Republic, LXXXIV (September 11, 1935), 123.

1936
C16 "Strange Distortion" ["Open House"]
Scribner's Magazine, XCIX (May 1936), 311.
C17 "Genesis"
Nation, CXLII (June 24, 1936), 807.
An early version appeared in *Portfolio* (*see* I, C211) and in *On the Poet and His Craft*, p. 32.
C18 " 'Long Live the Weeds' "
Poetry, XLVIII (July 1936), 203.

1937
C19 "In the Time of Change"
Atlantic, CLIX (January 1937), 47.
Roethke had a reprint of this made into a New Year's card.
Reprinted: *The Days We Celebrate*, comp. and ed. Robert Haven Schauffler. New York: Dodd, Mead and Company, 1940.
C20 "Lines upon Leaving a Sanitarium"
New Yorker, XIII (March 13, 1937), 30.
C21 "Meditation in Hydrotherapy"
New Yorker, XIII (May 15, 1937), 87.
C22 "Hay-Fever Lament"
New Yorker, XIII (August 14, 1937), 54.
Woman's Journal [London], June 1938, p. 10.
Initialed "T.R."
C23 "Prayer before Study"
New Yorker, XIII (August 28, 1937), 45.

C24 "Autumnal" (The ribs of leaves lie in the dust), "The Heron"
New Republic, XCII (September 1, 1937), 96.

C25 "Reply to Censure"
Poetry, LI (November 1937), 80.

C26 "Statement"
Commonweal, XXVII (December 3, 1937), 261.

C27 "In Praise of Prairie"
New Republic, XCIII (December 22, 1937), 203.

1938

C28 "Interlude"
New Republic, XCIII (February 2, 1938), 361.

C29 "Sign Though No Sign"
Sewanee Review, XLVI (January–March 1938), 3.

C30 "The Light Comes Brighter"
Atlantic, CLXI (March 1938), 340.

C31 "The Adamant"
New York Times, LXXXVII (March 22, 1938), 20.

C32 "Verse with Allusions"
Atlantic, CLXI (May 1938), 700.

C33 "The Bat"
New Republic, XCV (May 18, 1938), 51.

C34 "The Unextinguished"
Saturday Review of Literature, XVIII (July 23, 1938), 7.

C35 "Autumnal" (The late peach yields a subtle musk)
Christian Science Monitor, XXX (September 8, 1938), 9.

C36 "The Victims"
Twentieth Century Verse [London], n.s. 12–13 (October 1938), pp. 105–106.

C37 "Against Disaster," "The Bringer of Tidings," "The Pause," "Prognosis," "The Reckoning," "The Signals," "The Summons"
Poetry, LIII (December 1938), 138–143.

62

1939

C38 "For an Amorous Lady"
New Yorker, XIV (January 7, 1939), 25.

C39 "Random Political Reflections"
New Republic, XCVIII (March 1, 1939), 98.

C40 "Academic"
New Verse [London], n.s. I (May 1939), 41.
Partisan Review, VI (Winter 1939), 39.
A variation of the last stanza appeared in *West Coast Review* (*see* II, B12) and was erroneously described as a satire on Dylan Thomas.

C41 "The Auction"
Poetry, LIV (May 1939), 69.

C42 "Summer Wind"
New Yorker, XV (July 22, 1939), 58.

C43 "Idyll"
New Yorker, XV (August 26, 1939), 51.

C44 "After Loss"
New York Times, LXXXIX (September 27, 1939), 24.

C45 "Ballad of the Clairvoyant Widow"
Partisan Review, VI (Fall 1939), 18–19.
Roethke had a reprint of this appearance made into a Christmas card.

C46 "Slow Season"
Yale Review, n.s. XXIX (Autumn 1939), 89.

C47 "Poetaster"
New Republic, CI (November 29, 1939), 89.

C48 "Praise"
New Republic, CI (December 20, 1939), 254.

1940

C49 "Lull"
New Republic, CII (February 12, 1940), 209.

C50 "Vernal Sentiment"
New Yorker, XVI (March 30, 1940), 57.
C51 "Orders for the Day"
Poetry, LVI (May 1940), 75.
C52 "The Search"
American Prefaces, V (May 6, 1940), 118.
C53 "Highway: Michigan"
New Republic, CII (May 6, 1940), 608.
C54 "Night Journey"
New Yorker, XVI (June 8, 1940), 34.
C55 "The Pure Poets"
Childhood Education, XVII (November 1940), 134.

1941

C56 "Sale," "Second Shadow"
Poetry, LVII (February 1941), 292–293.
These poems appeared under the collective title "Two Poems."
New York Herald Tribune, March 5, 1941, p. 26.
See II, B49.
C57 "Poem with a Dash of Housman"
C58 "The Cycle"
Virginia Quarterly Review, XVI (Autumn 1941), 538.
C59 "City Limits"
Partisan Review, VIII (November–December 1941), 459.

1942

C60 "My Papa's Waltz"
Harper's Bazaar, LXXV (February 1942), 16.
The Times Literary Supplement [London], L (January 19, 1951), 30.
C61 "Wind over the City"
Harper's Bazaar, LXXV (April 1942), 114.

C62 "Dedicatory Poem"
Centre Daily Times [State College, Pa.], April 13, 1942, p. 1.
The poem also appeared in the program for the opening of the Mineral Industries Art Gallery (*see* II, B60). (PSC)

C63 "Episode Seven" (With Buck still tied to the saw, on comes the light)
Commonweal, XXXVI (June 12, 1942), 179.

C64 "The Minimal"
Harper's Bazaar, LXXXVI (November 1942), 103.

1943

C65 "Growth"
American Mercury, LVI (March 1943), 366.

C66 "Pickle Belt"
American Mercury, LVI (March 1943), 366.

C67 "Germinal"
New Yorker, XIX (April 3, 1943), 17.

C68 "Elegy" (Her leaf-like hands on the long branches of willow)
Poetry Quarterly [London], V (Summer 1943), 68.

C69 "River Incident"
New Yorker, XIX (September 11, 1943), 67.

C70 "Dolor," "Florist's Root Cellar," "The Gossips," "Summer School Marms"
Poetry, LXIII (November 1943), 68–70.
All of these poems appeared under the collective title "Four Poems."

1944

C71 "Night Crow"
Saturday Review of Literature, XXVII (November 11, 1944), 12.

1946

C72 "Old Florist"
  Harper's Magazine, CXVII (February 1946), 174.
C73 "Child on Top of a Greenhouse," "Flower Dump," "Fruit Bin"
  New Republic, CXIV (February 11, 1946), 181.
C74 "Carnations"
  New Republic, CXIV (February 18, 1946), 244.
  The Listener [London], XLII (September 29, 1949), 545.
C75 "Moss-Gathering"
  New Republic, CXIV (February 18, 1946), 244.
C76 "Weed Puller"
  New Republic, CXIV (February 25, 1946), 282.
C77 "Last Words" (Solace of kisses and cookies and cabbage)
  Harper's Bazaar, LXXX (April 1946), 239.
C78 "The Return" (I circled on leather paws)
  Poetry, LXVIII (August 1946), 250.
C79 "Forcing House"
  New York, XXII (October 5, 1946), 79.

1947

C80 "Judge Not," "The Lost Son"
  Sewanee Review, LV (Spring 1947), 252–259.
  Section V of "The Lost Son" is untitled.
C81 "The Long Alley"
  Poetry, LXX (July 1947), 198–201.
C82 "The Shape of the Fire"
  Partisan Review, XIV (September–October 1947), 486–488.
  Includes section 3 only.
    Reprinted: *Arena: New Zealand and Overseas Writers*,
  American Poetry No. 23. New Zealand, 1950, pp. 12–13. (UW)
  Sewanee Review, LVIII (Winter 1950), 68–108.
  This article contains an excerpt from an early version.

C83 "Big Wind"
American Scholar, XVII (Winter 1947–1948), 56–57.

1948

C84 "Cuttings" ["Cuttings *(later)*"]
Harper's Bazaar, LXXXII (February 1948), 227.
"Cuttings *(later)*" was entitled "Cuttings" in this appearance.
Reprinted: *Arena: New Zealand and Overseas Writing*,
American Poetry No. 23. New Zealand,1950, pp. 12-13. (UW)

C85 "A Field of Light"
The Tiger's Eye, I (March 1948), 15–16.
See I, A2.

C86 "Transplanting"
Mademoiselle, XXVI (April 1948), 148.
See I, A2.

C87 "Unfold! Unfold!"
Partisan Review, XVI (November 1949), 1098–1100.

1950

C88 "The Kitty-Cat Bird," "The Lamb," "The Monotony
Song," "The Sloth"
Flair, I (May 1950), 114–115.
All of the poems appeared under the collective title "Fables in
Song."

C89 "Elegy for Jane"
Kenyon Review, XII (Summer 1950), 476.
The Times Literary Supplement [London], LIII (September
17, 1954), liv.

C90 "I Cry, Love! Love!"
Hudson Review, III (Summer 1950), 217–218.

C91 "A Light Breather"
Kenyon Review, XII (Summer 1950), 475.

C92 "The Ceiling," "The Chair," "The Serpent"
Poetry, LXXVI (September 1950), 331–332.

C93 "The Cow"
Poetry, LXXVI (September 1950), 332.
The Times Literary Supplement [London], LVII (February 7, 1958), 72.

C94 "Praise to the End!"
Sewanee Review, LVIII (Winter 1950), 109–117.
This poem appeared with "The Visitant" and "Where Knock is Open Wide" under the collective title "Three Poems." *See* I, D14.
Reprinted: *Arena: New Zealand and Overseas Writing*, American Poetry No. 23. New Zealand, 1950, pp. 12–13. (UW)

C95 "Where Knock is Open Wide"
Sewanee Review, LVIII (Winter 1950), 109–117.
This poem appeared with "Praise to the End!" and "The Visitant" under the collective title "Three Poems."

C96 "The Visitant"
Sewanee Review, LVIII (Winter 1950), 109–110.
This poem appeared with "Praise to the End!" and "Where Knock is Open Wide" under the collective title "Three Poems."
Encounter [London], III (November 1954), 58.

1951

C97 "The Lady and the Bear"
Flair, II (January 1951), 119.

C98 "To an Anthologist," "Words in the Violent Ward"
Poetry, LXXVII (February 1951), 262.
These poems appeared under the collective title "Two Epigrams."
Reprinted: *Shenandoah*, XVI (Autumn 1964), 54. Entitled in this appearance "Heard in a Violent Ward."

C99 "O Lull Me, Lull Me!," "Sensibility! O La!"
Poetry, LXXVIII (September 1951), 311–315.
These poems appeared under the collective title "Two Poems."
These are probably the poems which were awarded the Levinson Prize by *Poetry* (*see* Biographical Notes 1951).

1952

C100 "Frau Bauman, Frau Schmidt, and Frau Schwartze"
New Yorker, XXVIII (March 29, 1952), 38.

C101 "The Bug"
New Yorker, XXVIII (August 9, 1952), 30.
C102 "The Partner" (from "Four for Sir John Davies")
Partisan Review, XIX (September–October 1952), 558.
C103 "O, Thou Opening, O"
Poetry, LXXI (October 1952), 64–67.
C104 "The Dance" (from "Four for Sir John Davies")
Atlantic, CXC (November 1952), 53.
New Statesman and Nation [London], XLVI (November
9, 1953), 568.
C105 "Old Lady's Winter Words"
Kenyon Review, XIV (Winter 1952), 60–62.
The Listener [London], LII (December 30, 1954), 1153.

1953

C106 "Dinky," "Song for a Squeeze-Box," "The Wraith"
(from "Four for Sir John Davies")
Hudson Review, V (Winter 1953), 516.
See I, B6.
C107 "Pastorale"
Nation, CLXXVI (May 9, 1953), 398.
See I, C130.
C108 "The Waking" (I wake to sleep)
The Times Literary Supplement [London], LIII (January
15, 1954), 35.
For first American appearance, see I, B7.

1954

C109 "Words for the Wind"
Encounter [London], II (March 1954), 16–17.
Harper's Bazaar, LXXXVIII (September 1955), 190–191.
Section III appeared as "Song" in New Poetry 1964 (Critical
Quarterly Poetry Supplement) [London], No. 5, 1964.

C110 "Poem"

The Times Literary Supplement [London], LIII (September 17, 1954), lxvi.

Harper's Bazaar, LXXXVIII (December 1954), 101.

C111 "The Follies of Adam"

Partisan Review, XXI (November–December 1954), 150–151.

1955

C112 "Love's Progress"

New Republic, CXXXII (April 11, 1955), 27.

C113 "All the Earth, All the Air"

Hudson Review, VII (Spring 1955), 58–59.

The Listener [London], LIV (September 8, 1955), 374.

C114 "The Beast"

Hudson Review, VIII (Spring 1955), 60.

New Statesman and Nation [London], LI (March 17, 1956), 248.

C115 "Song" (I met a ragged man)

Hudson Review, VIII (Spring 1955), 58–60.

Reprinted: *Best Poems of 1955: Borestone Mountain Poetry Awards, 1956.* Stanford, California: Stanford University Press, 1957, p. 80.

The Listener [London], LIV (September 8, 1955), 374.

C116 "The Dream" (I met her as a blossom on a stem)

New Yorker, XXXI (June 4, 1955), 34.

The Times Literary Snpplement [London], LV (August 17, 1956), xxi.

C117 "The Voice"

New Yorker, XXXI (July 9, 1955), 28.

C118 "The Slug"

New Republic, CXXXIII (August 1, 1955), 18.

C119 " 'The Shimmer of Evil' "

New Republic, CXXXIII (August 29, 1955), 19.

C120 "Old Woman's Meditation"
Partisan Review, xxii (Fall 1955), 491–494.
See I, C127.

C121 "Elegy" (Should every creature be as I have been)
New Republic, cxxv (September 12, 1955), 19.
The London Magazine, iv (July 1957), 13.

C122 "Snake" (I saw a young snake glide)
New Yorker, xxi (September 17, 1955), 48.
The London Magazine, v (March 1958), 13.

C123 "His Words," "The Wall," "What Now?" (from "The Dying Man")
Encounter [London], v (December 1955), 50–51.
These poems appeared under the collective title "The Dying Man."
Atlantic, cxcvii (May 1956), 48–49.
"His Words" appeared with "The Exulting" under the collective title "The Dying Man."

1956

C124 "The Sententious Man"
Poetry: London-New York, i (Winter 1956), 27–28.

C125 "Memory"
Atlantic, cxcvii (April 1956), 41.

C126 "The Exulting" (from "The Dying Man")
Atlantic, cxcvii (May 1956), 49.
The Times Literary Supplement [London], lvi (August 16, 1957), 414.

C127 "First Meditation" (from "Meditations of an Old Woman")
The London Magazine, iii (June 1956), 13–16.
See I, C120.

C128 "They Sing (A Dying Man Speaks)" (from "The Dying Man")
New Yorker, xxxii (August 18, 1956), 22.

C129 "The Small"
New Yorker, xxxii (September 8, 1956), 32.

C130 "The Siskins"
The Listener [London], LVI (October 18, 1956), 666.
See I, C107.

C131 "She" (I think the dead are tender, shall we kiss)
The Listener [London], LVI (November 29, 1956), 873.
Kenyon Review, XVIII (Winter 1956), 120.
Untitled in this appearance.
Toronto Daily Star [Canada], February 7, 1959, p. 30.

C132 "I'm Here (Old Lady on the Way to Sleep)" (from
"Meditations of an Old Woman")
New Yorker, XXXII (December 15, 1956), 39.

C133 "I Waited" (I waited for the wind to move the dust)
Kenyon Review, XVIII (Winter 1956), 121.
Untitled in this appearance.
New Statesman [London], LXVI (November 29, 1963),
789.

1957

C134 "What Can I Tell My Bones? (An Old Lady Musing)"
(from "Meditations of an Old Woman")
Partisan Review, XXIV (Summer 1957), 359–362.

C135 "An Old Lady Muses"
Harper's Bazaar, XC (September 1957), 246–247.

C136 "A Walk in Late Summer"
New Yorker, XXXIII (September 7, 1957), 36.
Reprinted: *Best Poems of 1957: Borestone Mountain Poetry
Award*. Stanford, California: Stanford University Press, 1958. The
poem was awarded second prize.

C137 "The Cantankerous One"
New Yorker, XXXIII (November 30, 1957), 50.
See I, C139.

C138 "Reply to a Lady Editor"
Poetry: London-New York, I (Winter 1957), 27.

1958

C139 "The Surly One"
The Observer [London], January 12, 1958, p. 14.
See I, C137. Reprinted from the English edition of *Words for the Wind*.

C140 "The Renewal"
New Yorker, xxxiv (April 26, 1958), 97.
New Statesman [London], lvi (September 6, 1958), 292.

C141 "The Pure Fury"
Partisan Review, xxv (Summer 1958), 97.

C142 "The Decision"
The Yale Review, xlviii (September 1958), 78.
The Observer [London], May 3, 1959, p. 23.

1959

C143 "Harsh Country"
New Yorker, xxv (April 18, 1959), 39.

C144 "The Early Flower"
New Yorker, xxv (April 25, 1959), 44.
The Listener [London], lxv (February 16, 1961), 317.

C145 "Dirge" (I would praise:—Those who will be compelled to dance)
The American Scholar, xxviii (Summer 1959), 293–295.

C146 "Many Arrivals"
New Yorker, xxv (July 25, 1959), 29.
See I, C157, 205.

C147 "Saturday Eight O'Clock"
Ladies Home Journal, cxxvi (November 1959), 130.
An early version of this poem appeared in *Penn State Alumni News*, liii (Fall 1967), 9; *Centre Daily Times* [State College, Pa.], lxiv (September 12, 1966); and *News: The Pennsylvania State University*, September 11, 1966, p. 3.

C148 "The Longing"
The Times Literary Supplement [London], lviii (November 6, 1959), xxxviii.

Saturday Review, XLIV (June 24, 1961), 46 (sections I and II only).

Saturday Review, XLV (August 11, 1962), 19 (complete).

1960

C149 "In a Dark Time"

New Yorker, XXV (January 16, 1960), 35.
Appeared with "In Evening Air" and "Sequel" under the collective title "Sequence."
Reprinted: *Best Poems of 1960: Borestone Mountain Poetry Award*. Palo Alto, California: Pacific Books, 1961.

Encounter [London], XVI (January 1961), 3.
Appeared with "Elegy" (Her face like a rain-beaten stone on the day she rolled off) and "Light Listened" under the collective title "Sequence."

C150 "In Evening Air"

New Yorker, XXXV (January 16, 1960), 35.
Appeared with "In a Dark Time" and "Sequel" under the collective title "Sequence."
Reprinted: *See* I, C149.

New Statesman [London], LXI (March 31, 1961), 514.

C151 "The Sequel"

New Yorker, XXXV (January 16, 1960), 35.
Appeared with "In a Dark Time" and "In Evening Air" under the collective title "Sequence."
Reprinted: *See* I, C149.

The Observer [London], October 16, 1960, p. 23.

C152 "Dirge," "Her Dream" (I went down to the river)

Hudson Review, XIII (Spring 1960), 30–32.

C153 "The Motion"

Hudson Review, XIII (Spring 1960), 31–32.

3 Arts Quarterly [London], No. 3 (Autumn 1960), pp. 12–13.

C154 "The Dancing Man"

Atlantic, CCVI (October 1960), 77.

C155 "Advice to One Committed"
  Esquire, LIV (November 1960), 138.
  Spectator [London], CCVI (March 24, 1961), 408.
C156 "Meditation at Oyster River"
  New Yorker, XXXVI (November 19, 1960), 54.
  The London Magazine, I (May 1961), 34–36.
C157 "Poem" (Many arrivals make us live: the tree becoming)
  The Listener [London], LXIV (December 1, 1960), 976.
  See I, C145, 205.
C158 "The Restored"
  New Yorker, XXXVI (December 10, 1960), 38.
  Spectator [London], CCVI (March 24, 1961), 408.

1961

C159 "Elegy" (Her face like a rain-beaten stone on the day
  she rolled off)
  Encounter [London], XVI (January 1961), 4.
  Appeared with "In a Dark Time" and "Light Listened" under the
  collective title "Sequence."
  Poetry Northwest, V (Summer 1964), 2.
C160 "Light Listened"
  Encounter [London], XVI (January 1961), 4.
  Appeared with "In a Dark Time" and "Elegy" (Her face like a
  rain-beaten stone on the day she rolled off) under the collective
  title "Sequence."
  Harper's Bazaar, February 1965, p. 139.
C161 "Journey to the Interior"
  New Yorker, XXXVI (January 7, 1961), 27.
  Encounter [London], XXII (June 1964), 50–51.
C162 "The Knowing"
  New Yorker, XXXVII (April 15, 1961), 38.
C163 "The Tree, the Bird"
  New Yorker, XXXVII (April 29, 1961), 40.
  New Statesman [London], LXII (September 29, 1961), 430.

Appeared with "The Lizard" (He too has eaten well) under the
collective title "Two Poems."

C164 "The Thing"
The Observer [London], May 14, 1961, p. 31.
Saturday Review, XLVI (March 9, 1963), 10.

C165 "The Lizard" (He too has eaten well)
New Yorker, XXXVII (June 7, 1961), 36.
New Statesman [London], LXII (September 29, 1961), 430.
Appeared with "The Tree, the Bird" under the collective "Two
Poems."
Reprinted: *Best Poems of 1961: Borestone Mountain Poetry
Award*. Palo Alto, California: Pacific Books, 1962.

C166 "The Reply"
New Yorker, XXXVII (July 1, 1961), 23.

C167 "Gob Music," "The Shy Man"
Poetry, XCVIII (August 27, 1961), 283–285.
Appeared with the title "Pub Songs."
The Dubliner [Ireland], No. 4 (July–August 1962),
pp. 51–53.

C168 "The Happy Three," "Her Words," "Her Wrath"
The Observer [London], August 27, 1961, p. 18.
Harper's Bazaar, April 1962, p. 130.

C169 "The Young Girl"
Ladies Home Journal, LXXVII (September 1961), 85.
The Observer [London], October 20, 1963, p. 24.

C170 "The Storm (Forio d'Ischia)"
New Yorker, XXXVIII (September 9, 1961), 48.
Listening and Writing [London], Autumn 1962, pp. 40–41.
(UW)
Entitled "Storm" in the English appearance.

C171 "Song" (My wrath, where's the edge)
The Observer [London], November 5, 1951, p. 29.
Harper's Magazine, CCXXVI (February 1963), 44.

C172 "From Whence?"
   Yale Review, LI (December 1961), 264.
   See I, C197

1962

C173 "The Saginaw Song"
   Encounter [London], XVIV (January 1962), 94.
   Michigan Quarterly Review, VI (October 1967), 139–240.
C174 [Epigram for Robert Frost]
   Seattle Times, January 19, 1962. (UWSC)
   Time, LXXIM (January 26, 1962), 40.
   See II, B178, 181.
      Reprinted: *The Glass House*, p. 276.
C175 "The Apparition"
   New Yorker, XXXVII (February 10, 1962), 43.
   The Observer [London], October 20, 1963, p. 24.
C176 "Two for Cynthia"
   Harper's Magazine, CXXIV (March 1962), 54.
C177 "The Marrow"
   New Yorker, XXXVIII (May 1962), 42.
   New Statesman [London], LXVI (August 9, 1963), 176.
   Appeared with "Advice" and "Song" (From whence cometh
   song?) under the collective title "Three Poems."
C178 "Once More, the Round"
   Encounter [London], XVIII (May 1962), 45.
   For the first American appearance, *see* I, B15.
C179 "The Long Waters"
   New Yorker, XXVIII (June 2, 1962), 34.
   Critical Quarterly [London], XV (Spring 1963), 20–22.
C180 "On the Quay (Inishbofin, Ireland)"
   New York Times, CXI (July 16, 1962), 22.
C181 "Her Longing"
   The Observer [London], September 16, 1962, p. 24.
   Atlantic, CCXII (October 1963), 101.

C182 "Villanelle"
The Observer [London], September 16, 1962, p. 22.
See I, C188.

C183 "The Abyss"
Encounter [London], October 1962, pp. 51–53.
Harper's Magazine, CCXXVII (November 1963), 82–83.

C184 "The Far Field"
Sewanee Review, LXX (October 1962), 609–612.
For the first American appearance, *see* I, B14.
    Reprinted: *Seattle Magazine*, I (April 1964), 12–13 (*see* II, F12).
The Times Literary Supplement [London], LXI (December 21, 1962), 992.
Reprinted: *American Poetry 1965* (*Critical Quarterly* Poetry Supplement) [London], No. 6, 1965.

C185 "Old Florist's Lament"
Spectator [London], CCIX (October 5, 1962), 530.
Erroneously described as "unpublished" in the *Selected Letters of Theodore Roethke*, page 226.

C186 [Occasional Poem]
University of Washington Daily [Seattle], October 18, 1962, p. 1.

1963

C187 "The Chums"
New Statesman [London], LXVI (February 8, 1963), 202.
Saturday Review, XLVI (December 21, 1963), 52.

C188 "The Right Thing"
Atlantic, XXI (March 1963), 51.
See I, C182.

C189 "All Morning"
The Observer [London], March 24, 1963, p. 22.
Harper's Bazaar, March 1964, pp. 92–93.

C190 "The Geranium"
Partisan Review, xxx (Spring 1963), 55.
Agenda [London], iii (December–January 1963–1964), 9.

C191 "Her Reticence"
Hudson Review, xvi (Spring 1963), 52.

C192 "His Foreboding"
Hudson Review, xvi (Spring 1963), 53.

C193 "Wish for a Young Wife"
Hudson Review, xvi (Spring 1963), 53.
Reprinted: *New Poetry 1964* (*Critical Quarterly* Poetry
Supplement) [London], No. 5, 1964.

C194 "Otto"
Partisan Review, xxx (Spring 1963), 56–57.
The Times Literary Supplement [London], lxiii (January
30, 1964), 189.

C195 "The Pike"
The Observer [London], May 5, 1963, p. 27.
Saturday Review, xlvi (November 9, 1963), 42.

C196 "The Rose"
New Yorker, xxxix (July 6, 1963), 26–27.
Agenda [London], iii (April 1964), 1–4.
Reprinted: *See* II, F13.

C197 "Advice" (A learned heathen told me this), "Song"
(From whence cometh song?)
New Statesman [London], lxvi (August 9, 1963), 176.
Appeared with "The Marrow" under the collective title "Three
Poems." *See* I, C172.

C198 "The Moment"
Encounter [London], xxi (October 1963), 68.
New Yorker, xxxix (October 19, 1963), 51.

C199 "Her Time"
New Yorker, xxxix (October 19, 1963), 50.
The Observer [London], October 20, 1963, p. 24.

C200 "Infirmity"
New Yorker, xxxix (October 19, 1963), 50.
C201 "The Meadow Mouse"
New Yorker, xxxix (October 19, 1963), 50–51.
Spectator [London], xxxi (November 29, 1963), 719.
C202 "The Tranced"
New Yorker, xxxix (October 19, 1963), 51.
C203 "Supper with Lindsay" (1962)
Poetry, ciii (October–November 1963), 85–86.
Encounter [London], xxvii (October 1966), 51–52.
C204 "Song" (Witch-me-tiddle-dee Mirabell), "Wheeze for Wystan"
Poetry, ciii (October–November 1963), 87–89.
C205 "The Manifestation"
New Statesman [London], lxvi (November 29, 1963), 789.
See I, C146, 157.

1964
C206 "Her Convalescence (An Old Lady Speaks)"
Ladies Home Journal, lxxxi (April 1964), 124.

1965
C207 "Light Poem" (Wren-song in trellis: A light ecstacy of butterflies courting)
New Yorker, xli (July 10, 1965), 21.

1968
C208 "Philander"
West Coast Review, iii (Spring 1968), 9.
This is an early version of the poem that first appeared in I Am! Says the Lamb (see I, A6).

Essays

C209 "A Junior Speech by a Junior (Theodore Roethke, Grade Pupil, Flint, Michigan)"

Junior Red Cross News, October 1922, p. 21. (UW)
Reprinted: *See* I, B24 and II, B32.

C210 "The English Reviews"
Michigan Chimes [Ann Arbor], October 14, 1926, p. 11.
Initialed "T.R." (UW)

C211 "Verse in Rehearsal"
Portfolio [Student publication of Pennsylvania State
College], I (September 1939), 3, 15–16. (PSU, UW)

C212 "The Teaching Poet"
Poetry, LXXIX (February 1952), 250–255.

C213 "Dylan Thomas: Memories and Appreciations"
Encounter [London], II (January 1954), 11.
An excerpt from this article appears in *The Glass House*,
pp. 192–193, and II, B13.

C214 "Last Class"
College English, XVIII (May 1957), 383–386. Signed
"Winterset Rothberg."

C215 "Theodore Roethke Writes . . ."
Poetry Book Society Bulletin [London], No. 16 (December
1957).

C216 "Tribute to Richard Selig—1929–1957"
Gemini: The Oxford and Cambridge Magazine, I (Winter
1957–1958), 62–63.

C217 "How to Write Like Somebody Else"
Yale Review, XLVIII (March 1959), 336–343.
The London Magazine, VII (October 1960), 49–55.

C218 "The Poetry of Louise Bogan"
Michigan Alumnus Quarterly Review, LXVII (Autumn
1960), 3–20.
Critical Quarterly [London], III (Summer 1961), 142–150.
Reprinted: *Michigan Quarterly Review*, VI (Fall 1967), 246–251;
To the Young Writer. Ann Arbor: University of Michigan Press,
1967.

C219 "Some Remarks on Rhythm"
Poetry, XCVII (October 1960), 35–46.
Reprinted: *Washington Alumnus* [Seattle], Winter 1966,
pp. 24–29; *The Structure of Verse*. New York: A Fawcett Premier
Book, 1966, p. 272 (with the title "What do I like?").
C220 "Tirade Turning"
Encounter [London], XXI (December 1963), 44–45.
Signed "Winterset Rothberg."
C221 "On 'Identity' "
Show, V (May 1965), 10–12, 15.
C222 "Some Self-Analysis"
Show, V (May 1965), 15.

Notes and Notebooks

C223 "Straw for the Fire"
Poetry, CV (November 1964), 113–118. Arranged by
David Wagoner.
C224 "In the Large Mind of Love"
Hudson Review, XIX (Summer 1966), 253–258. Arranged
with an introduction by David Wagoner.
See The Glass House, pp. 167–169.
C225 "The Plain Speech of a Crow"
Southern Review, II (October 1966), 609–910. Arranged
with an introduction by David Wagoner.
C226. "The Things I Steal from Sleep"
Poetry Northwest, IX (Spring 1968), 3–6. Arranged by
David Wagoner.
C227 "A Nest of Light (from the Notebooks of Theodore
Roethke, 1948–1949)"
Northwestern University Tri-Quarterly Review, XII (Spring
1968), 101–103. Arranged by David Wagoner.
C228 "Words for Young Writers—From the Notes of
Theodore Roethke"

Saturday Review, LI (June 29, 1968), 14–15, 42. Arranged by David Wagoner.

Excerpts from and comments on this article appeared in the following: Ed Miller. "From Ted Roethke's Classroom Lectures," *The Saginaw News*, July 18, 1968; Robert V. Bauer. "Roethke, a Poet and a Teacher," *Centre Daily Times* [State College, Pa], August 3, 1968; Robert V. Bauer. "About Roethke, a Poet as Critic," *Centre Daily Times* [State College, Pa.], August 10, 1968.

C229 "In the Lap of a Dream, from the Notebooks of Theodore Roethke, 1948–1949)"
Atlantic, CCXXII (November 1968), 58–62. Arranged by David Wagoner.

C230 "The Stony Garden (from the Poet's Notebook, 1949–1950)"
Poetry, CXIII (November 1968), 104–108. Arranged by David Wagoner.

C231 "The Proverbs of Purgatory (from the Notebooks of Theodore Roethke, 1948–1949)"
Shenandoah, XX (Autumn 1968), 30–31. Arranged by David Wagoner.

C232 "Father-Stem and Mother-Root (from the Notebooks, 1951–53)"
Denver Quarterly, III (Winter 1969), 81–84.

C233 "The Right to Say Maybe"
Seattle Magazine, VI (February 1969), 27–29. Arranged by David Wagoner.

C234 "The Wrath of Other Winds"
Malahat Review [Victoria, B.C.], No. 10 (April 1969), pp. 86–88. Arranged by David Wagoner.

C235 "First Class: From the Notebooks of Theodore Roethke 1950–1953"
Antioch Review, XXIX (Summer 1969), 212–217. Arranged by David Wagoner.

C236 "The Loveless Provinces"
Yale Review, LIX (October 1969), 99–103. Arranged by David Wagoner.

C237 "In the Bush of Her Bones (from the Notebooks 1948–1949)"
Southern Review, n.s. V (Winter 1969), pp. 1–3. Arranged by David Wagoner.

C238 "The Root of the Wind"
Mademoiselle, LXX (March 1970), 92–93. Arranged by David Wagoner.

C239 "I Teach Out of Love"
Shenandoah, XXI (Spring 1970), 141–149. Arranged by David Wagoner.

C240 "The Dance of the One-Legged Man"
Poetry Northwest, XI (Summer 1970), 3ff. Arranged by David Wagoner.

C241 "All the Semblance, All the Loss: from the Notebooks of Theodore Roethke (1948–1949)"
Michigan Quarterly Review, X (Winter 1971), 53–55, 63.

C242 "The Dark Angel (from the Notebooks of Theodore Roethke—1943–47)" and "The Poet's Business (from the Notebooks of Theodore Roethke—1950–53)"
Northwest Review, XI (Summer 1971), 32–41, 112–115. Arranged by David Wagoner.

C243 "Heart, You Have No House (from the Notebooks of Theodore Roethke—1951–1953)"
Voyages, IV (Spring 1972), 61–64.

C244 "The Beautiful Disorder (from the Notebooks of Theodore Roethke—1954–1963)"
Pebble, VIII (June 1972), 26–32.

Reviews

C245 "*Ideas of Order* by Wallace Stevens," *New Republic*, LXXXVII (July 15, 1936), 305.

C246 "*This Modern Poetry* by Babette Deutsch," *New Republic*, LXXXVII (July 22, 1936), 333. Signed with initials only.

C247 "*A Spectacle for Scholars* by Winifred Welles," *New Republic*, LXXXVII (August 26, 1936), 83–84. Signed with initials only.

C248 "*The Last Look and Other Poems* by Mark Van Doren," *New Republic*, XCIII (November 17, 1937), 52.

C249 "*Country Men* by James Hearst," *New Republic*, XCIII (December 29, 1937), 234.

C250 "Facing the Guns": *And Spain Sings: Fifty Loyalist Ballads* adapted by American poets, ed. M. J. Bernadete and Rolfe Humphries, *Poetry*, LII (April 1938), 43–46.

C251 "Ben Belitt's First Volume": *The Five-Fold Mesh* by Belitt, *Poetry*, LII (January 1939), 214–217.

C252 "Evidence of Growth": *Concerning the Young* by Williard Maas, *Poetry*, LIII (March 1939), 336–338.

C253 "*Personalities and the Arts from Another World: The Autobiography of Louis Untermeyer*," *The Headlight on Books at Penn State* [State College, Pa.], II (May 1940), 10.

C254 "Obiter Dicta": *The Alert* by Wilfred Gibson, *Poetry*, LX (May 1942), 109–110.

C255 "Obiter Dicta": *Gautama the Enlightened* by John Masefield, *Poetry*, LX (May 1942), 109–110.

C256 "Meditations of a Sensitive Man": *A Lost Season* by Roy Fuller, *Poetry*, LXVII (January 1946), 218–221.

C257 "Integrity of Spirit": *The Earth-Bound* by Janet Lewis, *Poetry*, LXIX (January 1947), 220–223.

C258 "One Ring-Tailed Roarer to Another": *Country Sleep and Other Poems*, by Dylan Thomas, *Poetry*, LXXXI (December 1952), 184–186. Signed "Winterset Rothberg."

Reprinted: *Dylan Thomas: The Legend and the Poet*. London: William Heinemann, Ltd., 1960.

Letter Excerpts

C259 "Jack Gilbert," *Genesis West*, I (Fall 1962), 70.
This is an excerpt from a letter written to Gordon Lish (for further information, *see* II, A7, p. 148).

C260 "Marguerite Caetani," *Atlantic*, CCXV (February 1965), 86.
This article contains two excerpts from two letters to Marguerite Caetani. The first was written about 1949 and appeared in its entirety in the *Selected Letters of Theodore Roethke*, p. 163 (*see* I, A12) and in part in *The Glass House*, p. 179 (*see* II, B26). The second excerpt remains unpublished in its entirety and is dated January 19, 1949 (for further information, *see* II, A7, p. 121).

Miscellaneous

C261 "Roethke on His Own Poetry," *Literary Cavalcade*, XV (April 1963), 15–17.
This article contains excerpts from the essays "Theodore Roethke" (I, B19); "Open Letter" (I, B17); and "An American Poet Introduces Himself and His Poems" (I, E6). This was the first published appearance of any part of the essay "An American Poet Introduces Himself and His Poems" (for the complete essay, *see On The Poet and His Craft*, pp. 7–13). Reprints of "Night Journey," "Child on Top of a Greenhouse," "Cuttings," "Cuttings (*later*)," "Dolor," and "Elegy for Jane" also appeared with illustrations. (UW)

C262 "Antidotes," *Harper's Bazaar*, July 1963, p. 75. Signed by Roethke.

D Foreign Appearances and Translations

This section lists foreign appearances of Roethke's poetry and prose in English (those in *Botteghe Oscure* being the first appearance of the poems in English anywhere) and in translation, published and unpublished. While this section cannot be considered complete (a sizable selection in Italian appeared in *Poeti Americani, 1900–1956* [Milano, 1958], pp. 731–765, but the volume could not be located for examination), it does suggest the range of the acceptance of his poetry in non-English-speaking areas of the world.

Theodore Roethke's foreign publication began in 1922 when he was fourteen; he wrote a speech for the Saginaw chapter of the Junior Red Cross which was subsequently translated into twenty-six languages (*see* I, B24, C209, and II, 832). Since that time, his poetry has been translated into most of the major languages of Europe and many non-European languages (Afrikaans, Bengali, Indonesian, Persian, and Urdu).

Books

D1 *Theodore Roethke Sequenza Nordamericana E Altre Poesie* (1966) Italian edition:

THEODORE ROETHKE [black] / SEQUENZA / NORDAMERICANA / E ALTRE POESIE [green] / A CURA DI AGOSTINO LOMBARDO / NOTE E TRADUZIONE DI MARIOLINA MELIADO / ARNOLDO / MONDADORI / EDITORE

19 × 12½. Published March 1966, at Lire 3500. Issued in brown cloth and stamped in white on the cover and

backstrip. Cover: THEODORE ROETHKE / SEQUENZA / NORDAMERICANA / E ALTRE POESIE. Backstrip, reading up from the foot: MONDADORI ROETHKE SEQUENZA NORDAMERICANA E ALTRE POESIE. All edges trimmed; dust jacket.

Collation: [1]–[454], as follows: [1]–[2] blank; [3] CO SPEECHIO / I POETI DEL NOSTRO TEMPO; [4] blank; [5] title page as above; [6] acknowledgment; [7]–[26] Introduction: LA POESIA DI THEODORE ROETHKE / di Agostinao Lombardo; [27]–39 NOTA DELLA TRADUTTRICE; [40] blank; [41] half title; [42] from OPEN HOUSE / 1941; [43] da CASA APERTA / 1941; 44–415 English and Italian text; [416] blank; [417]–441 APPENDICE; NOTIZIE BIOGRAFICHE, OPERE, TRADUZIONI ITALIANE, NOTE AL TESTO; [442]–[451] INDICE; [452] colophon; [453]–[454] blank.

Contents: From OPEN HOUSE (1941), da CASA APERTA (1941), "Open House," "Casa Aperta"; "To My Sister," "A mia sorella"; "Interlude," "Interludio"; "The Adamant," "Il diamante"; "Prayer," "Preghiera"; "The Heron," "L'airone"; "Vernal Sentiment," "Sentimento primaverile"

From THE LOST SON AND OTHER POEMS (1948), da Il FIGLIO PERDUTO E ALTRE POESIE (1948), "Orchids," "Orchidee"; "Moss-Gathering," "La raccolta del muschio"; "Frau Bauman, Frau Schmidt and Frau Schwartz," "Frau Bauman, Frau Schmidt e Frau Schwartze"; "Transplanting," "Trapianto"; "Child on Top of a Greenhouse," "Bambino sul tetto di una serra"; "Flower Dump," "Ammasso di fiori"; "Carnations," "Garotani"; "My Papa's Waltz," "Il valzer di papà"; "The Minmal," "Vita minima"; "The Cycle," "Il ciclo"

From *PRAISE TO THE END!* (1951), da *LODE ALLA FINE!* (1951), "Bring the Day!," "Datemi il giorno!"; "The Lost Son": (1 "The Flight," 2 "The Pit," 3 "The Gibber," 4 "The Return," 5 "It was beginning winter"), "Il figlio perduto": (1 "La fuga," 2 "La voragine," 3 "Il farfuglio," 4 "Il ritorno," 5 "Era l'inizio dell' inverno"); "A Field of Light," "Un campo di luce"; "Praise to the End!", "Lode alla fine!"; "I Cry, Love! Love!" "Io piango, amore! amore!"

From *THE WAKING* (1953), da *IL RISVEGLIO* (1953), "A Light Breather," "Un essere dal respiro lieve"; "Elegy for Jane," "Elegia per Jane"; "Four for Sir John Davies": (1 "The Dance," 2 "The Partner," 3 "The Wraith," 4 "The Vigil"), "Quattro per Sir John Davies": (1 "La danza," 2 "La compagna," 3 "L'apparizione," 4 "La veglia"); "The Waking," "Il risveglio"

From *WORDS FOR THE WIND* (1958), da *PAROLE PER IL VENTO* (1958), "The Dream," "Il sogno"; "All the Earth, All the Air," "Tutta la terra, tutta l'aria"; "Words for the Wind," "Parole per il vento"; "She," "Lei"; "The Beast," "La bestia"; "The Small," "Il piccoli"; "Snake," "Il serpe"; "The Dying Man": (1 "His Words," 2 "What Now?" 3 "The Wall," 4 "The Exulting," 5 "They Sing, They Sing"), "L' uomo morente": (1 "Le sue parole," 2 "E adesso?," 3 "Il muro," 4 "L'esultante," 5 "Cantano, cantano"); "Meditation of an Old Woman": ("First Meditation," "I'm here," "Fourth Meditation," "What can I tell my bones?"), "Meditazioni di una vecchia": ("Prima meditazione," "Sono qui," "Quarta meditazione," "Che cosa dira alle mie ossa?")

From *I AM! SAYS THE LAMB* (1962), da *IO SONO! DICE L'AGNELLO* (1962), "The Whale," "La balena"; "The Donkey," "Il somaro"; "The Ceiling," "Il soffitto";

"The Chair," "La sedia"; "The Cow," "La mucca"; "The Hippo," "L'ippopotamo"; "The Lamb," "L'agnello" From *THE FAR FIELD* (1964), da *IL CAMPO LONTANO* (1964), *NORTH AMERICAN SEQUENCE, SEQUENZA NORDAMERICANA*, "The Longing," "L'anelito"; "Meditation at Oyster River," "Meditazione ad Oyster River"; "Journey to the Interior," "Viaggio all'interno"; "The Long Waters," "Le lunghe acque"; "The Far Field," "Il campo lontano"; "The Rose," "La rosa"

From *Love Poems*, da *Poesie D' Amore*, "Her Time," "Lei: ilsuo momento"; "Song," "Canzone"

From *Mixed Sequence*, da *Sequence Mista*: "The Abyss," "L'abisso"; "Elegy," "Elegia"; "Otto," "Otto"; "The Lizard," "La lucertola"; "The Storm," "La tempesta"

From *Sequence, Sometimes Metaphysical*, da *Sequenza A Volte Metafisica*, "In a Dark Time," "In un'ora di buio"; "The Sequel," "Il corollario"; "The Motion," "Il moto"; "The Decision," "La de cisione"; "The Marrow," "Il midollo"; "The Tree, the bird"; "L'albero, l'uccello"; "The Restored," "Reintegrazione"; "The Right Thing," "La cosa giusta"; "Once More, the Round," "Ancora una volta il circolo"

Previous Publications in Italian: *See* I, D3, 9, 13–18, 21, 23, 24, 28, 31, 34, 39, 40, 43.

Colophon: "STAMPATO IN ITALIA – PRINTED IN ITALY – LSP 9040 / QUESTO VOLUME E STATO IMPRESSO / NEL MESE DO, ARZO DELL'ANNO MCMLXVI / NELLE OFFICINE GRAFICHE DI VERONA / DELLA ARNOLDO MONDADORI EDITORE"

The following translations are filed with the Roethke Papers at the University of Washington and appear to correspond with those above: "Ammasso di fiorio" (with notes by Roethke?); "Datemi il giorno!"; "Elegia"; "Io piango, amore! amore!"; and "Il serpe" (with notes by Mariolina Meliado). All of the above appear in manuscript and are probably by Mariolina Meliado.

The edition can be obtained from Arnoldo Mondadori Editore, Via Bianca di Savoia, 20, Milano 20122.

Words for the Wind was first published in England in 1957. *I Am! Says the Lamb* was published in 1961 rather than 1962 as given above in the contents.

"The Lost Son" and "A Field of Light" first appeared in *The Lost Son and Other Poems* rather than in *Praise to the End!* as suggested by the contents entry above. Perhaps the translator wished to retain the sense of sequence by listing them together. The listing of these poems as part of a sequence including others is visible in *Praise to the End!*, *The Waking*, and *Words for the Wind* but does not appear in the arrangement of *The Collected Poems of Theodore Roethke* (see I, A10).

D2 *Theodore Roethke Dalekie pole*

Polish edition:

THEODORE ROETHKE / Dalekie pole / [ornament in green] / WYBRALA I PRZELOZYLA / LUDMILA MARJANSKA / [green dot] / PANSTWOWY INSTYTUT *WYDAWNICZY*

18 × 11½. Published in 1971, at Cena ł 10, ———. Issued in green paper with black letter press. Cover [white ornament (bird)] / *THEODORE ROETHKE* / Dalekie pole / [publisher's device]. All edges trimmed; dust jacket.

Collation: [1] half title; [2] blank; [3] title page as above; [4 notice of copyright, acknowledgment; 5–[6] introduction; 7–45 text; 46 blank; 47–[48] index (spis Rzeczy); [49] blank; [50]–[51] other titles in series; [52] publication information as follows: "PRINTED IN POLAND / Państwowy Instytut Wydawniczy, Warzawa 1971. / Wydanie pierwsze / Naklad 1, 500 + 260 egz.

Ark. Wyd 1,5 Ark. druk. 3,25 / Oddanodo Skladania w
grudniu 1970 r. / Podpisano do druku w lutym 1971 r. /
Druk ukończono w Kwietniu 1971 r. / Zaklady Graficzne
w Koszalinie / Nr zam. D–14 G–2 / Cena zł 10,——."

Contents: Wstep [introduction by Ludmila Marjańska]; Z,,
SEKWENCJI POLNOCNO-AMERYKANSKIEJ"
[NORTH AMERICAN SEQUENCE]: "Pragnienie"
["The Longing"], "Rozmýslania nad Rzeka Ostrygowa"
["Meditation at Oyster River"], "Dalekie pole" ["The Far
Field], "Róza" ["The Rose"]; Z,, WIERSZY
MILOSNYCH" [LOVE POEMS]: "Jej slowa" ["Her
Words"], "Jej pozadanie" ["Her Longing"], "Szczésliwa
trójka" ["The Happy Three"], "Jej gniew" ["Her
Wrath"], "Zyczenie mlodej zony" ["Wish for a Young
Wife"]; Z,, SEKEWENCJI MIESZANEJ" [MIXED
SEQUENCE]: "Otchlań" ["The Abyss"], "Mysz polna"
["The Meadow Mouse"], "Szczupak" ["The Pike"],
"Przez caly ranek" ["All Morning"], "Piosenka" ["The
Song"], "Chwila" ["The Moment"], "Odkrycie"
["The Manifestation"]; Z,, SEKWENCJI NIEKIEOY
METAFIZYCZNEJ" [SEQUENCE, SOMETIMES
METAPHYSICAL]: "W ciemny czas" ["In a Dark
Time"], "Choroba" ["The Infirmity"], "Decyz ja" ["The
Decision"], "Ten ptak, to drzewo" ["The Tree, the Bird"],
"Jeszcze jeden obrót" ["Once More, the Round"]

See I, A12, pp. 261–262, and I, D12.

Appearances in Books and Pamphlets

D3 *Nuovissima Poesia Americana E Neqra*, ed. Carlo Izzo.
Guanda, Italia: Parma, 1953.

Contents: "O Lull Me, Lull Me" and "Unfold! Unfold!"
appear as "O, cullami, cullami" and "Schuiditi! Schuiditi!"

The text of this book was not available for description. Reference is made to it in the *Annual Bibliography* (Department of English, University of Washington [*see* II, G2]), which was prepared by Roethke himself, and is listed on page 423 of I, D1 above.

D4 PERSPECITVAS / DOS / ESTADOS UNIDOS / AS ARTES-EAS LETRAS / Introducao de / John Niell / Traducao de / Adolfo Casais Monteiro / e / JOERGE DE SENA / [ornament] / PORTUGALIA EDITORA / LISBOA

12 × 19. 1–324. Probably published in 1954, no price. Issued in white paper with dark blue rule surrounding white, red, and black lettering on the front cover. All edges trimmed.

Contents: "A Field of Light" appears as "Un campo de luz" on page 257.

D5 *PANORAMA* / DE LA / LITTÉRATURE CONTEMPORAINE / AUX E'TATS UNIS / introduction / illustrations / documents / Par / John BROWN / [the title extends the breadth of the recto and verso pages]

14 × 19. 1–656. Published by Librarie Gallimard on August 20, 1954, at 1.350 fr. Issued in dark blue paper with end flaps. All edges trimmed.

Contents: "A Field of Light" [sections I and 2 only] appears as "Champ de lumiere" on pages 546–547. A biographical note appears on pages 293–294.

Colophon: "ACHEVE D'IMPRIMER LE 20 AOUT 1954 / SUR LES PRESSES DE L'IMPRIMERIE / GEORGE LANG A PARIS / N.D. EDITION: 4323 / DEP, LEGAL 3E TRIM. 1954 / IMPRIME EN FRANCE."

D6 A. A. ROGGIANO—JULIAN PALLEY / DIEZ PORTAS [black] / NORTEAMERICANOS [gold] /

CUADERNOS [ornament] / [ornament] Julio Herr era y Reissig / MONTEVIDEO URUGUAY [the above is the description of the front cover, since there is no title page]

13¾ × 19¾. [ii] + 10 unnumbered pages. Published February 20, 1956, no price. Issued in white paper with end flaps and front cover as described above. All edges trimmed.

Contents: "Elegy for Jane" appears as "Elegia para Jane (Mi alumna, caida de un caballo)" on page [7]. A brief biographical note also appears.

Colophon: Este Cuaderno se termino de imprimir el 20 / de febrero de 1956 en los talleres de la / Impresora Libertad-Treinta y Tres 1528.

The following information on this edition appears on the back cover: "Numero 40 de / La serie 1955 de 'Cuadernos Julio Herrera 4 Reissigo.' "

D7 ALAIN BOSQUET / ANTHOLOGIE / DE LA / POESIE AMERICAINE / DES ORIGINES A NOS JOURS / 1956 / [broad black rule with thin rule below] / LIBRAIRIE STOCK / DELAMAIN ET BOUTELLEAU / 6, rue Casimir DeLarigne, 6 / PARIS

13½ × 19½. [i]–[320]. Published March 30, 1956, no price. Issued in stiff sepia paper. All edges trimmed.

Contents: "A Field of Light" appears as "Champ de lumiere" on pages 230–232. "The Waking" ("I strolled across") appears as "Le reveil" on pages 232–233. A biographical note appears on pages 303.

Colophon: "ACHEVE D'IMPRIMER SUR LES / PRESSES DE L'IMPIMERIE / CRETE A CORBEIL-ESSONNES / LE 30 MARS

1956. / No d'edition 978. / De 'pôt Legal: Ier
trimestre 1956."

"Le reveil" also appeared in *Combat*, April 19, 1956, p. 6.

D8 CZAS NIEPOKOJU / ANTHOLOGIA WSPO'CZESNEJI
/ BRYTYJSKIEJ I AMERYKAN'SKIEJ / Wybrati
opracowat / PAWEL MAYEWSKI / Wstep napisal /
KARL SHAPIRO / Wydane. staraniem / THE EAST
EUROPE INSTITUTE / prezez / CRITERION BOOKS /
NOWY YORK: 1958

12½ × 19. xviii–382. Published in 1958, no price. Issued
in tan cloth. Backstrip, reading downward in two lines:
PAWEL *antologia wspo'łczesnej* / MAYEWSKI *brytyjskiej
i amerykan'skiej* [publisher's device] Criterion. All pages
trimmed.

Contents: "The Song" (I met a ragged man) appears as
"Piesen" on pages 330–331.

D9 *Poesia Stranie Ra Del 900*, ed. Attilio Bertolucci and trans.
Guidacci. Milan, Italy, 1958.

Contents :"The Shape of the Fire" appears with the
translation on pages 516–517.

This book was not available for examination. Reference is made to
it in the *Annual Bibliography* (Department of English, University
of Washington), which was prepared by Roethke (*see* II, G2).

D10 TRENTE-CINQ / JEUNES POETES / AMERICAINS
/ Traduction, preface et choix par / ALAIN BOSQUET
/ NRF / GALLIMARD / 5, rue Sebastien—Bottin,
Paris Vlle

20½ × 14. [1]–464. Published in 1960, at 1.600 fr. Issued
in sepia paper with black and red lettering on the cover
and backstrip. All edges uneven and untrimmed.

Contents: "Orchids" appears as "Orchidées" on pages
92–93; "Bring the day!" appears as "Apporte le jour!"
on pages 94–97; "The Visitant" appears as "La visiteuse"
on pages 98–101; "The Dying Man": (1 "His Words," 2
"What Now?," 3 "The Wall," 4 "The Exulting," 5 "They
Sing, They Sing,") appears as "Le moribund": (1
"Sesmots," 2 "Et maintenant," 3 "Le mur," 4 "L'exultation,"
5 "Ils chantent, ils chantent") on pages 102–111; "What
Can I Tell My Bones?" appears as "Que puis-je dire a mes
os?" on pages 112–114. (UWSC)

D11 *Fifty Poems from Contemporary American Poetry* [the
title is in Arabic], ed. Tawfig Sayagh. Beirut, Lebanon,
1963.

24½ × 17. Published by Dar El-Yaqza in February 1963,
at 5 L. L. [$1.65]. 3,000 copies were issued in stiff white
paper with black lettering on the front cover backstrips. The
back cover has an abstract design in orange, blue, gray,
and brown with black lettering. Cover design by Waddah
Faris. All pages trimmed.

Contents: "The Dying Man," "The Lost Son" [an excerpt],
and "The Shape of the Fire" appear in Arabic on
pages 129–140. A biographical note entitled "Theodore
Roethke" appears on page 141 in Arabic.

All titles are in Arabic and English.
   Three copies of this book are located with Roethke's library in
storage in Seattle.

D12 *An Anthology of English and American Poetry.* Warzawa:
Panstwowy Instytut Wydawniczy, ca. 1964 or 1965.

Contents: "Elegy for Jane," "The Waking" (I wake to
sleep), and others. Translated by Ludmila Marjańska.

See the *Selected Letters of Theodore Roethke*, pp. 261–262. The
poem titles and the book title are probably in Polish.

Appearances in Periodicals: Poetry

1948

D13 "Lode alla fine" ("Praise to the End!")

Translated by H. Furst. *Poeti Inglesi E Americani* (*Botteghe Oscure* Supplement) [Rome], II (1948), 46–49.

D14 "Praise to the End!"

Botteghe Obscure [Rome], II (1948), 288–291.

This is the first appearance of this poem in English.

1951

D15 "Bring the Day!," "Give Way, Ye Gates," "I Need, I Need"

Botteghe Oscure [Rome], VI (1951), 443–449.

All the poems appeared with the collective title "Give Way, Ye Gates" and with a brief introductory comment by Roethke: "I wish to have these three poems considered as an entity, the group making one poem from childhood into a violent adolescence, caterwauling."
This is also the first appearance of these poems in English.

D16 "Song" (This fair parcel of summer's)
Botteghe Oscure [Rome], VIII (1951), 282–283.

This is the first appearance of this poem in English.

1952

D17 "Campo di luce" ("A Field of Light")

Translated by Antonio Russi. *Perspettive* [Firenzie], No. 1 (Autumn 1952), pp. 144–147. [English and Italian]

A biographical note and photo appear on page 225.

D18 "The Changeling"

Botteghe Oscure [Rome], X, (Fall 1952), 239–241.

This is the first appearance of this poem in English.

D19 "Champ de lumiere" ("A Field of Light")

Translated by Alain Bosquet, *Profiles* [Paris], No. 1 (October 1952), pp. 136–138. [English and French]

A manuscript with the same title and translator is filed with the Roethke papers at the University of Washington. (UW)
A biographical note and photo appear on page 234.

D20 "Ein feld lichtes" ("A Field of Light")

Translated by Deutsch Von Alexander Koval. *Perspecktiven*, No. 1 (October 1952], pp. 170–173. [English and German]

A biographical note and photo appear on page 236. (UW)

1953

D21 "Words for the Wind"

Botteghe Oscure [Rome], XII (1953), 211–214.

This is the first appearance of this poem in English.

D22 "Pole swiatla" ("A Field of Light")

Translated by J. D. Przetayl. *Kulture*, No. 7/69–8/70 (July–August 1953), pp. 78–81. [English and Polish?] (UW)

1954

D23 "Elegy" (Should every creature be as I have been), "Love's Progress," " 'The Shimmer of Evil'—Louise Bogan"

Botteghe Oscure [Rome], XIV (1954), 224–226.

This is the first appearance of these poems in English.

D24 "The Minimal," "Open House," "Vernal Sentiment"

Lo Spettatore Italiano, VII (February 1954), 73–74. [English] (UW)

D25 "Intermede" ("Interlude")

Le Journal des Poetes, XXIV (June 1954), 9. (UW)

D26 "Elegie für Jane" ("Elegy for Jane"), "Der Besuch" ("The Visitant"), "Kind auf deim Dach eines Treibhauses" ("Child on Top of a Greenhouse")

Translated with an introduction by Hans Sahl. *Die Heune Zeitung*, July 18, 1954.

Reprinted in *Sueddeutsche Zeitung* [Munich]. (UW)

1955

D27 "Börja dagen" ("Bring the Day!"), "Eldens gestalt" ("The Shape of the Fire"), "Sangen" ("Song" [I met a ragged man])

Translated by G. Printz-Pahlson and Kjell Espmark. *Upptakt* [Stockholm], No. 6 (1955), pp. 11–17. (UW)

1956

D28 "The Other"

Botteghe Oscure [Rome], XVIII (1956), 235–236.

This is the first appearance of this poem in English.

D29 "Flucht" ("The Flight" from "The Lost Son" [section 1]), "Where Knock Is Open Wide" (section 5 only)

Translated by Heinrich Stammler. *Merkur*, X (November) 1073–1076. (UW)

1957

D30 "Fra ildens skikkelse" ("The Shape of the Fire" [sections 4 and 5 only])

Translated by Erling Christie. *Vinduet: Glydendals Tidsskrift for Litterature* [Sweden], XI (1957), 74. (UW)

D31 "Third Meditation" (from "Meditations of an Old Woman")

Botteghe Oscure [Rome], XIX (Spring 1957), 207–210.

This is the first appearance of this poem in English.

D32 "Apporte le jour" ("Bring the day!"), "Orchidées" ("Orchids"), "La Visiteuse" ("The Visitant")

Translated by Alain Bosquet. *Présence*, VII (Winter 1957/1958), 38–40. (UW)

1958

D33 "Apporte le jour" ("Bring the Day!"), "Orchidées" ("Orchids"), "La visiteuse" ("The Visitant")

Translated by Alain Bosquet. *Correspondances: Revue Bimestrielle*, XXII (1958), 181–183. (UW)

D34 "Her Becoming (An Old Lady Muses)" (from "Meditations of an Old Woman")

Botteghe Oscure [Rome], XXI (Spring 1958), 183–186.

This is the first appearance of this poem in English.

1959

D35 "My Papa's Waltz" [the first and last stanzas only in Russian]

Translated under the supervision of Karl Shapiro. *American Ilustrated* [*Amerika*], n.s. No. 28 (Yeha 5 [1959]), p. 10. [English and Russian]

The poem appears with a critical note on Roethke in Shapiro's article, "Recent American Poetry" (*see* II, D20). *See* the introduction to this section for further comment.

D36 "Child on Top of a Greenhouse," "Cuttings (*later*)," "The Dream," "I Knew a Woman," "My Papa's Waltz,"

"Old Florist," "Orchids," "The Pure Fury," "She,"
"The Waking" (I wake to sleep)

Today's Japan [Tokyo], IV (March 1959), 45–51.
[English]

D37 "Orchidées" ("Orchids"), "Le réveil" ("The Waking"
[I strolled across])

Translated by René Char. *Preuves*, No. 100 (June 1959),
pp. 61–62.

Manuscripts with the same title and translator are located at the
University of Washington Manuscript Division A galley for this
appearance is located with a letter from Char at the University
of Washington Manuscript Division (*see* II, A7, p. 213).

1960

D38 "The Longing" [the title probably appears in Bengali]

Translated by Mihir Gupta. *Uttarsuri* [Bengal, India]
[early 1960?].

According to a letter from Gupta, this translation was to appear,
but the published text could not be located (*see* II, A7, p. 218).
     A manuscript in English with the same title and translator is
located at the University of Washington Manuscript Division.

D39 "Casa aperta" ("Open House"), "Che cosa raccontare
alle mie ossa?" ("What Can I Tell My Bones?"), "Il
ciclo" ("The Cycle"), "Conoscevo una dona" ("I Knew a
Woman"), "Elegy" ("Her face like a rain-beaten stone on
the day she rolled off" [English only]), "Il figlio perduto"
("The Lost Son"), "Garofani" ("Carnations"),
"Intermezzo" ("Interlude"), "Lei" ("She"), "Orchidee"
("Orchids"), "Parole per il vento" ("Words for the
Wind"), "Passeggiata nella tarda estate" ("A Walk in
Late Summer"), "Il puro furore" ("The Pure Fury"), "Il
risveglio" ("The Waking" ["I wake to sleep"]), "Il sogno"

("The Dream"), "Tutta la terra, tutta l'aria" ("All the Earth, All the Air"), "Il valzer del Babbo" ("My Papa's Waltz"), "La voce" ("The Voice")

Translated by Ada Jahn, Raffaels Petrillo, and Lina Angioletti, and edited by Renato Poggioli. "Poesie Da *Words for the Wind* Di Theodore Roethke," *Inventario*, Instituto Editoriale Italiano, xv (gennaio–disembre 1960), 1–25.

Manuscripts for "Il figlio perduto," "Tutta la terra, tutta l'aria," and "Orchidee" [with notes by Roethke?] are located at the University of Washington Manuscript Division. For other manuscripts of translations above, *see* I, D1. (UW)

1963

D40 "L'airone" ("The Heron")

Translated by Renato Poggioli. *Cesare Barbieri Courier*, v (Spring 1963), 17. (UW)

D41 "Jag behöver, jag behöver" ("I Need, I Need")

Translated by Rönnog Seaberg. *Ord Och Bild: Kulturtidskrift för de Nordiska Länderna* [Stockholm], Härte 5, 1963, p. 409. (UW)

D42 "Die dans" ("The Dance" [from "Four for Sir John Davies"]), "Die jong meisie" ("The Young Girl"), "Die verlore seun" ("The Lost Son"), "My papie se wals" ("My Papa's Waltz"), "Steggies" ("Cuttings"), "Wat sal ek my beendere vertel?" ("What Can I Tell My Bones?")

Tydskrift vir Letterkunda [Johannesburg], ii (May 1936), 37–41. (UW)

1964

D43 "Child on Top of a Greenhouse," "The Lamb," "A Light Breather," "Open House," "Praise to the End!", "Snake" (I saw a young snake glide)

Studi Americani [Rome], IX (1964), 425, 431, 437, 439, 450, 453. [English] (UWR)

This appearance also includes excerpts from "Open Letter" and "Some Remarks on Rhythm" (*see* I, D49).

D44 "Supper with Lindsay"

Tematy [1964?].

The assistant editor wrote Henry Rago of *Poetry* on July 27, 1964, asking permission to translate this poem into Polish for inclusion in a special edition of the magazine (*see* II, G32).

Appearances in Periodicals: Prose

1950

D45 "Last Class"

Botteghe Oscure [Rome], V (1950), 400–406.

This appearance was signed "Winterset Rothberg."
This is the first appearance of this piece in English.

D46 "Ultimo corso" ("Last Class")

Translated by Salvatore Rosati. *Poeti E Narratorie Inglesi E Americani* (*Botteghe Oscure* Supplement) [Rome], 1950, pp. 98–104.

This appearance was signed "Winterset Rothberg."

1951

D47 [Comment on "Give Way, Ye Gates" sequence]

Botteghe Oscure [Rome], VI (1951), 443. [English]

This is the first and only appearance of this comment. *See* I, D15 for the text of the comment.

1955

D48 "Tra dikter" [an excerpt from "Open Letter"]

Translated by G. Printz-Pahlson. *Upptakt* [Stockholm], No. 6 (1955), p. 11. (UW)

This appearance served as an introduction to Roethke's poems appearing in *Upptakt* (*see* I, D27).

1964

D49 "Open Letter," "Some Remarks on Rhythm" [excerpts appearing in English]

Studi Americani [Rome], IX (1964), v.p. (UWR)

These appear in an article in Italian (*see* II, D15).

Translations in Manuscript

D50 "The Dream"

A manuscript in French translated by René Char [unpublished?]. (UW)

For Roethke's comment on Char's influence, *see* pp. 222–223.

D51 "La forme du feu" ("The Shape of the Fire"), "Un pré de clarté" ("A Field of Light")

Typescripts in French translated by Bernard Citrogen [unpublished?]. (UW)

D52 "Kind auf eine Glaushaus" ("Child on Top of a Greenhouse")

A typescript in German translated by Erick Fried about 1961 [unpublished?]. (UW)

D53 "Natt kraka" ("Night Crow")

A manuscript in Swedish translated by Robert Sund [unpublished?]. (UW)

E Film and Recordings

This section, while probably incomplete, lists recordings and a film by Theodore Roethke, which are valuable as a reflection of Roethke's interest in the auditory nature of his poetry and as a reflection of his personality.

Film

E1 "The Abyss" [an excerpt], "The Adamant," "Cuttings (*later*)," "Dolor," "Elegy for Jane," "For an Amorous Lady," "Gob Music" [Roethke sings this poem], "In a Dark Time," "Light Listened," "My Papa's Waltz," "Once More, the Round," "A Rouse for Stevens," "The Sloth," "The Waking" (I wake to sleep)

In a Dark Time, directed by David Meyer. New York and San Francisco: Contemporary Films, Inc. (16 mm, black and white, sound, 27½ minutes), 1963. Produced with the cooperation of the students of San Francisco State College. (UW)

The University of Washington has a rental copy ($6.00) and a research copy (filed with the Roethke papers). The film is also available through Contemporary Films, Inc., 267 West 25th St., New York, for rental ($15.00) or purchase ($165.00). A copy was also released by National Educational Television in February, 1966, with the title: *U.S.A. Poetry: Theodore Roethke*.

A pamphlet entitled *Contemporary Films Present In A Dark Time: A Film about Theodore Roethke by David Meyer* appeared in 1963. It includes a note, "The Poet" (*see* II, C115), by James Schevill and Mark Linethal. Schevill's comments on this film appear in two unpublished letters (September 14, 1963, and October 26, 1963) to Henry Rago, editor of *Poetry* (*see* II, G32). The pamphlet also includes the text for each poem read and critical comments on the film by Stanley Kunitz, Professor Patrick D. Hazard, Robert Lowell, Ray B. West, Jr., Richard Wilbur, Peter Vierick, John Ciardi, and others. (UW)

The film includes scenes shot at Roethke's home at 3802 East John Street in Seattle, Parrington Hall at the University of Washington, and the studio of Elizabeth Bayley Willis (mother of Mary Randlett, whose photographs of Roethke have appeared frequently) on Bainbridge Island near Seattle. According to Elizabeth Willis, Roethke was particularly fond of the studio and the adjacent woods. It is with scenes from these woods that the film opens with a reading of "In a Dark Time."

For further information, *see* Biographical Notes 1963, II, B26, 201–203, and II, E2.

Recordings: Poetry

1947

E2 "The Adamant," "Ballad of the Clairvoyant Widow," "The Bat," "The Cycle," "Interlude" (two readings), "Judge Not," "The Lost Son," "My Papa's Waltz," "Night Journey," "Vernal Sentiment"

[Untitled.] The Library of Congress, LWO No. 2689 (reel 9), 1947. (LC)

Recorded in the Recording Laboratory of the Library of Congress on January 3, 1947.

E3 "The Long Alley," "The Shape of the Fire"

[Untitled.] Harvard Vocarium Records, 1947. (HC)
See I, A12, p. 127.

1948

E4 "The Lost Son"

Twentieth Century Poetry in English: Theodore Roethke. Library of Congress, Album P8 and Record P39 (12", 78 rpm, 2 sides), 1948. (LC)

Recorded in the Recording Laboratory at the Library of Congress in 1948 and released in August, 1950. The album is available at $4.50 from the Reference Department, Music Division, Recording Laboratories of the Library of Congress.

A printed leaflet including biographical and bibliographic notes bearing the title above is located with the Roethke papers at the University of Washington. (UW)

1953

E5 "Academic," "The Bat," "Big Wind," "The Cow," "The Donkey," "Elegy for Jane," "A Field of Light," "Four for Sir John Davies," "The Heron," "Interlude," "The Lady and the Bear," "The Lizard" (The Time to Tickle a Lizard), "My Papa's Waltz," "The Old Florist," "The Shape of the Fire," "The Sloth," "Vernal Sentiment," "The Waking" (I wake to sleep), "The Whale"

"Simmons Lecture Series." Pennsylvania State University (1 tape, 3 ¾ speed, full track), February 18, 1953. (PSC) Roethke also read poems by Elizabeth Hutchins, Katherine McLaughlin, and David Wagoner. The reading was introduced by Dr. P. A. Shelley of the Department of German.

This is the first public appearance of "The Donkey," "The Whale," and "The Lizard," which were not published until 1961.

Review: Edmund Reiss. "Roethke Poems Delight Audience," *Daily Collegian* [State College, Pa.], L (February 19, 1953), 2.

E6 "Big Wind," "Four for Sir John Davies," "The Heron," "I Cry Love! Love!," "I Need, I Need," "The Waking" (I wake to sleep)

"An American Poet Introduces Himself and His Poems." British Broadcasting Corporation, Disc No. 34254, 1953.

Recorded and broadcasted in London on July 30, 1953. *See* I, A11, pp. 7–13 (incomplete) and UW, UWE for text.

1954

E7 "Bring the Day," "A Field of Light," "Give Way, Ye Gates," "I Need, I Need," "The Long Alley," "The Lost

Son," "O Lull Me, Lull Me," "Sensibility! O La!,"
"The Shape of the Fire," "Where Knock Is Open Wide"

" 'I Cry, Love! Love!' " Station KPFA, Berkeley, California
(2 tapes, 3¾ speed), 1954. (UW, UW, KPFA)

Recorded and broadcasted by Station KPFA on March 24, 1954
(9:10–9:40 P.M.), March 25, 1954 (8:45–9:10 P.M.), and April
4, 1954 (11:45 A.M.), For an excerpt from this tape, see II, A6.
    Roethke makes comments on the sequence and individual poems
(see II, C82, pp. 88–89).

1957

E8 "Academic," "Big Wind," "The Dance" [from "Four
    for Sir John Davies"], "The Exulting" [from "The Dying
    Man"], "I Need, I Need," "The Long Alley," "My Papa's
    Waltz," "The Sloth," "They Sing, They Sing" [from
    "The Dying Man"], "Vernal Sentiment," "The Waking"
    (I wake to sleep). *Theodore Roethke Reading His Own*
    Works and Others. Western Electric Records (12",
    33 1/3 rpm, 2 sides), May 1957. (UW, RC)

Recorded in May 1957 at Reed College, Portland, Oregon (see
Biographical Notes, May 1957). Roethke also read poems by
Louise Bogan, W. H. Auden, Stanley Kunitz, and Thomas Hardy.
An epigram for W. H. Auden (which is a play on words of some
lines from Auden's "The Sea and the Mirror") makes its only
only appearance in this reading: "Auden, Auden, that Dirty Dick's
with a floppy nose, that drank his Liquor straight."
    For Roethke's comment on this reading, see I, A12, p. 213.

1959

E9 "Academic," "Big Wind," "Child on Top of a Green-
    house," "For an Amorous Lady," "Elegy for Jane,"
    "The Heron," "I Need, I Need" [an excerpt], ("It was
    beginning Winter") [from "The Lost Son"], "The Lamb,"
    "My Papa's Waltz," "Night Crow," "The Return" [from

"The Lost Son"], "The Sloth," "Vernal Sentiment,"
"Where Knock Is Open Wide"

[Untitled.] The Library of Congress, LWO No. 2863
(1 reel), 1959. (LC)

Recorded at the YM-YWHA Poetry Center in New York City in
July 1959. Roethke also read poems by Léonie Adams, Janet
Lewis, W. B. Yeats, Louise Bogan, Allen Tate, Gerard Manley
Hopkins, Stanley Kunitz, and Rolfe Humphries.

E10 "The Bat," "Big Wind," "Elegy" (Few the Academes
we can), "I Knew a Woman," "I Need, I Need," "In a
Dark Time," "The Longing," "The Lost Son," "Method,"
"Moss-Gathering," "The Motion," "My Papa's Waltz,"
"Night Crow," "Pickle Belt," "Reply to a Lady Editor"
[Roethke sings this poem], "A Rouse for Stevens,"
"Saturday Eight O'Clock," "The Sequel," "The Shape of
the Fire," "Vernal Sentiment"

[Untitled.] University of Washington Health Science
Auditorium, Seattle (2 tapes, 7½ speed, 1 side only),
August, 1959. (UW)

This is a humorous and informal reading with numerous comments
on the poems read. "Elegy" is an unpublished poem appearing
only in this reading. "The Longing" appears here with a minor
revision. "Saturday Eight O'Clock" was not published until
November 1959 even though it was written years before at Penn
State.
     Reviews: Jack DeYounge. "Roethke Gives Warm Informal
Reading," *Seattle Times*, August 21, 1959, p. 27 (UWSC);
George W. Taylor. "Books and Readers," *The Argus* [Seattle],
September 1, 1959. (UW)

E11 "I Knew a Woman," " 'The Shimmer of Evil'—
Louise Bogan"

An Album of Modern Poetry; *An Anthology Read by the
Poets*, ed. Oscar Williams. Columbia Broadcasting System,
LWO No. 2859, 1959.

E12 "Elegy for Jane," " 'The Shimmer of Evil'—*Louise Bogan*," "I Knew a Woman"

An Album of Modern Poetry, III. Listening Library, PM 72-13 (12", 33 1/3 rpm), 1959.

1960

E13 "After a Betrayal of Confidence," "The Decision," "Elegy" (Her face like a rain-beaten stone on the day she rolled off), "From Whence?," "Gob Music" [Roethke sings this poem], "In a Dark Time," "In Evening Air," "Light Listened," "The Longing," "The Motion," "The Old Florist's Lament," "The Sequel," "The Shy Man"

"The Living Poet: Theodore Roethke." British Broadcasting Corporation, No. TLO 34582, 1961.

Recorded November 3, 1960 (12:00–13:00 in Studio PP2) and broadcasted over the BBC in London on February 8, 1961. A copy of the script is filed with the Roethke papers at the University of Washington.
     Review: Paul Fenis. *Observer* [London], February 12, 1961. (UW)

1961

E14 "Journey to the Interior," "Journeys," "The Long Waters," "Meditation at Oyster River"

"Four Poems by Theodore Roethke." British Broadcasting Corporation, No. TLO 45311, 1961.

Recorded for an unscheduled broadcast for the Third Program (11:15 A.M.–12:00 P.M.) on February 13, 1961. A copy of the script is filed with the Roethke papers at the University of Washington.

E15 "The Return" [from "The Lost Son"], "The Wraith" [from "Four for Sir John Davies"]

Anthology of Contemporary American Poetry. Folkways
Records, FL No. 9735 (12", 33 1/3 rpm), 1961.

The text is included with the album.

1962

E16 "All the Earth, All the Air," "Bring the Day!," "Dinky,"
"The Dream" (I met her as a blossom on a stem), "Elegy
for Jane," "Four for Sir John Davies," "Give Way, Ye
Gates," "I Knew a Woman," "I Need, I Need," "The Lady
and the Bear," "The Long Alley," "The Lost Son,"
"Love's Progress," "Memory," "My Papa's Waltz," "The
Other," "The Pure Fury," "The Renewal," "Reply to a
Lady Editor," "The Sensualists," "She," "Song for
the Squeeze Box," "The Surly One," "The Swan," "The
Voice," "The Waking" (I wake to sleep), "Words
for the Wind"

*Words for the Wind; Selections from the Poetry of
Theodore Roethke.* Folkways Records, FL No. 9736 (12",
33 1/3 rpm), 1962.

Also issued by Listening Library, PM 35 (12", 33½ rpm) as
Theodore Roethke.
   Reviews: David A. Lupher. "Lost Son: Theodore Roethke,"
Yale Literary Magazine, cxxxv (March 1967), 11; John Wain,
Observer Weekend Review [London], October 14, 1962. (UW)

1965

E17 "The Lost Son"

"Tribute to Theodore Roethke." WUOM, Ann Arbor,
Michigan (tape), 1965. (UM)

Recorded and broadcasted at the University of Michigan in May,
1965.

1966

E18 "The Return," "The Wraith"

Anthology of Contemporary American Poetry. Folkways
Records, FL No. 9735 (12", 33 1/3 rpm), 1966.

1968

E19 "Dinky," "Elegy for Jane," "The Lady and the Bear,"
"My Papa's Waltz," "The Sloth," "The Shape of a Rat?"
[excerpt from "The Lost Son"]

The Light and Serious Side of Theodore Roethke.
Scholastic Records, CC No. 0604 (7", 33 1/3 rpm), 1968.

Recorded at the University of Washington in Seattle.

E20 "Big Wind," "Elegy for Jane," "I Knew a Woman,"
"The Lady and the Bear," "My Papa's Waltz," "Night
Crow," " 'The Shimmer of Evil,'—*Louise Bogan*"

Theodore Roethke. Spoken Arts (part of a 15-volume
anthology), 1968.

1970

E21 "The Bat" (vol. I), "The Lady and the Bear" (vol. II),
"Mid-Country Blow" (vol. III), "The Heron" (vol. IV)

A Gathering of Great Poetry for Children. Caedmon
Records, TC 1236, 1237, 1238 (12", 33 1/3 rpm), 1970.

1971

E22 "The Cycle," "Dinky," "The Donkey," "Give Way, Ye
Gates," "My Papa's Waltz," "Pickle Belt," "Where Knock
Is Open Wide," and others

Theodore Roethke Reads His Poetry. Caedmon Recordings,
TC 1351 (12", 33 1/3 rpm), 1971..

Recordings: Prose

E23 "An American Poet Introduces Himself and His Poems"
British Broadcasting Corporation, Disc No. SLO 34254,
1953. (UW, UWE)

Recording broadcasted in London on July 30, 1953 (*see* I, E6).

E24 "The Poetry of Louise Bogan"
WUOM, Ann Arbor, Michigan (tape), 1960.
(UM tape, UW script)

Recording of the Hopwood Lecture at the University of Michigan on May 19, 1960 (*see* I, A11, pp. 133–148, and I, C218).

E25 "Some Remarks on Rhythm: Conversations on the Craft of Poetry" Cleanth Brooks and Robert Penn Warren, eds. Holt, Rinehart, and Winston (3 3/4 speed, tape No. 2), 1961. (UM)

Recorded supplement to the anthology *Understanding Poetry*. New York: Holt, Rinehart and Winston, 1961 (*see* I, A11, pp. 71–84, and I, C219).

E26 "James Dickey Poetry Reading"
Poetry Northwest Series, Seattle (tape), 1963. (UM)

Recorded introduction by Roethke to the Dickey reading at the University of Washington in Seattle (*see* II, B11).

Roethke's Poetry Read by Others

(*see also* I, F7, 10, 11, 12, 16, 18)

E27 "The Geranium," "The Saginaw Song"
John Ciardi. "An Evening with Ted Roethke." WUOM, University of Michigan, Ann Arbor, 1967. (UM)

Recorded at the Arthur Hill High School in Saginaw on May 24, 1967, to inaugurate the Theodore Roethke Memorial Foundation. For the text, *see* II, B10.

E28 "The Bat"
Paul and Ellen Holly Hecht. *Reflections on a Gift of Watermelon Pickle.* Folkways/Scholastic Records, No. 21007 (12", 33 1/3 rpm), 1968.

E29 "Academic," "After Munich" (1939), ["Words for the Hesitant"] (1937), "The Bringer of Tidings," ["This Light"] (1937), ["On the Road to Woodlawn"], ["The Pursued"] (1941), "Pastoral," "Specialist," "Summer Wind," "Three Poems on F. Prokosch," "The Undoing," ["Sign Though No Sign"] (1935).

Rolfe Humphries. "The Early Theodore Roethke: Reminiscences and Reading. University of Washington, Seattle. (1 tape, speed 3¾), 1966 (see II, E6).

Dates in parenthesis denote probable date of composition. Titles in brackets indicate poems were not titled. For additional information, see II, A7.

E30 "What Can I Tell My Bones?"

Rolfe Humphries. "Theodore Roethke Memorial Reading, May 25, 1966." University of Washington, Seattle (1 tape, speed 3¾), 1966 (see II, E7).

Includes a dedicatory poem by Humphries (see II, F42).

E31 "The Cow," "Cuttings (*later*)," "The Lost Son"

Stanley Kunitz. "An Evening with Ted Roethke," WUOM, University of Michigan, Ann Arbor, 1967. (UW)

Recorded at the Arthur Hill High School in Saginaw on May 24, 1967, to inaugurate the Theodore Roethke Memorial Foundation. For text, see II, B10.

E32 "Academic"

Solomon Katz. "Theodore Roethke Memorial Reading, May 25, 1967." University of Washington, Seattle (1 tape, speed 3¾), 1967. (UWE)

Katz reads this poem in the introduction to the reading by Archibald MacLeish (see II, E10).

E33 "The Geranium," "The Heron," "In a Dark Time," "The Lizard" (He too has eaten well), "The Lost Son," "The Shape of the Fire" [section V]

Robert Lowell. "Theodore Roethke Memorial Reading, May 25, 1965." University of Washington, Seattle (2 tapes, speed 7½), 1965. (UWE)

See II, E9.

E34 "Death Piece"

Archibald MacLeish. "Theodore Roethke Memorial Reading, May 25, 1967." University of Washington, Seattle (1 tape, speed 3¾), 1967. (UWE)

See II, E10.

E35 "All the Earth, All the Air," "The Song" (I met a ragged man)

Richard Murphy. "New Verse." British Broadcasting Corporation, Third Programme Series, 1955.

Recorded in London on August 17, 1955.

E36 "The Boy and the Bush," "The Ceiling," "The Hippo," "The Lamb," "The Lizard," "The Meadow Mouse," "Myrtle," "Night Journey," "Philander"

Jean Richards. *The Light and Serious Side of Theodore Roethke.* Scholastic Records, No. 0604 (7", 33 1/3 rpm), 1968.

See I, E19.

E37 "Big Wind," "The Meadow Mouse," "Method"

Allan Seager. "An Evening with Ted Roethke." WUOM, University of Michigan, Ann Arbor, 1967.

For text, *see* II, B10.

E38 "The Dance" [from "Four for Sir John Davies"], "I Waited," "A Light Breather"
William Taylor. *Sounds of Pacific Northwest Poetry.* Washington State Poetry Foundation (No. W 4 RM—8758, 12", 33 1/3 rpm), n.d.

Includes a dedicatory poem by Edgar H. Dickson (*see* II, F29).

E39 "The Long Alley," "The Lost Son," "The Shape of the Fire"
Dylan Thomas. [Untitled.] British Broadcasting Corporation, 1952.

Recorded in London on October 8, 1952. For Roethke's comment, *see* I, A12, p. 182.
   Review: Martin Armstrong. *The Listener* [London], XI (October 16, 1952), 655.

F Musical Settings and Backgrounds

This section cannot be considered complete; it merely lists chronologically musical settings and backgrounds present with Roethke's papers and elsewhere. "Song" (O, I love red and green), "Old Song," and "Words for the Bard" appear to be the only poems written specifically for a musical setting.

Undated

F1 "The Long Alley

Ruth Lewis. n.p., n.d. (UW)

This setting is a madrigal based on two stanzas from "The Long Alley."

1947

F2 "Old Song" (I come to the willow alone)

Douglas Moore. *Old Song*. New York: Carl Fischer, Inc., 1950. (UW)

This lyric was especially written for the setting and does not appear elsewhere.

1950

F3 "The Kitty-Cat Bird"

Gail Kubik. [Unpublished?] Saratoga Springs, New York (Yaddo Writer's Colony), June 10, 1950. (UW)

F4 "Song" (O, I love red and green)

Ben Weber (arranged by J. Glosel). [Unpublished?] n.p., September 15, 1950. (UW)

This lyric was probably especially written for the setting since it does not appear elsewhere.

F5 "The Cycle," "No Bird," "The Waking" (I strolled across)

Paul Tufts. *Three Songs.* [Unpublished?] Seattle, December 2, 1950. (UW)

1952

F6 "The Monotony Song"
Gail Kubik. *The Monotony Song: American Folk Song.* New York: G. Ricordi and Company, 1960. (DC, UW)

Performed at the Dartmouth College Carnival Concert on February 6–7 and April 2, 1953. The setting was commissioned by Dartmouth College and dedicated to the Glee Club. This setting was completed in 1952.

1953

F7 "The Lady and the Bear"

Bernard Wolfman. [Unpublished?] New York, January 20, 22, and 25, 1953.

Performed over radio station WABF and WJZ channel 7 in New York City by Bernard Wolfman (guitar) on January 20 and 22. A recording of this song by Wolfman was played on January 25 at the Circle-in-the-Square Theatre (*see* Biographical Notes, January 1953, and I, F8).

F8 "The Kitty-Cat Bird"

Larry Pratt. [Unpublished?] New York, January 25, 1953.

Performed at the Circle-in-the-Square. Roethke was accompanied by Larry Pratt (accordion), Wilder Hobson (trombone), and Verna Hobson (tuba). *See* Biographical Notes, January 1953, and I, F7.
  Review: *New York Times Book Review*, February 8, 1953, p. 8. (UW)

1959

F9 "I Strolled Across an Open Field" ["The Waking"]
"Orchids"

Ned Rorem. *Two Poems of Theodore Roethke.* New York:
Boosey and Hawkes, 1969.

The setting was completed in 1959. *See* Biographical Notes,
April 1960.

F10 "My Papa's Waltz"

Ned Rorem. *My Papa's Waltz.* New York: Henmar Press,
Inc. 1963;
David Diamond. *My Papa's Waltz.* New York: Southern
Music Publication Company.
Recordings: *Songs of Ned Rorem.* Columbia, MS 6561,
1963; *Ned Rorem Songs.* Odyssey, 32 16 0274. Sung
by Donald Gramm, Bass-baritone.

The setting was completed in 1959. *see* Biographical Notes,
April 1960.

F11 "Root Cellar"

Ned Rorem. *Root Cellar.* New York: C. F. Peters,
1961–1963. *Recordings: Songs of Ned Rorem.* Columbia,
MS 6561, 1963; *Ned Rorem Songs.* Odyssey, 32 16 0274.
Sung by Donald Gramm, Bass-baritone.

The setting was completed in 1959. *See* Biographical Notes,
April 1960.

F12 "Snake" (I saw a young snake)

Ned Rorem. *Snake.* New York: C.F. Peters, 1963.
Recordings: *Songs of Ned Rorem.* Columbia, MS 6561,
1963; *Ned Rorem Songs.* Odyssey, 32 16 0274. Sung
by Gianna D'Angelo, Soprano.

The setting was completed in 1959. *See* Biographical Notes,
April 1960.

F13 "In a Dark Time"

Leo Smit. [Unpublished?] Los Angeles, May 12, 1959.

Sung by Soprano Catherine Gayer at the University of California at Los Angeles at Schoenberg Hall. A copy of the program is filed with a letter from Leo Smit at the University of Washington Manuscript Division (*see* II, A7, p. 232).
Review: *Seattle Post-Intelligencer*, March 14, 1960, p. 6.

F14 "Memory"

Ned Rorem. *Memory.* New York: Henmar Press, Inc., 1961. (UW)

The setting was completed in New York on May 27, 1959. *See* Biographical Notes, April 1960.

F15 "The Waking" (I wake to sleep)

Ned Rorem. *The Waking.* New York: Henmar Press, Inc., 1961. (UW)

The setting was completed at Saratoga Springs, New York (Yaddo Writers' Colony), June 9–11, 1959. *See* Biographical Notes, April 1960.

F16 "Night Crow"

Ned Rorem. *Night Crow.* New York: Henmar Press, Inc., 1963.

Recording: *Some Trees.* Composer Recordings, CRI-S-238.

The setting was completed on August 22, 1959. *See* Biographical Notes, April 1960.

1961

F17 " 'The Shimmer of Evil' "

Richard G. Swift. [Unpublished?] Davis, California, February 14, 1961.

Performed at the University of California at Davis.

1963

F18 "The Apparition," "Interlude"

Ned Rorem. *The Apparition* and *Interlude.* New York: Boosey and Hawkes, 1963.

Recordings: *Poems of Love and the Rain.* Desto Records, DC 6480, and Composer Recordings, CRI 202, 1963. Sung by Regina Surfaty and Beverly Wolff, mezzo-sopranos, with Ned Rorem at the piano.

The settings were completed sometime during 1963.

F19 "The Voice"

Hope Leroy Baumgartner. *Selected Words for Unaccompanied Chorus,* I. New Haven: A-R Editions, Inc., 1963. (UW)

F20 "Words for the Bard"

Stanley N. Keen. Unpublished. Seattle, June 1963. (UW)

This lyric was written specially for this setting and was described as a tongue-in-cheek assault on the White House position of "Poet Laureate."

F21 "The O'Connell's Daughter," "The Shy Man"

Stanley N. Keen. Unpublished. Seattle, July 1963.

This Irish ballad was written for Beatrice Roethke. A manuscript by Roethke and the setting are in the possession of Stanley Keen. The poem was first published in August 1961 (*see* I, C167).

1965

F22 "The Boy and the Bush," "The Ceiling," "The Chair," "The Cow," "Dinky," "The Donkey," "The Gnu," "The Hippo," "The Kitty-Cat Bird," "The Lady and the Bear," "The Lamb," "The Lizard," "The Monotony Song," "Myrtle," "Philander," "The Serpent," "The Wagtail," "The Whale," "The Yak"

Stanley N. Keen. *Improvisations on 'The Nonsense Poems'
of Theodore Roethke.* Unpublished. Seattle, April 1, 1965.

All of the poems were narrated and mimicked against a background
of illustrations and music (except "The Kitty-Cat Bird," which
was a setting). The musicians were Stan Keen (jazz piano),
Floyd Standifer (trumpet), and Ronald Simon (bass fiddle). The
narrator was Ben Bradford, and the mimicker was Diane Adler.
The artist was Jerrold Balline. The program was presented by the
Music and Art Foundation of Seattle for the benefit of the Cornish
School of Allied Arts.

Review: "Theodore Roethke's Poems Unify Music and Dance,"
Seattle Times, April 2, 1965; *see also* Awards, Memorials,
Reminiscences, Tributes 1965.

1966

F23 "What Can I Tell My Bones?"

Ned Rorem. *Sun.* New York: Boosey and Hawkes, 1966.

The final verses of the poem appear as part of a cycle for voice and
orchestra entitled *Sun.* The setting was completed in 1966.

1971

F24 "The Serpent" (There was a serpent who liked to sing)
Ned Rorem. *The Serpent.* New York: Boosey and
Hawkes, 1971.

II Works and Materials about Theodore Roethke

A Bibliographies, Checklists, and Other Reference Works

This section includes published bibliographies, checklists, and other reference works; additional unpublished bibliographies are listed in II, G1–9.

Theodore Roethke: A Manuscript Checklist (II, A7) is a listing of Roethke's manuscripts, letters, and other writings in twenty repositories throughout the United States and Canada. Information not included in the *Checklist* concerning recently collected Roethke materials with the papers of Allan Seager at The Bancroft Library of the University of California, Berkeley, is cited in I, B24 and II, A1, B26, and G33.

A1 "Allan Seager Papers," *Bancroftiana*, No. 47 (October 1970), p. 5. (UWNW)

> The Seager papers at The Bancroft Library of the University of California at Berkeley include: letters of Roethke (1931–1960); photocopies of Roethke's notebooks, poems, miscellaneous writings, and other papers; a list of books belonging to him; clippings and reviews regarding his work; bibliography and chronology (*see also*: II, B26 and II,G33). (UCB)

A1a Courtney, Winifred F., ed. *The Reader's Adviser*: *A Guide to the Best in Literature*. 11th ed. New York: R. R. Bowker Company, 1968, I, 223.

A2 Hastings, John. "Bibliography of the Published Work of Theodore Roethke," *The Browse* [State College, Pa.], No. 8 (March 8, 1941), pp. 3–4.

A3 Hollenberg, Susan Weidman. "Theodore Roethke," *Twentieth Century Literature*, XII (January 1967), 216–221.

A4 Lane, Gary, ed. *A Concordance to The Poems of Theodore Roethke*. Metuchen, New Jersey: The Scarecrow Press, Inc., 1972.

Programmed by Roland Dedekind.

A5 *Library of Congress National Union Catalogue of Manuscript Collections, 1965–1966.*

This collection contains early letters and poems 1934–1941; including 27 letters from Roethke to Rolfe Humphries and 32 poems, several of which contain corrections and reworkings in the author's hand. The letters contain references to W. H. Auden, Stephen Spender, Malcolm Cowley, Louis Untermeyer, and Humphries. For further comment on the collection, *see*: Paul G. Sifton, "Acquisition Notes: Theodore Roethke Manuscripts," *Library of Congress Bulletin*, XXIV (December 6, 1965)), and "Recent Acquisition," *Wilson Library Bulletin*, February 1966, p. 484.

A6 McLeod, James R. "Bibliographic Notes on the Creative Process and Sources of Roethke's 'The Lost Son' Sequence," *Northwwest Review*, XI (Summer 1971), 97–111.

A7 ———. *Theodore Roethke: A Manuscript Checklist.* Kent, Ohio: Kent State University Press, 1971.

For further comments on the collections listed in this checklist, *see* II, A1 and A3 for the Library of Congress; I, B1 and B67 and Awards, Memorials, Reminiscences, Tributes 1966 for Pennsylvania State University; II, B46 for the State University of New York at Buffalo; Awards, Memorials, Reminiscences, Tributes 1964 for

Tufts University; II, G9 and G31 and Awards, Memorials, Reminiscences, Tributes 1964 for the University of Washington; and I, A9.

Reviews: Charles W. Mann, Jr. *Library Journal*, LXXVI (December 15, 1971), 4083; Kenyon C. Rosenberg. "Theodore Roethke," in *American Reference Books Annual*, 3rd edition. Littleton, Colorado: Libraries Unlimited, 1971.

A8 Malkoff, Karl. "Bibliography," in *Theodore Roethke; An Introduction to the Poetry*. New York: Columbia University Press, 1966, pp. 226–234.

A9 Mills, Ralph J., Jr. "Selected Bibliography," in *Theodore Roethke*. Minneapolis: University of Minnesota Press, 1963, pp. 46–47.

A10 Walker, Ursula Genung. *Notes on Theodore Roethke*. Charlottesville: Bibliographical Society of the University of Virginia, 1968.

Review: *See* II, C86.

A11 White, William. *John Ciardi: A Bibliography*. Detroit: Wayne State Press, 1959, p. 56.

Includes a list of Roethke's manuscripts located with Ciardi's papers in the Feinberg Collection. The manuscripts are for those poems appearing in *Mid-Century American Poets* (*see* I, B17).

B Biographical Studies and Commentaries

The first part of this section lists general studies or random commentaries, whereas the second part lists chronologically items with specific significance. Most of the early citations in the second part were gleaned from the Saginaw scrapbooks located at the University of Washington or were selected from the great mass of clippings in the special collections of the University of Washington (UW, UWE, UWR, UWSC) and Pennsylvania State University (PSC, PSU); therefore, in several instances the citations are not complete.

General Biographical Studies

B1 Anon. " 'And So Much I Have Missed,' " *Penn State Alumni News*, LIII (February 1967), 18–19.
See I, C147.

B2 Anon. "Faculty Profile," *Washington Alumnus* [Seattle], V (Spring 1962), 9–10.

B3 Anon. "Five Music Men of Words . . . Who They Are . . . As They Began and Today," *Newsweek*, LI (March 17, 1958), 110.

B4 Anon. "Theodore Roethke," in *The Americana Annual of 1964, An Encyclopedia of the Events of 1963*. New York: American Corporation, 1964, p. 744.

B5 Bourbon, Joseph A. "Lone Scout," *Saturday Review*, LIV (March 13, 1971), 19.

B6 Brinnin, John Malcom. *Dylan Thomas in America.* Boston and Toronto: Little, Brown and Company, 1955, p. 8.

B7 Callaghan, Margaret B. "Seattle's Surrealistic Poet," *Seattle Times Magazine,* March 16, 1952, p. 7. (UWR, UWSC)

B8 Ciardi, John. "Comments on Theodore Roethke," *Cimarron Review,* No. 8 (March 1969), pp. 6–8.

Includes Ciardi's "Was a Man" (*see* II, F24).

B9 ———. "Theodore Roethke," *Saturday Review,* LI (June 29, 1968), 14.

This a brief introduction to "Words for Young Writers" (*see* I, C228).

B10 Ciardi, John, Stanley Kunitz, and Allan Seager. "An Evening with Ted Roethke," *Michigan Quarterly Review,* VI (October 1967), 227–245.

Reprinted: *see* II, C59.

B11 Dickey, James. "The Greatest American Poet," *Atlantic,* CCXXII (November 1968), 53–58.

Reactions to this article by Frank Kermode, Howard Nemerov, James Schevill, W. D. Snodgrass, Stanley Kunitz, Robert Bly, Denise Levertov, Richard Seamon, William Stafford, Malcolm Cowley, X. J. Kennedy, Kenneth Burke, and Beatrice Roethke appeared in "The Mail," *Atlantic,* CCXXII (December 1968), 5–11. (UWSC)

B12 Everette, Oliver. "Theodore Roethke: The Poet as a Teacher," *West Coast Review,* III (Spring 1968), 5–11. (UWSC)

Includes an early version of "Philander" (*see* I, C208).

B13 FitzGibbon, Constantine. *The Life of Dylan Thomas.* London: J.M. Dent, 1965.

Includes reference to Roethke's relationship to Thomas and excerpts from Roethke's essay "Dylan Thomas: Memories and Appreciations" (*see* I, C213).
Reprinted: *The Life of Dylan Thomas.* Boston and Toronto: Atlantic Monthly Press, 1965; and London: Sphere Books Ltd., 1968.

B14 Fuller, John G. "Another Poet," *Saturday Review,* XLII (March 7, 1959), 10–11.

Reference to this article appeared in the *Centre Daily Times* [State College, Pennsylvania], XLII (April 7, 1959), 4. (PSC)

B15 Hart, Dorothy. "Theodore Roethke 'Blew' for Seattle," *Northwest Today* (*Seattle Post-Intelligencer*), May 28, 1967, p. 7. (UWR, UWSC)

B16 Hart, James D., ed. "Theodore Roethke," in *Oxford Companion to American Literature.* 4th ed. New York: Oxford University Press, 1965, p. 721.

B17 Heilman, Robert B. "Theodore Roethke: Personal Notes," *Shenandoah,* XVI (Autumn 1964), 55–64.

Reprinted: "Roethke: A Candid Reminiscence," *Seattle Magazine,* II (June 1, 1965), 38–44.

B18 Herzberg, Max J., ed. "Theodore Roethke," in *The Reader's Encyclopedia of American Literature.* New York: Thomas J. Crowell Company, 1962, pp. 969–970.

B19 Kizer, Carolyn. "Poetry: School of the Pacific Northwest," *New Republic,* CXXXV (July 16, 1956), 18–19.

Reprinted: *Congressional Record,* July 12, 1956, section A, p. 5490.

B20 Kunitz, Stanley. "Theodore Roethke," *New York Review of Books,* I (October 17, 1963), 21–22.

Includes "His Foreboding" (*see* I, C192).

B21 ———. "Roethke Remembered," *Show*, v (May 1965), 10–11.

Essentially the same article as in B20 above.

B21a ———. "Theodore Roethke," in *Atlantic Brief Lives: A Biographical Companion to the Arts*, ed. Louis Kronenberger. Boston, Toronto: Little, Brown and Company, 1971, pp. 649–651.

B22 McManis, Jack. "Theodore Roethke as a Poetry Teacher at Penn State, 1936–1947," *Penn State English Notes*, xi (Spring 1966), 19–21.

B23 Magnison, Kristin. "Poets-Teachers Blend Verse and Lectures in Dual Role," *University of Washington Daily* [Seattle], April 17, 1969, p. 12.

B24 Origio, Iris. "Marguerite Caetani," *Atlantic*, ccxv (February 1965), 86 ff.

See I, C260.

B25 Roethke, Beatrice. "About Theodore Roethke," in *Theodore Roethke: Second Memorial Program*. New York: YM-YWHA Poetry Center, January 17, 1966, unpaginated. (UW, PSC)

See Awards, Memorials, Reminiscences, Tributes 1966.

B26 Seager, Allan. *The Glass House: The Life of Theodore Roethke*. New York: McGraw-Hill, 1968.

The Seager Papers of The Bancroft Library, University of California at Berkeley, include Seager's interviews with people who knew Roethke and notes for *The Glass House*; comment by Beatrice Roethke on *The Glass House*; photocopies of various drafts of *The Glass House*; printer's copy, galleys and corrected galleys; reviews of *The Glass House*; and letters to Seager commenting on *The Glass House.* (UCB) *See* I, B24 and II, A1, B11, G14, 15.

Reviews: Anon. *Virginia Kirkus Service,* XXXVI (August 1968), 875; Anon. *Publisher's Weekly,* CIXIV (August 26, 1968), 270; O'Gorman, Ned. "Theodore Roethke and Paddy Flynn," *Columbia University Forum,* XII (Spring 1969), 34–36; James Atlas. "Roethke's Boswell," *Poetry,* CXIV (August 1969), 327–330; Robert Boyers. "The Roethke Puzzle," *New Republic,* CLX (January 8, 1969), 32–34; David Brewster. "Glimpse into a Poet's Life," *Seattle Times Magazine,* December 29, 1968, p. 19; Kenneth Burke. "Cult of the Breakthrough," *New Republic,* CLIX (September 21, 1968), 25–26; Jon Clark. "On the Diagonal," *Michigan Quarterly Review,* VIII (Winter 1969), 1–2; L. S. Dembro. *American Literature,* XLI (May 1969), 305; Julia C. DeVang. *Spirit: A Magazine of Poetry,* XXXVI (Spring 1969), 37–39; Coburn Freer. *Arizona Quarterly,* XXV (1969), 83–84; Ben W. Fuson. *Library Journal,* XCII (September I, 1968), 3006; Michael Harrington. "No 'Half-baked Bacchus' from Saginaw," *Commonweal,* LXXXIX (February 21, 1969), 656–657; Thomas Lask. "Life Was as Difficult as the Art," *New York Times,* January 1, 1969, p. 19; Elwood McClellan. *Michigan History,* LIII (1969), 319–322; Karl Malkoff. *Southwest Review,* LIV (1969), 329–332; M. L. Rosenthal. "Poet's Story: The Glass House," *New York Times Book Review,* November 24, 1968, pp. 12, 16, 18; Karl Shapiro. "Case History of a Poet's Crackup," *Book World (Chicago Tribune and Washington Post),* II (October 13, 1968), 7; Paul Sherman. "Making It as a Poet," *Nation,* CCVIII (January 6, 1969), 27–28; Arnold Stein. "Roethke: Man and Poet," *Virginia Quarterly Review,* XLV (Spring 1969), 361; Louis Untermeyer. "Multifaced Portrait of a Multifaced Poet," *Saturday Review,* LI (November 1968), 36, 39; Margaret Vanderhaar. *New Orleans Review,* I (1969), 285–286; S. M. Anthony Weinig. *Best Sellers,* XXVIII (January 1, 1969), 417; Jerald Bullis. *Massachusetts Review,* XI (1970), 209–212; Donald Sheehan. *Modern Philology,* LXVIII (1970) 123–126.

B27 Tate, Allen. "In Memoriam—Theodore Roethke, 1908–1963," *Encounter* [London], XXI (October 1963), 68.

Includes "The Moment" (*see I,* C198).

B28 Untermeyer, Louis, ed. "Theodore Roethke," in *The Britannica Library of Great American Writing*, II. Chicago: Britannica Press, pp. 1745–1746.

B29 Walker, Ursula Genung. *Notes on Theodore Roethke.* Charlottesville: Bibliographic Society of the University of Virginia, 1968.

B30 White, Bernke, ed. "Theodore Roethke," in *Who's Who in Washington* (Century 21 Edition). Olympia: Hugh L. White Publishers, 1963, p. 309.

B31 Williams, William Carlos. *The Autobiography of William Carlos Williams.* New York: Random House, 1951, p. 310.

A brief excerpt from this volume appears on the dust jacket of *The Lost Son* (*see* I, A2).

Biographical Commentaries with Specific Significance

1922

B32 Anon. "Saginaw Youth's Address Now in World Languages," *The Saginaw News Courier*, October 22, 1922, p. 6. (UW)
See I, C209.

1934

B33 Anon. "Theodore Roethke Selected to Head College Publicity," *The Lafayette* [Easton, Pa.], October 16, 1934, p. 14. (UW)

B34 Anon. "Poetry of Theodore Roethke Featured Recently by American Poetry Journal," *The Lafayette* [Easton, Pa.], December 14, 1934, pp. 1, 3. (UW)
See I, C12.

132

B35 Anon. "English Department Member Called Promising
Young Poet," *Daily Collegian* [State College, Pa.],
XXXIII (December 18, 1936), 1. (PSC)

1937

B36 Anon. "Penn State Author Praised Very Highly," *Centre
Daily Times* [State College, Pa.], January 5, 1937. (UW)

B37 Anon. "Roethke Will Address Bell Staff Tomorrow,"
Daily Collegian [State College, Pa.], XXXIV (October 12,
1937). (UW)

B38 Anon. "Roethke to Judge in College Poetry Contest,"
Daily Collegian [State College, Pa.], XXXIV
(December 13, 1937). (UW)

1938

B39 Anon. "Women's Club to Hear Poet," *Centre Daily
Times* [State College, Pa.], February 11, 1938. (UW)

B40 Anon. "Roethke to Deliver Liberal Arts Lecture," *Centre
Daily Times* [State College, Pa.], February 21, 1938.
(PSC)

B41 Anon. "Roethke to Give Third Liberal Arts Lecture,"
Daily Collegian [State College, Pa.], XXXV (February 22,
1938). (PSC)

B42 Anon. "Book Marks for Today," *New York World
Telegram*, December 6, 1938. (UW)

1939

B43 Werner, William L. "The Bookworm," *Centre Daily
Times* [State College, Pa.], January 13, 1939. (UW)

B44 Anon. "Dink Stover Replaced by Ex-mentor," *Daily Collegian* [State College, Pa.], xxxvi (March 28, 1939), 3. (PSC)

B45 Anon. "Tennis Coach Bemoans Wet Weather Man," *Centre Daily Times* [State College, Pa.], April 22, 1939. (PSC)

1940

B46 Anon. "Eight Roethke Poems Preserved in Collection at Buffalo Library," *Daily Collegian* [State College, Pa.], xxxvii (March 19, 1940). (PSC)

B47 Anon. "Roethke Starts Third Year as Tennis Coach Here," *Daily Collegian* [State College, Pa.], xxxvii (September 12, 1940), 12. (PSC)

1941

B48 Anon. "Roethke and Auden," *Portfolio* [State College, Pa.], February 1941 [inside front cover]. (UW)

B49 Lanely, Al. "Roethke, Penn State Tennis Coach, Author of Book of Verses," *New York Herald Tribune*, March 5, 1941, p. 26. (UWE)

Includes "Poem with a Dash of Housman" (*see* I, C57).

B50 Anon. "Saginawian Publishes Collection of Poems, Wins Praise of Critic," *The Saginaw News*, March 9, 1941, p. 4. (UW)

B51 Anon. "Theodore Roethke Has Book of Poems Published," *Centre Daily Times* [State College, Pa.], March 11, 1941. (PSC)

B52 Werner, William L. "The Bookworm," *Centre Daily Times* [State College, Pa.], March 12, 1941. (PSC)

B53 Mulder, Arnold. "A Michigan Poet," *Bay City Times* [Michigan], March 23, 1941. (UW)

B54 Bergman, Harold. "Poet Theodore Roethke Prefers Drinking Beer to Talking Shop," *The Burlington Free Press and Times* [Breadloaf, Vermont], September 10, 1941, p. 2. (UW)

B55 Whittaker, Betty A. "Roethke on Review," *Portfolio* [State College, Pa.], December 1941, pp. 2, 8. (UW)

B56 Anon. "Roethke Humor," *Portfolio* [State College, Pa.], December 1941, p. 8. (UW)

1942

B57 Anon. " 'Ted' Roethke Chosen Lecturer at Harvard," *Centre Daily Times* [State College, Pa.], February 27, 1942. (PSC)

B58 Werner, William L. "The Bookworm," *Centre Daily Times* [State College, Pa.], March 24, 1942. (PSC)

B59 Baily, Ben. "Tennis Situation Presents Problem," *Daily Collegian* [State College, Pa.], xxxviii (April 11, 1942), 3. (PSC)

B60 Anon. "Mineral Industries Art Gallery Formally Opened," *Centre Daily Times* [State College, Pa.], April 13, 1942, pp. 1, 6.
Includes "Dedicatory Poem" (*see* I, C62).

B61 Anon. "The Daily Half-Colyum," *Centre Daily Times* [State College, Pa.], June 12, 1942. Signed A. R. W. (PSC)

B62 Anon. "Poet-Coach Again Breaks Into Print," *Daily Collegian* [State College, Pa.], xxxviii (November 18, 1942), 2. (PCS)

Includes a drawing of Roethke by Mary Kunkel (*see* II, A7, pp. 144–146).

1943

B63 Dolinger, Milton. "A Lean and Hungry Look," *Daily Collegian* [State College, Pa.], March 24, 1943. (PSC)

B64 Miller, Art. "Collegian Sports," *Daily Collegian* [State College, Pa.], March 25, 1943, p. 3. (PSC)

B65 Anon. "Roethke, Lion Tennis Coach Leaves College; Dickinson New Mentor," *Centre Daily Times* [State College, Pa.], March 31, 1943, p. 2. (PSC)

B66 Anon. "Lean and Hungry Look," *Daily Collegian* [State College, Pa.], XL (April 7, 1943), 2. (PSC)

B67 Anon. "Old Main Columns," *Penn State Alumni News*, XXIX (May 1943), 12. (PSC)

Regarding gift of manuscript of *Open House* to Penn State.

1945

B68 Anon. "Guggenhein Fellowship Won," *Penn State Alumni News*, XXXI (May 1945), 15. (PSC)

1946

B69 Werner, William L. "The Bookworm," *Centre Daily Times* [State College, Pa.], February 12, 1946. (UW)

B70 Sherman, Leo. "The Shoutings about at Bennington," *Junior Bazaar*, October 1946, p. 223.

1948

B71 Perry, Ralph. "Prof's Career Moves from Athletics to Verse," *University of Washington Daily* [Seattle], February 3, 1948. (UWNW)

B72 Anon. "Native Saginaw Poet Listed for State Talk,"
The Saginaw News, March 28, 1948. (UW)

B73 Persons, Margaret. "MacDonalds, MacInresses and other
Seattle Authors," *Worcester Telegram* [Massachusetts],
May 23, 1948.

B74 Martin, Suzanne. "Counterpoint," *Seattle Post-
Intelligencer Magazine*, August 15, 1948. (UW)

B75 Anon. "Professor Buys Poetry Volumes for Parrington,"
University of Washington Daily [Seattle], September
30, 1948. (UWSC)

1950

B76 Werner, William L. "The Bookworm," *Centre Daily
Times* [State College, Pa.], May 31, 1950. (UW)

B77 Anon. "Roethke Represents West Coast Poets," *University
of Washington Daily* [Seattle], November 9, 1950.
(UWR)

1951

B78 Anon. "Works of Roethke in Poetry Article by London
Times," *University of Washington Daily* [Seattle],
February 15, 1951, p. 1. (UWSC)
See II, C1.

B79 Anon. "Roethke Leaves for New York Lecture,"
University of Washington Daily [Seattle], March 8,
1951. Signed K.S. (UWSC)

B80 Anon. "Professor Theodore Roethke," *Centre Daily
Times* [State College, Pa.], November 6, 1951. (PSC)

1952

B81 Werner, William L. "The Bookworm," *Centre Daily
Times* [State College, Pa.], January 15, 1952. (UW)

B82 Anon. "Washington Workshop," *Poetry*, LXXIX (February 1952), 249. (UW)

B83 Anon. "Teaching Poets," *Time*, LIX (February 25, 1952), 46, 49. (UW)

B84 Anon. "University of Washington Teacher, Ten Student Poets Honored," *Seattle Times*, February 25, 1952. (UWSC)

B85 Anon. "Time Quotes Prof. Roethke," *University of Washington Daily* [Seattle], February 27, 1952. (UWSC)

B86 Anon. "Roethke Gets Recognition in Journal," *University of Washington Daily* [Seattle], February 28, 1952. (UWSC)

B87 Anon. "Theodore Roethke," *Seattle Times*, March 9, 1952. (UW)

B88 Anon. "Two Profs Win Grant," *University of Washington Daily* [Seattle], April 1, 1952. (UWSC)

B89 Anon. "Roethke Wins $1,000 Grant and Fellowship," *University of Washington Daily* [Seattle], May 5, 1952. (UWSC)

B90 Anon. "Arts-and-Letters Grant Won by University of Washington Professor," *Seattle Times*, May 15, 1952. (UWSC)

B91 Anon. "Roethke Wins $1,000 Grant," *University of Washington Daily* [Seattle], May 23, 1952. (UW)

B92 Anon. "High Honors Accruing to Ex-Saginaw Poet," *The Saginaw News*, June 1, 1952, p. 25. (UW)

B93 Werner, William L. "The Bookworm," *Centre Daily Times* [State College, Pa.] November 25, 1952. (UW)

1953

B94 Anon. "Wild and Lively," *New Hope Gazette* [Pennsylvania], January 29, 1953, p. 3. (UW)

B95 Anon. "Former English Professor Opens Simmons Series Reading Poems," *Centre Daily Times* [State College, Pa.], LV (February 13, 1953), 5. (PSC)

B96 Anon. "Noted Poet to Present Readings," *Daily Collegian* [State College, Pa.], LIII (February 17, 1953), 1. (PSC)

B97 Anon. "Saginawia," *The Saginaw News*, May 5, 1953. (UW)

B98 Frame, Marallyn. "Work of English Professor Gets Praise of Critic," *University of Washington Daily* [Seattle], October 21, 1953. (UWR)

B99 Anon. "Ex-Saginawian's Poems Collected in Book Form," *The Saginaw News*, December 22, 1953. (UW)

1954

B100 Anon. "Notes on the Margin," *San Francisco Chronicle*, February 21, 1954. (UW)

B101 Anon. "University Professor Wins Pulitzer Poetry Prize," *Seattle Times*, May 3, 1954. (UWSC)

B102 Anon. "Columbia Names Seven Pulitzer Prize Winners," *Daily Collegian* [State College, Pa.], LIV (May 4, 1954), 3.

B103 Anon. "Ex-Saganawian Wins Coveted Pulitzer Prize," *The Saginaw News*, May 4, 1954, p. 1. (UW)

B104 Anon. "Pulitzer Prize Won by Roethke," *Centre Daily Times* [State College, Pa.], LVII (May 4, 1954), 1. (PSC)

B105 Anon. "Pulitzer Poetry Prize Won by University of Washington Professor," *Seattle Post-Intelligencer*, May 4, 1954, p. 1. (UWR, UWSC)

B106 Anon. "Pulitzer Prize Won for Volume of Poems 'The Waking,' " *Daily Collegian* [State College, Pa.], LIV (May 4, 1954), 3. (PSC)

B107 Anon. "Theodore Roethke," *St. Louis Post-Dispatch*, May 4, 1954. (UWSC)

B108 Anon. "University Poet, Roethke, Given Pulitzer Prize," *University of Washington Daily* [Seattle], May 4, 1954.

B109 Beaham, Paddy. "Former Prof Wins Prize for Poetry," *Daily Collegian* [State College, Pa.], LIV (May 6, 1954), 8. (PSC)

B110 Anon. "Reason to be Proud of State University," *Seattle Times*, May 17, 1954, p. 6.

B111 Anon. "University of Washington Poet Wears Honors Modestly," *Seattle Times*, August 4, 1954. (UWR)

B112 Werner, William L. "The Bookworm," *Centre Daily Times* [State College, Pa.], LVII (September 28, 1954), 4. (PSC)

B113 Canty, Dave. "London *Times* Lauds Professors for Outstanding Literary Feats," *University of Washington Daily* [Seattle], October 22, 1954. (UWR)
See II, C4.

1955

B114 Werner, William L. "Five Professors to Get Funds for Lectures," *Centre Daily Times* [State College, Pa.], LVII (April 26, 1955), 4. (PSC)

Roethke represented by three poems in Untermeyer's American and British anthology: *Treasury of Great Poems, English and American.* New York: Simon and Schuster, 1955.

B115 Anon. "Roethke's Work Included in American Poetry Book," *Seattle Times*, June 18, 1955. (UWR)

See II, B114 above.

1956

B116 Anon. "Institute of Arts Adds 13 Members," *New York Times*, February 7, 1956, p. 38.

B117 Anon. "Ex-Saginaw Poet Wins High Honors," *The Saginaw News*, February 28, 1956, p. 17. (UW)

B118 Werner, William L. "The Bookworm," *Centre Daily Times* [State College, Pa.], LVIII (March 27, 1956), 4. (PSC)

Roethke elected member of National Institute of Arts and Letters.

B119 Anon. "Two Art Groups Make 24 Awards," *New York Times*, May 24, 1956, p. 25.

B120 Anon. "Roethke Honored by Literary Group," *University of Washington Daily* [Seattle], May 25, 1956. (UWSC)

B121 Werner, William L. "The Bookworm," *Centre Daily Times* [State College, Pa.], LVIII (July 3, 1956), 4. (PSC)

Roethke teaches a course in modern American poetry in Florence, Italy (*see* Biographical Notes 1955).

1958

B122 Anon. "Poetry Society Honors Book by Professor,"
University of Washington Daily [Seattle], January 8,
1958. (UWR)

Words for the Wind is the "Christmas Choice" of the Poetry Book
Society of England.

B123 Anon. "Magazine Cites Poet Ex-Professor," *Daily
Collegian* [State College, Pa.], LVIII (March 22, 1958),
2. (PSC)

B124 Werner, William L. "The Bookworm," *Centre Daily
Times* [State College, Pa.], LX (March 25, 1958), 4.
(PSC)

Roethke praised in *Newsweek* as one of America's four outstanding
poets (*see* II, B3).

B125 Anon. "Seattle Genius," *Seattle Post-Intelligencer*,
December 6, 1958, p. 13. (UW)

1959

B126 Anon. "Awarded Yale's Bollingen Prize," *New York
Herald Tribune*, January 12, 1959. (UW)

B127 Anon. "University of Washington Professor Awarded
Top Poetry Prize," *Seattle Post-Intelligencer*, January 12,
1959, p. 9. (UW)

B128 Anon. "Yale's Bollingen Prize Won by Professor Poet,"
New York Times, January 12, 1959, p. 12.

B129 Anon. "Professor Roethke Wins Top Yale Poetry
Award," *University of Washington Daily* [Seattle],
January 13, 1959. (UWR, UWSC)

B130 Anon. "Roethke Wins Poetry Prize," *Centre Daily
Times* [State College, Pa.], LXI (January 14, 1959), 11.
(PSC)

B131 Anon. "Roethke Wins 1958 Bollingen Prize in Poetry," *Faculty Bulletin* [State College, Pa.], XLVI (January 16, 1959), 3. (PSC)

B132 Anon. "University of Washington Poet Gets Second Major Award," *Seattle Times*, January 23, 1959, p. 19. (UW)

B133 Anon. "Professor Roethke Wins Second Major Award," *University of Washington Daily* [Seattle], January 27, 1959. (UWR, UWSC)

B134 Werner, William L. "The Bookworm," *Center Daily Times* [State College, Pa.], LXI (January 27, 1959), 4. (PSC)

Roethke awarded Edna St. Vincent Millay Prize of $200 by Poetry Society of America.

B135 Anon. "Prize Winner," *Seattle Post-Intelligencer*, January 30, 1959, p. 12. (UW)

B136 Anon. "Former Professor Gets Bollingen Poetry Award," *Daily Collegian* [State College, Pa.], LIX (February 5, 1959), 8. (PSC)

B137 Anon. "Bollingen Prize," *Library Journal*, LXXXIV (February 15, 1959). (UW)

B138 Anon. "Ford Foundation Honors Theodore Roethke," *Seattle Post-Intelligencer*, February 15, 1959, p. 18. (UWSC)

B139 Anon. "Roethke Wins Grant from Ford Foundation," *Seattle Times*, February 16, 1959, p. 11. (UWR)

B140 Reuter. "$150,000 for U.S. Writers: Concentration on Creative Works," *The Times* [London], February 16, 1959, p. 8d.
Times [State College, Pa.], LXI (February 24, 1959), 4.

B141 Werner, William L. "The Bookworm," *Centre Daily Times* [State College, Pa.], LXI (February 24, 1959), 4. (PSC)
Roethke given Ford Foundation grant.

B142 Anon. "Roethke Wins Two National Awards for Latest Poetry Book," *University Record* [Seattle], January–February 1959, p. 6. (UWSC)

B143 Anon. "Roethke National Book Award Winner: Saginaw–Born Poet Adds Another Literary Honor," *The Saginaw News*, March 4, 1959. (UW)

B144 Anon. "Former Faculty Member Wins Award for Poetry," *Penn State Alumni News*, XIV (April 1959), 13. (PSC)

B145 Anon. "In the Argus Eyes: Theodore Roethke," *The Argus* [Seattle], LXVI (April 3, 1959), 1. (UWE)

B146 Werner, William L. "Anecdote, Poem and Letters," *Centre Daily Times* [State College, Pa.], LXII (April 7, 1959), 4. (PSC)

B147 Richards, Mary and Courteny Johnston. "Roethke Rates Local Writers Among Nation's Top Young Poets," *University of Washington Daily* [Seattle], June 3, 1959, p. 1. (UWSC)

B148 Anon. "This is the Poet Today," *Newsweek*, LIII (June 5, 1959), 106, 108, 110. (UW)

B149 Anon. "Pulitzer Poet to Give 2 Readings," *San Francisco Chronicle*, July 8, 1959, p. 36.

B150 Anon. "Theodore Roethke," *Daily Gater* [San Francisco], July 9, 1959, p. 1.

B151 Anon. "University of Washington Professor Wins Northwest Writer's Award," *Seattle Times*, August 3, 1959, p. 9. (UW)

B152 Anon. "Writer's Award Won by Roethke," *University of Washington Daily* [Seattle], August 6, 1959. (UWSC)

1960

B153 Anon. "In the Argus Eyes of 1959," *The Argus* [Seattle], LXVIII (January 1, 1960), 5. (UWE)

B154 Anon. "University of Washington Poet Wins Award (Theodore Roethke)," *University of Washington Daily* [Seattle], January 20, 1960. (UWSC)

B156 Anon. "Ten Americans to Watch in 1960: Literature: Theodore Roethke," *Pageant Magazine*, February 1960, p. 27. (UW)

B157 Werner, William L. "The Bookworm," *Centre Daily Times* [State College, Pa.], LXII (February 2, 1960), 6. (PSC)

Roethke is chosen as one of *Pageant Magazine*'s Ten Americans to Watch in 1960.

B158 ———. "The Bookworm," *Centre Daily Times* [State College, Pa.], LXII (March 15, 1960), 2. (PSC)

Roethke is the subject of an article in *College English* (*see* II, C123).

B159 Jacobs, Mary Jane. "Notes . . . and Notables . . . Professor and Mrs. Theodore Roethke," *Seattle Times*, March 27, 1960, section IV, p. 4. (UW)

B160 Anon. "Lecture Tour Takes Professor to Eastern U.S.," *University of Washington Daily* [Seattle], March 30, 1960. (UWSC)

B161 Petto, Dick. "Roethke: Area Prodigy," *University of Washington Daily* [Seattle], April 7, 1960, p. 3. (UWR, UWSC)

B162 Anon. "Morris Gray Poetry Reading," *Harvard University Gazette*, April 23, 1960, p. 179.

B163 Anon. "Distinguished Alumnus: Arthur Hill Honors Prize-Winning Poet," *The Saginaw News*, May 24, 1960, p. 1. (UW)

B164 Anon. "Famed Poet Greets Hill Students," *The Saginaw News*, May 25, 1960, p. 9. (UW)

B165 Anon. "Theodore Roethke '25' 10th Honor Alumnus," *Arthur Hill News*, May 25, 1960, pp. 1, 5. (UW)

B166 Anon. "University of Washington Prof Receives Award," *Seattle Times*, May 27, 1960, p. 11. (UW)

B167 Anon. "Poet Honored at Home Town Commencement," *University of Washington Daily* [Seattle], June 1, 1960. (UWSC)

1961

B168 Ghose, Zulfikar. "Roethke: I Ran with the Roaring Boys: Cherubic Image," *Western Daily Press* [Bristol], January 18, 1961. (UW)

Reprinted: *The Glass House*, pp. 268–270 (*see* I, B26).

B169 Chambers, Peter. "Poets without Appointments," *Daily Express* [London], January 28, 1961. (UW)

B170 Anon. "Poet's Visit," *Oxford Mail*, February 16, 1961. (UW)

B171 Keely, Carol. "Pulitzer Prize Winner Reads in Hub Thursday," *Daily Campus* [Connecticut College], March 15, 1961, p. 1.

B172 Anon. "Roethke to Recite Poetry at Trinity," *Hartford Times*, March 16, 1961. (UW)

B173 Keely, Carol. "Roethke Reads Works in Ballroom Tonight," *Daily Campus* [Connecticut College], March 16, 1961, p. 1. (UW)

B174 Anon. "Roethke to Give 'Journeys' as Feature of Arts Festival," *The DePauw*, May 2, 1961, p. 2.

B175 Anon. "Old Greenhouse No Longer Exists," *The Saginaw News*, August 3, 1961. (UW)

B176 Anon. "Roethke Named for Award," *Seattle Times*, August 10, 1961, p. 25.

1962

B177 Anon. "Professor Wins Shelley Award for Poetry," *University of Washington Daily* [Seattle], January 19, 1962. (UWSC)

B178 Guzzo, Louis R.. "Roethke Wins $1,280 Shelley Award," *Seattle Times*, January 19, 1962, p. 13.
   See I, C174 and II, B179, 180, 181.

B179 Terte, Robert F. "Cherne's Bust of Frost Unveiled at Poetry Awards Dinner Here," *New York Times*, January 19, 1962, p. 29. (UW)

B180 Werner, William L. "A New Museum and an Award for Poet," *Centre Daily Times* [State College, Pa.], LXIV (January 23, 1962), 6. (PSC)

B181 Anon. "People," *Time*, LXXIX (January 23, 1962), 40.

B182 Anon. "Notes on the Margin," *San Francisco Chronicle*, April 29, 1962. (UW)

B183 Wegars, Don. "Bookmarking," *San Francisco Examiner*, April 29, 1962. (UW)

B184 Anon. "Poetry Reading," *Daily California* [Berkeley], May 7, 1962, p. 11.

B185 Anon. "University of Michigan to Honor Poet from Saginaw," *The Saginaw News*, June 7, 1962, p. 4.

B186 Anon. "Roethke to be Honored at University of Michigan," *Seattle Times*, June 12, 1962, p. 16.

B187 Anon. "Honorary Degree's Given," *New York Times*, June 17, 1962, p. 27.

B188 Anon. "Michigan Fetes Roethke for Poetry Contributions," *University of Washington Daily* [Seattle], June 18, 1962, p. 1. (UWSC)

B189 Anon. "Prof Roethke, Poet, Given Honorary Title," *Seattle Times*, June 23, 1962. (UWSC)

B190 Bennett, Nancy and Bob Peterson. "Prof Roethke Receives Titles from Regents," *University of Washington Daily* [Seattle], June 28, 1962, pp. 1, 2. (UWR, UWSC)

B191 Brazier, Dorothy Brant. "Introduction to a Poet's Wife," *Seattle Times*, October 9, 1962, p. 19. (UW)

B192 Anon. "Prof Roethke to Read Own Works at Fair," *University of Washington Daily* [Seattle], October 12, 1962. (UWNW)

B193 Anon. "Roethke to Read Poetry," *Seattle Times*, October 14, 1962. (UW)

B194 Anon. "Roethke, C[ontra] C[osta] C[ollege] Poets Set for Art Festivals October 26," *The Advocate* [Contra Costa, California], October 19, 1962, pp. 1, 3.

B195 Anon. "Noted American Poet Will Read Own Works at U[niversity] of C[alifornia] at R[iverside]," *Riverside Press*, October 22, 1962, p. 1.

B196 Anon. "Poet Roethke Recites Selection of Own Poems," *The Highlander* [Riverside], October 24, 1962, p. 1.

B197 Anon. "Art Festival Hosts Roethke and Poets," *The Advocate* [Contra Costa, California], October 26, 1962, p. 1.

B198 Anon. "Famous American Poet Will Read Works at Oxy Tuesday," *The Occidental* [Los Angeles], October 26, 1962, p. 1.

B199 Anon. "Pulitzer Poet at U[niversity] of C[alifornia] at R[iverside] Soon," *Riverside Press*, October 26, 1962, p. 1.

B200 Anon. "Dimensions: Poetry—North, West, South, and East," *University of Washington Daily* [Seattle], November 30, 1962, pp. 7–10. (UW)

1963

B201 Anon. "Prize-Winning University of Washington Poet is Movie Subject," *Seattle Times*, January 15, 1963, p. 7.

B202 Robbins, Tom. "San Francisco Director Making Film about Roethke," *Seattle Times*, January 17, 1963. (UWSC)

B203 Anon. "Film of Roethke Shows Poet in His Classroom," *University of Washington Daily* [Seattle], January 20, 1963, p. 1. (UWSC)

B204 Anon. "Roethke Says: Robert Frost 'Symbol of Courage,' " *University of Washington Daily* [Seattle], January 20, 1963, p. 1. (UWSC)

B205 Anon. "U.S. Native Poetry Best, Roethke Says," *Daily Northwestern* [Chicago], February 12, 1963, p. 4.

B206 Cummings, Gray. "Divergent Views of Mans' Self Merge in Panel," *Daily Northwestern* [Chicago], February 12, 1963, p. 4.

B207 Anon. "Williams Poetry Will Endure Says Roethke," *University of Washington Daily* [Seattle], March 7, 1963. (UWSC)

B208 Anon. "Student Symposium on 'Spectrum of Perspectives," *The Northwestern University Alumni News*, April 1963, pp. 8–11.

B209 Anon. "Burglary, Runaway Auto: Roethke Has Double Trouble," *Seattle Times*, April 20, 1963. (UWSC)

B210 Anon. "Dirty Dinky Bites Bard that Bore Him," *Seattle Post-Intelligencer*, April 20, 1963, p. 20. (UW)

B211 Anon. "In and Out of Books: Numbers," *New York Times Book Review*, May 19, 1963, p. 9.

B212 Anon. "Roethke Top Poet," *Seattle Times Magazine*, July 28, 1963, p. 23. (UWSC)

B213 Anon. "Professor Roethke Acclaimed as Poet, Dies," *Seattle Times*, August 2, 1963, p. 41. (UWSC)

B214 Anon. "Theodore Roethke Dies at 55; Poet Won Pulitzer in '54," *New World Telegram*, August 2, 1963. (UW)

B215 Anon. "Theodore Roethke, 55, Is Dead; Poet Won 1954 Pulitzer Prize," *New York Times*, August 2, 1963, p. 27. (UWSC)

B216 Anon. "Dr. Roethke Services to be Held Monday," *Seattle Post-Intelligencer*, August 3, 1963. (UWSC)

B217 Anon. "Memorial Rites for Dr. Roethke," *Seattle Times*, August 3, 1963. (UWSC)

B218 Anon. "Mr. Theodore Roethke: Notable American Poet," *The Times* [London], August 3, 1963, p. 8e. (UW)

B219 Anon. "Theodore Roethke, Poet, Pulitzer Prize Winner," *New York Herald Tribune*, August 3, 1963. (UW)

B220 Anon. "Theodore Roethke," *Seattle Times*, August 5, 1963, p. 8. (UWE, UWSC)

B221 Watson, Emmett. "Passing of Giant," *Seattle Post-Intelligencer*, August 6, 1963. (UWE)

B222 Werner, William L. "Roethke a Rebel in a World He Didn't Conceive," *Centre Daily Times* [State College, Pa.], LXVI (August 6, 1963), 5. (PSC)

Controversy regarding this article appeared as follows: John Haag. "Letter to the Editor: Profitable Meditation," *Centre Daily Times*, LXVI (August 13, 1963), 4; Harold F. Graves. "More on Roethke" (August 16, 1963); John Haag. "More Personal" (August 20, 1963); William L. Werner. "Words of Thanks, Clarification, and Literature" (August 27, 1963), 2; Harry B.

Henderson. "James' Meaning" (August 28, 1963); John Haag. "Letters to the Editors: On Roethke Again" (September 4, 1963), 4.

B223 Rice. "Roethke—Death of a Poet," *University of Washington Daily* [Seattle], August 8, 1963, p. 2. (UWE, UWSC)

B224 Arnold, Martin. "Poet Roethke 'In First Sleep,' Mourned," *University of Washington Daily* [Seattle], August 8, 1963, pp. 1–2. (UWSC)

B225 Anon. "Milestones: Died," *Time*, LXXXII (August 9, 1963), 58.

B226 Donohoe, Ed. "Tilting the Windmill," *The Washington Teamster*, August 9, 1963. (UWE)

B227 Anon. "Theodore Roethke," *Publisher's Weekly*, CLXXXIV (August 12, 1963), 40.

B228 Anon. "Transition: Theodore Huebner Roethke," *Newsweek*, LXII (August 12, 1963), 52.

B229 Elliot, Gerald A. "State's Greatest Poet: Too Few Knew the Work of Saginaw's Theodore Roethke, Dead at 55," *Grand Rapids Press* [Michigan], August 18, 1963. (UW)

B230 Anon. "Professor Roethke Leaves Effects—Worth $40,000," *Seattle Times*, August 22, 1963, p. 5. (UW)

B231 Conquest, Robert. "A Dying Light," *Spectator* [London], September 6, 1963. (UW)

B232 Lipton, Lawrence. "Theodore Roethke—Hail and Farewell," *Los Angeles Times Calendar*, September 22, 1963, pp. 1, 9. (UW)

B233 Anon. "Theodore Roethke," *Wilson Library Bulletin*, XXXVIII (October 1963), 115.

C Critical Studies, Commentaries, and Reviews

This list of criticism is selective. Many relatively minor reviews appearing in newspapers throughout the United States are preserved with the Roethke papers at the University of Washington, but they are not cited here (with the exception of a few concerning *I Am! Says the Lamb, Party at the Zoo*, and some foreign appearances in English).

Several special issues devoted to Roethke's work have appeared since his death. Among these were the *Michigan Quarterly Review*, the *Minnesota Review*, and the *Northwest Review*. The *Michigan Quarterly Review* published a panel discussion by John Ciardi, Stanley Kunitz, and Allan Seager in October 1967 (II, C28) which included a large number of dedicatory poems for Roethke (*see* II, F4). The *Minnesota Review* followed with several articles in 1968 (II, C60, 121, 130), and in 1971 the *Northwest Review* published eight essays (II, C41, 43, 55, 74, 81, 107, 127) and excerpts from Roethke's notebooks arranged by David Wagoner (I, C242).

Critical Studies and Commentaries

C1 Anon. "American Poetry Today," *The Times Literary Supplement* [London], L (January 19, 1951), 29–31.
Includes an excerpt from "Open Letter" (*see* I, B17 and II, B78.)

C2 Anon. "The American Workshop," *The Times Literary Supplement* [London], LI (August 29, 1952), xxvii.

C3 Anon. "Bentley Terms University 'Trail Blazer in Poetry,' " *University of Washington Daily* [Seattle], May 29, 1959, p. 3. (UW)

Nelson Bentley comments on Roethke and his poetry.

C4 Anon. "Expressive Voices: The Emergence of a National Style," *The Times Literary Supplement* [London], LIII (September 17, 1954), xii.

C5 Anon. "Poetic Background: A Period of Consolidation," *The Times Literary Supplement* [London], LIII (September 17, 1954), ii.

C6 Anon. "Poetry in English: 1945–1962," *Time*, LXXIX (March 9, 1962), 93, 95.

C7 Anon. "Poetry: Men at Work," *Newsweek*, CII (March 17, 1958), 108, 110.

C8 Anon. "Roethke: A Look in His Greenhouse," *University of Washington Daily* [Seattle], October 10, 1963, p. 1.

Nelson Bentley, Arnold Stein, and David Wagoner comment on Roethke and his poetry.

C9 Anon. "The Three Realms of the Young Poet," *The Times Literary Supplement* [London], LIII (September 17, 1954), iv.

C10 Anon. "View from Parnassus," *Time*, LXXX (November 9, 1962), 100.

C11 Alexander, Floyce M. "Roethke, Two Years Later," *Western Humanities Review*, XX (Winter 1966), 76–78.

C12 Alvarez, Alfred. *The Shaping Spirit: Studies in Modern English and American Poets*. London: Chatto and Windus, 1958.

C13 Arnett, Carroll. "Minimal to Maximal: Theodore Roethke's Dialectic," *College English*, XVIII (May 1957), 414–416.

C14 Bell, Lou. "Once Over Lightly," *Centre Daily Times* [State College, Pa.], LVII (May 7, 1954), 400 L. (PSC)
Includes Roethke's comment on "The Heron."

C15 Bentley, Nelson. "Roethke: American Poet," *Puget Sound English Notes* [Seattle], XXVI (Fall 1963), 3–6.

C16 Berryman, John. "From the Middle and Senior Generations," *American Scholar*, XXVIII (Summer 1959), 384–390.

C17 Bluestone, George. "Roethke: Milestone of Greatness," *The Argus* [Seattle], LXX (August 9, 1963), 1, 3.

C18 Bode, Carl. "The Poem Across the Way," *Time and Tide*, XL (August 29, 1959), 933.

C19 Bogan, Louise. "Stitched on Bone," in *Trial Balances*, ed. Ann Winslow. New York: Macmillan, 1935, pp. 138–139.
See I, B2.

C20 Bowerman, Donald. "Theodore Roethke: "A Housman Echo," *Notes and Queries*, n.s. XVI (July 1969), 266.

C21 Boyd, J.D. "Texture and Form in Theodore Roethke's Greenhouse Poems," *Modern Language Quarterly*, XXXII (December 1971), 409–424.

C22 Breit, Harvey. "Pulitzer Poet," *New York Times Book Review*, LIX (May 16, 1954), 8.

C23 Buffel, Helen T. " 'I Knew a Woman,' " *Explicator*, XXIV (May 1966), item No. 78.

C24 Burke, Kenneth. "The Vegetal Radicalism of Theodore Roethke," *Sewanee Review*, LVIII (Winter 1950), 68–108.

Includes an early version of "The Shape of the Fire" on page 100. Reprinted: *see* II, C59.

C25 Ciardi, John. "My Papa's Waltz," in *How Does A Poem Mean?* Boston: Houghton-Mifflin, 1959.

C26 ———. *Mid-Century American Poets.* New York: Twayne, 1950.

See I, B17.

C27 ———. "Theodore Roethke: A Passion and a Maker," *Saturday Review*, XLVI (August 31, 1963), 13.

C28 Ciardi, John, Stanley Kunitz, and Allan Seager. "An Evening with Ted Roethke," *Michigan Quarterly Review*, II (October 1967), 227–242.

Reprinted: *see* II, C59.

C29 Cohen, J. M. *Poetry of this Age, 1908–1958.* London: Arrow Books, 1959, pp. 247–249; and *Poetry of this Age, 1908–1965.* London: Arrow Books, 1966.

C30 Coleman, Alice. *A Class Study of Theodore Roethke's 'The Waking.'* New York: College Entrance Examination Board, 1965.

See II, E1.

C31 Colussi, D. L. "Roethke's 'The Gentle,' " *Explicator*, XXVII (May 1969), item No. 73.

C32 Cott, Jonathan. "Two Dream Poets," in *On Contemporary Literature.* New York: Avon, 1964, pp. 530–531.

C33 Deutsch, Babette. "The Poet and His Critics: A Symposium," *New World Writing*, ed. Anthony Ostroff, XIX (1961), 201–206.

This is an essay on Roethke's "In a Dark Time."

C34 ———. "The Auditory Imagination," in *The Poetry in Our Time*. New York: Columbia University Press, 1952; and *The Poetry in Our Time*. New York: Doubleday, 1964.

C35 Dickey, James. *Babel to Byzantium*. New York: Farrar, Strauss, and Giroux, 1968.

C36 ———. "The Greatest American Poet," *Atlantic*, CCXXII (November 1968), 53–58.

Reactions to this article by Frank Kermode, Howard Nemerov, James Schevill, W. D. Snodgrass, Stanley Kunitz, Robert Bly, Denise Levertov, Richard Seamon, William Stafford, Malcolm Cowley, X. J. Kennedy, Kenneth Burke, and Beatrice Roethke appear in "The Mail," *Atlantic*, CCXXII (December 1968), 34–38.
Reprinted: *Sorties: Journals and New Essays*. Garden City, New York: Doubleday and Company, 1971, pp. 214–224.

C37 Donoghue, Denis. "Theodore Roethke," in *Connoisseurs of Chaos: Ideas of Order in Modern American Poetry*. New York: Macmillan, 1965.

Reprinted: "Roethke's Broken Music," in *Theodore Roethke: Essays on the Poetry*, ed. Arnold Stein. Seattle and London: University of Washington Press, 1965.

C38 Eberhart, Richard. "On Theodore Roethke's Poetry," *Southern Review*, n.s. I (July 1965), 612–620.

C39 Fiedler, Leslie A. "A Kind of Solution: The Situation of Poetry Now," *Kenyon Review*, XXVI (Winter 1964), 63–64.

C40 Frankenberg, Lloyd. *Invitation to Poetry*. Garden City, New York: Doubleday and Company, 1956, p. 255.

Frankenberg comments on "Big Wind."

C41 Freer, Coburn. "Theodore Roethke's Love Poetry," *Northwest Review*, XI (Summer 1971), 42–66.

C42 French, Warren. "Theodore Roethke: 'in a slow up-sway,' " in *The Fifties: Fiction, Poetry, Drama*. Deland, Florida: Everett/Edwards, 1971, pp. 199–207.

C43 Galvin, Brendan. "Kenneth Burke and Theodore Roethke's 'Lost Son' Poems," *Northwest Review*, XI (Summer 1971), 67–69.

C44 ———. "Theodore Roethke's Proverbs," *Concerning Poetry*, V (Spring 1972), 35–47.

C45 Gangewere, R. J. "Theodore Roethke: The Future of Reputation," *Carnegie Series in English*, II (1970), 65–73.

C46 Garmon, Gerald M. "Roethke's 'Open House,' " *Explicator*, XXVIII (November 1969), item No. 27.

C47 Ghose, Zulfikar. "The World's Best — Young and Old," *Western Daily Press* [Bristol], June 21, 1961. (UW)

C48 Gross, Harvey. *Sound and Form in Modern Poetry*. Ann Arbor: University of Michigan Press, 1964.

C49 G[unn,], T[hom]. "Theodore Roethke," in *The Concise Encyclopedia of English and American Poets and Poetry*, ed. Stephen Spender and Donald Hall. New York: Hawthorn Books, Inc., 1963, pp. 277–278.

C50 Gustafson, Richard. "In Roethkeland," *Midwest Quarterly*, VII (Autumn 1965), 167–174.

C51 Hall, Donald. "American Poets Since the War," *World Review*, n.s. XLVII (January 1953), 48–49.

C52 ———. "The New Poetry: Notes on the Past Fifteen Years in America," *New World Writing*, VIII (1955), 236–237.

C53 ———. *A Poetry Sampler*. New York: Franklin Watts, 1962.

C54 Hamilton, Ian. "Theodore Roethke," *Agenda* [London], III (April 1964), 5–10.

C55 Hayden, Mary H. "Open House: Poetry of the Constricted Self," *Northwest Review*, XI (Summer 1971), 116–138.

C56 Henry, Nat. "Roethke's 'I Knew a Woman,' " *Explicator*, XXVII (January 1969), item No. 31.

C57 Heron, Philip E. "The Vision of Meaning: Theodore Roethke's 'Frau Bauman, Frau Schmidt, and Frau Schwartze,' " *Western Speech*, XXXIV (Winter 1970), 29–33.

C58 Heyen, William. "The Divine Abyss: Theodore Roethke's Mysticism," *Texas Studies in Literature and Language*, XI (Winter 1969), 1051–1068.

C59 ———. *Profile of Theodore Roethke*. Columbus, Ohio: Charles E. Merrill Co., 1971.

Includes biographical comment by John Ciardi, Stanley Kunitz, and Allan Seager (II, B10) and essays by Kenneth Burke (II, C24), Jerome Mazzaro (II, C87), Delmore Schwartz (II, C250), Stanley Kunitz (II, C70), James McMichael (II, C80), David Ferry (II, C355), and William Heyen (II, C58).

C60 ———. "Theodore Roethke's Minimals," *Minnesota Review*, VIII (1968), 359–375.

C61 Hobbs, John. "The Poet as His Own Interpreter: Roethke on 'In a Dark Time,' " *College English*, XXXIII (October 1971), 55–66.

C62 Hoffman, Frederick J. "Theodore Roethke: The Poetic Shape of Death," in *Theodore Roethke: Essays on the Poetry*, ed. Arnold Stein. Seattle and London: University of Washington Press, 1965.

Reprinted: *Modern American Poetry: Essays in Criticism*, ed. Jerome Mazzaro. New York: McKay, 1970, pp. 301–320.

C63 Holmes, John A. "Forward Look at Poetry Plus Anniversary Remarks," *Boston Evening Transcript*, October 5, 1938. (UW)

C64 ———. "Our Youngest American Poets," *Boston Evening Transcript*, October 5, 1935. (UW)

C65 ———. "Theodore Roethke," *American Poetry Journal*, XVII (November 1934), 2. (UW)

C66 Hughes, Ted. "Wind and Weather," *Listening and Writing* [London], Autumn 1965, pp. 30–38.

C67 Keil, H. Charles. "Among the Happy Poets," *Cadence*, XII (Winter 1958), 7–9.

C68 Kizer, Carolyn. "Poetry of the Fifties in America," in *International Literary Annual*, ed. John Wain. London, 1958.

See I, A11, p. 179.

C69 Kramer, Hilton. "The Poetry of Theodore Roethke," *Western Review*, XVIII (Winter 1954), 131–146.

C70 Kunitz, Stanley. "Roethke: Poet of Transformations," *New Republic*, CLII (January 23, 1965), 23–29.

C71 ———. "Roethke Remembered," *Show*, V (May 1965), 10–12, 15.

C72 ———. "The Taste of Self," *New World Writing*, ed. Anthony Ostroff, XIX (1961), 206–214.

This is an essay on "In a Dark Time."
Reprinted: *The Contemporary Poet as Artist and Critic: Eight Symposia*. Boston: Little, Brown and Company, 1964.

C73 ———. "Theodore Roethke," *New York Review of Books*, I (October 17, 1963), 21–22.

C74 LaBelle, Jenijoy. "Theodore Roethke and Tradition: 'The Pure Serene of Memory in One Man,' " *Northwest Review*, XI (Summer 1971), 1–18.

C75 Lee, Charlotte I. "The Line as a Rhythmic Unit in the Poetry of Theodore Roethke," *Speech Monographs*, XXX (March 1963), 15–22.

Concerned basically with an analysis of "The Lost Son."

C76 Levi, Peter S. J. "Theodore Roethke," *Agenda* [London], III (April 1964), 11–14.

C77 Lucas, John. "The Poetry of Theodore Roethke," *The Oxford Review*, VII (Trinity 1968), 39–64.

C78 Lupher, David A. "Lost Son: Theodore Roethke," *Yale Literary Magazine*, CXXXV (March 1967), 9–12.

C79 McLatchy, J. D. "Sweating Light from a Stone, Identifying Theodore Roethke," *Modern Poetry Studies*, III (1972), 1–24.

C80 McMichael, James. "The Poetry of Theodore Roethke," *The Southern Review*, n.s. V (Winter 1969), 4–25.

Reprinted: *see* II, C5.

C81 ———. "Roethke's North America," *Northwest Review*, XI (Summer 1971), 149–159.

C82 Malkoff, Karl. *Theodore Roethke: An Introduction to the Poetry*. New York and London: Columbia University Press, 1966.

See II, G25.

Reviews: Anon. "Prose and Poetry," *Saturday Review*, LIV (May 22, 1971), 35; Floyce Alexander. *Western Humanities Review*, XXIII (1969), 82. Dorothy Curley. *Library Journal*, XCI (October 1, 1966), 4664–4666; Denis Donoghue. "Aboriginal Poet," *New York Review of Books*, VII (September 22, 1966), 14–16; David Ferry. "Roethke: Poetry," *Virginia Quarterly Review*, XLIII (Winter 1967), 169–173; R. W. Flint. "Poet of the Isolated Self," *New York Times Book Review*, LXXII (January 15, 1967), 4, 41; Eugene Goodheart. "The Frailty of the 'I,' " *Sewanee Review*, LXXVI (Summer 1968), 516–519; Thomas A. Kuhlman. *American Literature Abstracts*, II (1968), 158–159; David A. Lupher. "Lost Son: Theodore Roethke," *Yale Literary Magazine*, CXXXV (March 1967), 9–12; Dale Nelson. " 'Free in a Tearing Wind,' " *Northwest Today (Seattle Post-Intelligencer)*, February 26, 1967, p. 23. For comments on textual errors, *see* II, C86.

C83 Martin, Suzanne. "Counterpoint," *Seattle Post-Intelligencer Magazine*, August 5, 1948. (UW)

C84 Martz, Louis L. "Theodore Roethke: A Greenhouse Eden," in *The Poem of the Mind*. New York: Oxford University Press, 1960, pp. 162–182.

Reprinted: "A Greenhouse Eden," in *Theodore Roethke: Essays on the Poetry*, ed. Arnold Stein. Seattle and London: University of Washington Press, 1965.

C85 Martz, William J. *The Achievement of Theodore Roethke*. Glenview, Illinois: Scott, Foresman and Company, 1966.

C86 Maxwell, J. C. "Notes on Theodore Roethke," *Notes and Queries*, n.s. XVI (July 1969), 265–266.

C87 Mazzaro, Jerome. "Theodore Roethke and the Failures of Language," *Modern Poetry Studies*, I (July 1970), 73–96.

Reprinted: *see* II, C59.

C88 Meredith, William. "A Steady Storm of Correspondences: Theodore Roethke's Long Journey Out of the Self," *Shenandoah*, XVI (Autumn 1964), 41–54.

Reprinted: "A Steady Storm of Correspondences: Theodore Roethke's Long Journey Out of the Self," in *Theodore Roethke: Essays on the Poetry*, ed. Arnold Stein. Seattle and London: University of Washington Press, 1965.

C89 Mills, Ralph J., Jr. *Creation's Very Self; On the Personal Element in Recent American Poetry*, with a foreword by William Burford. Fort Worth: Texas Christian University Press, 1969.

C90 ———. "A Note on the Personal Element in Recent American Poetry," *Chicago Circle Studies*, I (December 1965), 7–11.

C91 ———. "In the Way of Becoming: Roethke's Last Poems," in *Theodore Roethke: Essays on the Poetry*, ed. Arnold Stein. Seattle and London: University of Washington Press, 1965.

C92 ———. "Theodore Roethke," in *Contemporary American Poetry*. New York: Random House, 1965.

C93 ———. *Theodore Roethke*. Minneapolis: University of Minnesota Press, 1963.

Reviews: *see* II, C78 and II, D9.

C94 ———. "Theodore Roethke 1908–1963: A Tribute," *Northwestern University Tri-Quarterly Review*, VI (Winter 1964), 13–15.

See I, B12.

C95 ———. "Theodore Roethke: The Lyric of the Self," in *Poets in Progress*, ed. Edward B. Hungerford. Evanston, Illinois: Northwestern University Press, 1962.

C96 ———. "Toward a Condition of Joy: Patterns in the Poetry of Theodore Roethke," *Northwestern University Tri-Quarterly Review*, I (Fall 1958), 25–29.

C97 ———, ed. *On the Poet and His Craft: Selected Prose of Theodore Roethke*. Seattle and London: University of Washington Press, 1965.

C98 ———, ed. *Selected Letters of Theodore Roethke*. Seattle and London: University of Washington Press, 1968.

C99 Morris, H. C. and I. Ribner, eds. *Poetry: A Critical and Historical Introduction*. Chicago: Scott Foresman, 1962, p. 405.

C100 Murphy, Richard. "Three Modern Poets," *Listener* [London], LIV (September 8, 1955), 373–375.

C101 Nelson, Dale. "Spirit of Roethke Moves, Yet Still Remains," *Northwest Today* (*Seattle Post-Intelligencer*), July 24, 1966, p. 20.

C102 Nyren, Dorothy, ed. "Roethke, Theodore (1908–1963)," in *A Library of Literary Criticism*. New York: Frederick Ungar Publishing Company, 1960.

This is a collection of excerpts from reviews by W. H. Auden, Eugene Davidson, Stanley Kunitz, Frederick Brantley, Rolfe Humphries, Kenneth Burke, Babette Deutsch, John Ciardi, Gerald Previn Meyer, Donald Hall, and Delmore Schwartz.

C103 Ostroff, Anthony, ed. "The Poet and His Critics: A Symposium," *New World Writing*, XIX (1961), 189–219.

> Includes essays on Roethke's "In a Dark Time."
> Reprinted: *The Contemporary Poet as Artist and Critic: Eight Symposia*. Boston: Little, Brown and Company, 1965.

C104 Pearce, Roy Harvey. "On the Continuity of American Poetry," *Hudson Review*, X (Winter 1957–1958), 538.

C105 ———. "Theodore Roethke: The Power of Sympathy," in *Theodore Roethke: Essays on the Poetry*, ed. Arnold Stein. Seattle and London: University of Washington Press, 1965.

> Reprinted: *Historicism Once More*. Princeton: Princeton University Press, 1969, pp. 294–326.

C106 Peck, Virginia. "Roethke's 'I Knew a Woman,' " *Explicator*, XXII (March 1964), item. No. 66.

C107 Porter, Kenneth. "Roethke at Harvard, 1930–1931 and the Decade After," *Northwest Review*, XI (Summer 1971), 139–148.

C108 Raleigh, Sally. "Take Children, Creative Work, Stir Well, All Happy," *Seattle Post-Intelligencer*, February 2, 1958, p. 2. (UW)

> Carolyn Kizer comments on Roethke and his poetry.

C109 Ransom, John Crowe. "On Theodore Roethke's 'In a Dark Time,' " *New World Writing*, ed. Anthony Ostroff, XIX (1961).

> Reprinted: *The Contemporary Poet as Artist and Critic*. Boston: Little, Brown and Company, 1964.

C110 Reichertz, Ronald. " 'Where Knock Is Open Wide,' " *Explicator*, XXVI (December 1967), item No. 34.

C111 Rosenthal, Macha Louis. "The American Influence on the Roots of Hamstead Heath, 1960–61," *Antioch Review*, XXII (Summer 1962), 192.

C112 ———. *The Modern Poets: A Critical Introduction*. New York: Oxford University Press, 1965.

C113 ———. "Other Confessional Poets: Theodore Roethke, John Berryman, Anne Sexton," in *The New Poets: American and British Poetry Since World War II*. New York: Oxford University Press, 1967.

C114 Ryan, Dennis. "Poetess Moore to Read," *University of Washington Daily* [Seattle], October 10, 1958, p. 7. (UW)

C115 Schevill, James and Mark Linethal. "The Poet," in *In a Dark Time*. New York and San Francisco: Contemporary Films, Inc., 1963, unpaginated [pp. 2–3]. (UWSC)
This is a pamphlet announcing the release of the film (*see* I, E1).

C116 Scott, Nathan A. "The Example of Roethke," in *The Wild Prayer of Longing and the Sacred*. New Haven: Yale University Press, 1971, pp. 76–118.

C117 Seymour-Smith, Martin. "Where is Mr. Roethke?" *Black Mountain Review*, I (Spring 1954), 40–47.

C118 Sitwell, Edith. "Preface," in *The American Genius*. London: J. H. Lehmann, 1951.

C119 ———. "The Rising Generation," *The Times Literary Supplement* [London], LIII (September 17, 1954), i.

C120 Skelton, Robin. *Five Poets of the Pacific Northwest*. Seattle: University of Washington Press, 1964, p. xv.

C121 Slaughter, William R. "Roethke's 'Song,'" *Minnesota Review*, VIII (1968), 342–344.

See I, C115.

C122 Snodgrass, W. D. "'That Anguish of Concreteness' —Theodore Roethke's Career," in *Theodore Roethke: Essays on the Poetry*, ed. Arnold Stein. Seattle and London: University of Washington Press, 1965.

C123 Southworth, James G. "The Poetry of Theodore Roethke," *College English*, XXI (March 1960), 326–330, 335–338.

See II, B158.

C124 Spender, Stephen. "The Objective Ego," in *Theodore Roethke: Essays on the Poetry*, ed. Arnold Stein. Seattle London: University of Washington Press, 1965.

C125 ———. "Rhythms that Ring in American Verse," *New York Times Magazine*, September 3, 1950, p. 3.

C126 Staples, Hugh B. "Rose in the Sea-Wind: A Reading of Theodore Roethke's 'North American Sequence,'" *American Literature*, XXXVI (May 1964), 189–203.

C127 Stein, Arnold. "Roethke's Memory: Actions, Visions, and Revisions," *Northwest Review*, XI (Summer 1971), 19–31.

C128 ———, ed. *Theodore Roethke: Essays on the Poetry*. Seattle and London: University of Washington Press, 1965.

Reviews: Anon. "*Theodore Roethke: Essays on the Poetry*," *Choice*, III (March 1966), 35; Dorothy Curley. *Library Journal*, XCI (January 1, 1966), 112; Eugene Goodheart. "The Frailty of the 'I,'" *Sewanee Review*, LXXVI (Summer 1968), 516–519; Karl Malkoff. *New Mexico Quarterly*, XXI (Winter 1965–1966),

379–380; David A. Lupher. "Lost Son: Theodore Roethke," *Yale Literary Magazine*, cxxxv (March 1967), 9–12; Ralph J. Mills, Jr. "Recognition," *New York Times Book Review*, lxxi (July 17, 1966), 30; Sanford Pinsker. "Nine Roads Lead to Theodore Roethke," *University of Washington Daily* [Seattle], March 8, 1966, p. 11; Grosvenor E. Powell. "Robert Lowell and Theodore Roethke: Two Kinds of Knowing," *Southern Review*, n.s. iii (Winter 1967), 180–195; Feliz Stefanile. "Profiles and Presences," *Poetry*, cix (December 1966), 198–200; Hyatt H. Waggoner. *American Literature*, xxxviii (November 1966), 417.

C129 Tate, Allen. "In Memoriam — Theodore Roethke, 1908–1963," *Encounter* [London], xxi (October 1963), 68.

C130 Truesdale, C. W. "Theodore Roethke and the Landscape of American Poetry," *Minnesota Review*, viii (1968), 345–358.

C131 Vernon, John. "Theodore Roethke's Praise to the End! Poems," *The Iowa Review*, ii (Fall 1971), 60–79.

C132 Waggoner, Hyatt H. *American Poets: From the Puritans to the Present*. Boston: Houghton-Mifflin, 1968.

C133 Wain, John. "Theodore Roethke," *Critical Quarterly*, vi (Winter 1964), 322–328.

Reprinted: "The Monocle of My Sea-Faced Uncle," in *Theodore Roethke: Essays on the Poetry*, ed. Arnold Stein. Seattle and London: University of Washington Press, 1965.

C134 Warfel, Harry R. "Language Patterns and Literature: A Note on Roethke's Poetry," *Topic: A Journal of the Liberal Arts*, vi (Fall 1966), 21–29.

Reprinted: *New Perspectives in American Literature*. Washington, Pennsylvania: Washington and Jefferson College Press, 1966.

C135 Werner, William L. "The Bookman," *Centre Daily Times* [State College, Pa.], LXI (November 11, 1958), 4. (PSC)

Richard Eberhart comments on Roethke and his poetry.

C136 Wesling, Donald. "The Inevitable Ear: Freedom and Necessity in Lyric Form, Wordsworth and After," *ELH: Journal of English Literary History* (Johns Hopkins University), XXXVI (1969), 544–561.

Reviews

Open House (1941)

C137 Anon. "Publishes New Book," *Penn State Alumni News*, XXVII (March 1941), 14. (PSC)

C138 Anon. "Roethke, Theodore," *Booklist*, XXXVII (June 1, 1941), 461.

C139 Anon. "Roethke, Theodore," *Bookmark*, II (November 1941), 10.

C140 Anon. "Open House," *San Francisco Chronicle*, April 27, 1941. (UW)

C141 Anon. "Open House," *Voices*, Autumn 1941, p. 62.

C142 Auden, W. H. "Open House," *The Browse* [State College, Pa.], No. 7 (March 8, 1941), pp. 1–2. (PSC)

C143 ———. "Verse and the Times," *Saturday Review of Literature*, XXIII (April 5, 1941), 30–31.

C144 Baldanza, Stephen. "Poetry," *Commonweal*, XXXIV (June 13, 1941), 188.

C145 Belitt, Ben. "Six Poets," *Virginia Quarterly Review*, XVII (Summer 1941), 462–463.

C146 [Bogan, Louise]. "Verse," *New Yorker*, XVII (March 29, 1941), 72.

C147 Boie, Mildred. *Boston Herald*, April 9, 1941, p. 28.

C148 Bonner, Amy. "The Poems of Theodore Roethke," *New York Times Book Review*, XLVI (October 5, 1941), 9, 12.

C149 Burklund, Carl E. "Open House," *Michigan Alumnus Quarterly Review*, XLVII (Spring 1941), 287.

C150 Deutsch, Babette. "Three Generations in Poetry," *Decision*, II (August 1941), 60–61.

C151 Drew, Elizabeth. "Bookshelf," *Atlantic*, CLXVIII (August 1941), unpaginated section.

C152 Forster, Louis, Jr. "A Lyric Realist," *Poetry*, LVIII (July 1941), 222–225.

C153 Holmes, John. "Poems and Things," *Boston Evening Transcript*, March 24, 1941, p. 9. (UWE)

C154 Humphries, Rolfe. "Inside Story," *New Republic*, CV (July 14, 1941), 62.

C155 Sweeney, John L. "New Poetry," *Yale Review*, XXX (June 1941), 817–818.

C156 Walton, Edna Lou. " 'Bridges of Iron Lace,' " *New York Herald Tribune Book Review*, XVII (August 10, 1941), 4.

C157 West, Maxine. "Poet in Residence," *Headlight on Books at Penn State*, X (May 1941), 2. (PSC)

C158 Whittaker, Betty A. "Roethke on Review," *Portfolio* [Student Publication at Penn State], III (December 1941), 2, 8. (UW, PSC)

C159 Winters, Yvor. "The Poems of Theodore Roethke," *Kenyon Review*, III (Autumn 1941), 514–516.

The Lost Son (1948 and 1949)

C160 Anon. "The Listener's Book Chronicle," *Listener* [London], LXII (September 29, 1949), 545.

C161 Anon. "*The Lost Son and Other Poems*," *Argus* [South Wales], October 4, 1949. (UW)

C162 Anon. "*The Lost Son and Other Poems*," *Sydney Sun* [Australia], October 29, 1949. (UW)

C163 Anon. "*The Lost Son and Other Poems*," *Irish Press*, October 13, 1949. Signed F. Macm. (UW)

C164 Anon. "Poets Turn from Obscurity," *Cape Argus* [Capetown, South Africa], February 18, 1950. (UW)

C165 Anon. "Roethke, Theodore," *Virginia Kirkus Service*, XVI (February 1, 1948), 78.

C166 Anon. "Theodore Roethke's Poetic Works," *Rhodesian Herald* [Africa], September 30, 1949. (UW)

C167 Anon. "Two American Poets," *The Times Literary Supplement* [London], XLIX (February 17, 1950), 107.

C168 Anon. "University Poet Writes 'More for Ear than Eye,'" *Seattle Times*, April 4, 1948. (UWSC)

C169 Anon. "Youthful American Poets Show Ability," *Los Angeles Times*, July 4, 1948. (UW)

C170 Bader, Arno L. *"The Lost Son." Michigan Alumnus Quarterly Review*, LIV (Summer 1948), 367–368.

C171 Bayliss, John. "Americans," *The Poetry Review*, XLI (September–October 1950), 280–281.

C172 Bogan, Louise. "Verse," *New Yorker*, XXIV (May 15, 1948), 118–119.

C173 Davidson, Eugene. "Poet's Shelf," *Yale Review* XXXVII (June 1948), 747.

C174 Davidson, Gustav. "Original Talent," *The Courant* [Hartford], April 29, 1948. (UW)

C175 Deutsch, Babette. "Fusing Word with Image," *New York Herald Tribune Book Review*, XXIV (July 25, 1948), 4.

C176 Ferril, Thomas. *"The Lost Son," San Francisco Chronicle Magazine*, June 13, 1948, p. 18. (UW)

C177 Fitzgerald, Robert. "Patter, Distraction, and Poetry," *New Republic*, CXXI (August 8, 1949), 17.

C178 Flint, F. Cudworth. "Nearing the Hour of the Phoenix," *Virginia Quarterly Review*, XXIV (June 1948), 476–477.

C179 Flint, R. W. "Ten Poets," *Kenyon Review*, XII (Autumn 1950), 707–708.

C180 Fraser, G. S. "The Riddling Style," *New Statesman and Nation* [London], XLVI (September 24, 1949), 335–336.

C181 Gibb, Hugh. "Symbols of Spiritual Growth," *New York Times Book Review*, LIII (August 1, 1948), 14.

C182 Griffin, Howard. "Exciting Low Voices," *Saturday Review of Literature*, XXXI (July 10, 1948), 21, 26.

C183 Hall, James. "Between Two Worlds," *Voices*, No. 134 (Summer 1948), pp. 57–58.

C184 Jump, J. D. "Collected Poems," *Manchester Guardian*, October 4, 1949, p. 4. (UWR)

C185 Kunitz, Stanley. "News of the Root," *Poetry*, LXXIII (January 1949), 222–225.

C186 Morgan, Frederick. "Recent Verse," *Hudson Review*, I (Summer 1948), 261–262.

C187 Mowrer, Deane. "Reviews of Some Current Poetry," *New Mexico Quarterly*, XVIII (Summer 1948), 255–256.

C188 Nicholson, Norman. "Poetry Today," *Time and Tide*, XXX (October 29, 1949), 1086–1087.

C189 Parkinson, Thomas. "Some Recent Pacific Coast Poetry," *Pacific Spectator*, IV (Summer 1950), 302–303.

C190 Perry, Ralph. "New Professor of Poetry Publishes Second Volume," *University of Washington Daily* [Seattle], March 10, 1948. (UW)

C191 Peschmann, Hermann. "Poetry, Simple and Profound," *Public Opinion* [London], March 17, 1950. (UW)

C192 Viereck, Peter. "Five Good Poets in a Bad Year," *Atlantic*, CLXXXII (November 1948), 95.

C193 Zillman, Lawrence. "*The Lost Son and Other Poems*, by Theodore Roethke," *Seattle Post-Intelligencer*, July 18, 1948. (UW)

Praise to the End! (1951)

C194 Anon. "Among the New Books," *San Francisco Chronicle*, January 20, 1952, p. 11. Signed L. G.

C195 Anon. "Praise to the End!" *Virginia Kirkus Service,* XIX (September 1, 1951), 523.

C196 Arrowsmith, William. "Five Poets," *Hudson Review,* IV (Winter 1952), 619–620.

C197 Bogan, Louise. "Verse," *New Yorker,* XXVII (February 16, 1952), 108.

Reprinted: "The Minor Shudder," in *Selected Criticism: Prose and Poetry.* New York: The Noonday Press, 1955, pp. 383–384.

C198 Brantley, Frederick. "Poets and Their Worlds," *Yale Review,* XLI (Spring 1952), 476–477.

C199 Callahan, Margaret B. "Seattle's Surrealist Poet," *Seattle Times Magazine,* March 16, 1952, p. 7. (UWR)

C200 Chang, Diana. "The Modern Idiom," *Voices,* No. 148 (May–August 1952), pp. 41–43.

C201 Eberhart, Richard. "Deep Lyrical Feelings," *New York Times Book Review,* LVI (December 16, 1951), 4.

C202 Frankenberg, Lloyd. "The Year in Poetry," *Harper's Magazine,* CCV (October 1952), 106.

C203 Humphries, Rolfe. "Verse Chronicle," *Nation,* CLXXIV (March 22, 1952), 284.

C204 Rodman, Seldon. "Intuitive Poet," *New York Herald Tribune Book Review,* XXVIII (December 2, 1951), 32.

C205 Sawyer, Kenneth B. "Praises and Crutches," *Hopkins Review,* V (Summer 1952), 126.

C206 Shapiro, Harvey. "Praise to the End!" *Furioso,* VII (Fall 1952), 126.

C207 Vazakas, Byron. "Eleven Contemporary Poets,"
New Mexico Quarterly, XXII (Summer 1952), 224–225.

C208 Viereck, Peter. "Technique and Inspiration," *Atlantic*,
CLXXXIX (January 1952), 81–83.

The Waking: Poems 1933–1953 (1953)

C209 Anon. "Poetry," *U.S. Quarterly Book Review*, X
(March 1954), 55.

C210 Anon. "Recent Poetry in Review," *San Francisco
Chronicle*, January 10, 1954, p. 17. Signed L. F.

C211 Anon. "Roethke, Theodore," *Booklist*, L (October 15,
1953), 74.

C212 Anon. "*The Waking*," *Virginia Kirkus Service*, XXI
(July 15, 1953), 464.

C213 Bennett, Joseph. "Recent Verse," *Hudson Review*,
VII (Summer 1954), 304–305.

C214 Bogan, Louise. "Verse," *New Yorker*, XXIX (October
24, 1953), 158–159.

C215 Carruth, Hayden. "The Idiom is Personal," *New York
Times Book Review*, LVIII (September 13, 1953), 14.

C216 Ciardi, John. "Poets of the Inner Landscape," *Nation*,
CLXXVII (November 14, 1953), 410.

C217 Cole, Thomas. "The Poetry of Theodore Roethke,"
Voices, No. 155 (September–December 1954), pp. 37–40.

C218 Husband, John Dillon. "Some Readings in Recent
Poetry," *New Mexico Quarterly*, XXIV (Winter 1954),
446–447.

C219 Meyer, Gerald Previn. "Logic of the North," *Saturday Review of Literature*, XXXVII (January 16, 1954), 18–19.

C220 Nemerov, Howard. "Three in One," *Kenyon Review*, XV (Winter 1954), 148–154.

Reprinted: "On Shapiro, Roethke, Winters," in *Poetry and Fiction: Essays*. New Brunswick, New Jersey: Rutgers University Press, 1963.

C221 Pearce, Donald. *Michigan Alumnus Quarterly Review*, LXI (Spring 1955), 273–275.

Words for the Wind (1957 and 1958)

C222 Anon. "Both Free and Formal," *Christian Science Monitor*, December 24, 1958, p. 7. Signed P. B.

C223 Anon. "Kin to the Bat," *Time*, LXXII (December 29, 1958), 55.

C224 Anon. "The Listener's Book Chronicle," *Listener* [London], LIX (February 27, 1958), 375.

C225 Anon. "A Modern Poet," *Madras Mail* [India], March 15, 1958. (UW)

C226 Anon. "Points of Origin," *The Times Literary Supplement* [London], LVII (February 7, 1958), 72.

C227 Anon. "Roethke Pulitzer Winner Has New Book of Poems Out," *Seattle Times*, November 30, 1958. (UW)

C228 Anon. "*Words for the Wind*," *Calcutta Statesman* [India], March 30, 1958. (UW)

C229 Anon. "*Words for the Wind*," *Punch* [London], February 26, 1958. Signed J. S.

C230 Anon. *"Words for the Wind,"* *Wings,* Spring 1959, pp. 22–24.

C231 Alvarez, Alfred. "To Be or Not to Be a Poet," *Observer* [London], January 5, 1958.

C232 Bogan, Louise. "Verse," *New Yorker,* xxxv (October 24, 1959), 187–188.

C233 Conquest, Robert. "The Language of Men," *Spectator,* cc (February 14, 1958), 210–211.

C234 Deutsch, Babette. "Roethke's Clear Signature," *New York Herald Tribune Book Review,* xxxiv (December 7, 1958), 3.

C235 Dickey, James. "Correspondences and Essences," *Virginia Quarterly Review,* xxxvii (Autumn 1961), 635–640.

Includes a review of *I Am! Says the Lamb.*

C236 Donnelly, Dorothy. *"Words for the Wind,"* *Michigan Quarterly Review,* i (Summer 1962), 212.

C237 Eberhart, Richard. "Creative Splendor," *New York Times Book Review,* lxiii (November 9, 1958), 34.

C238 Engle, Paul. *"Poetry: Humblest of All the Arts,"* *Chicago Tribune,* December 14, 1958.

C239 Flint, F. Cudworth. "Seeing, Thinking, Saying, Singing," *Virginia Quarterly Review,* xxxc (Spring 1959), 312–313.

C240 Gunn, Thom. "Poets English and American," *Yale Review,* n.s. xlviii (June 1959), 623–626.

C241 Hall, Donald. "*Words for the Wind*," *Michigan Alumnus Quarterly Review*, LXV (May 23, 1959), 270–271.

C242 MacGillivray, Arthur S. J. "Roethke, Theodore, *Words for the Wind*," *Best Sellers*, XVIII (February 1, 1959), 422–423.

C243 McPherson, Hugo. "In a Greenhouse the Poet Found Images of Love," *Toronto Daily Star* [Canada], February 7, 1959, p. 30. (UW)

C244 Mills, Ralph J., Jr. "Keeping the Spirit Spare," *Chicago Review*, XIII (Winter 1959), 114–122.

C245 Muir, Edwin. "New Verse," *New Statesman* [London], LV (January 18, 1958), 76–77.

C246 Napier, John. "Poetry in the Vernacular and Otherwise," *Voices*, No. 176 (September–December 1961), p. 54.

C247 Phillips, Douglas. "Over the Imagination's Far Frontier," *Western Mail* [London], December 14, 1957. (UW)

C248 Rosenthal, Macha Louis. "Closing in on the Self," *Nation*, CLXXVIII (March 21, 1959), 258–260.

C249 Ross, Alan. "Book Reviews," *The London Magazine*, March 1958, pp. 75, 77–79.

C250 Schwartz, Delmore. "The Cunning and the Craft of the Unconscious and Preconscious," *Poetry*, XCIV (June 1959), 203–205.

Reprinted: *Selected Essays of Delmore Schwartz*. Chicago: University of Chicago Press, 1971, pp. 197–199; *see also* II, C59.

C251 Scott, Winfred Townley. "Has Anyone Seen A Trend?" *Saturday Review*, XLII (January 3, 1959), 13.

C252 Seymour-Smith, Martin. "Form and Substance," *Time and Tide*, XXXIX (February 8, 1958), 167.

C253 Skelton, Robin. "Poets' Ways of Speech," *Manchester Guardian*, February 4, 1958, p. 4.

C254 Snodgrass, W. D. "Spring Verse Chronicle," *Hudson Review*, XII (Spring 1959), 114–117.

C255 Spender, Stephen. "*Words for the Wind*," *New Republic*, CXLI (August 10, 1959), 21–22.

C256 Thorpe, Bernice. "Roethke's Exciting Verse," *University of Washington Daily* [Seattle], January 15, 1959. (UW)

C257 Wain, John. "Half-way to Greatness," *Encounter* [London], X (April 1958), 82, 84.

C258 Weil, James L. "*Words for the Wind*," *American Weave*, Spring 1959, p. 35.

C259 Werner, William L. "The Bookworm," *Penn State Alumni News*, XIV (January 1959), 5. (PSC)

C260 Witt-Diamant, Ruth. "The Poems of a Singular Poet," *San Francisco Examiner*, November 23, 1958, p. 30.

I Am! Says the Lamb (1961)

C261 Anon. "*I Am! Says the Lamb*," *Virginia Kirkus Service*, XXIX (May 1, 1961), 423.

C262 Anon. "Rhymes by Roethke," *Christian Science Monitor*, August 3, 1961, p. 7.

C263 Anon. "Roethke Surprises Admirers with Book of Nonsense Poems," *Seattle Times Magazine*, August 6, 1961, p. 22. (UW)

C264 Dickey, James. "Correspondence and Essences," *Virginia Quarterly Review*, XXXVII (Autumn 1961), 640–645.
Includes a review of *Words for the Wind*.

C265 Ehrig, Victor. "Roethke's Nonsense Verse Delightfully Different," *St. Louis Globe-Democrat*, August 13, 1961. (UW)

C266 Henderson, James W. "*I Am! Says the Lamb*, Nonsense Nostalgia in Roethke Volume," *The Saginaw News*, August 3, 1961. (UW)

C267 Maxwell, Emily. "The Smallest Giant in the World, and the Tallest Midget," *New Yorker*, XXXVII (November 18, 1961), 237.

C268 Mills, Ralph J., Jr. "Roethke's Garden," *Poetry*, C (April 1962), 54–59.

C269 Patterson, Elizabeth L. "Theodore Roethke Writes Verse for Everybody," *Seattle Post-Intelligencer*, July 22, 1961. (UW)

C270 Pendon, Armando. " 'Find Out How the Ceiling's Feeling,' " *Oakland Tribune*, August 6, 1961. (UW)

C271 Scoggins, Margaret C. "Outlook Tower," *Horn Book*, XXXVII (December 1961), 567.

C272 Smith, Ray. "Poetry," *Library Journal*, June 15, 1961, p. 2320.

C273 Werner, William L. "The Bookworm," *Centre Daily Times* [State College, Pa.], LXIV (August 1, 1961), 3. (PSC)

Sequence, Sometimes Metaphysical (1963)

C274 Dickey, James. "Theodore Roethke," *Poetry*, CV
(November 1964), 119–122.

C275 Rexroth, Kenneth. "There's Poetry in a Ragged Hitch-
Hiker," *New York Times Book Review*, LXIX
(July 5, 1964), 5.

C276 Snodgrass, W. D. "The Last Poems of Theodore
Roethke," *New York Review of Books*, III (October 8,
1964), 5–6.

Party at the Zoo (1963)

C277 Anon. "Roethke Finishes Poetry," *University of
Washington Daily* [Seattle], June 21, 1963. (UW)

C278 Reddings, John J. "Book Dedicated to Roethke's God
Child," *Seattle Times*, September 6, 1963, p. A.
(UW, UWR, UWSC)

The Far Field (1964 and 1965)

C279 Anon. "Last Poems: 'The Far Field,' " *Time*, LXXXIV
(July 10, 1964), 98.

C280 Anon. "Poems for the Good-Hearted," *The London
Times*, November 4, 1965, p. 15b. (UW)

C281 Anon. "Roethke, Theodore," *Booklist*, LXI (September 1,
1964), 29.

C282 Anon. "Theodore Roethke's Verse Published Posthumously," *Seattle Times Magazine*, September 13,
1964, p. 19.

C283 Alvarez, Alfred. "New Poetry: *The Far Field* by Theodore Roethke," *Observer* [London], October 24, 1965, p. 27.

C284 Bogan, Louise. "Verse," *New Yorker*, XL (November 7, 1964), 243.

C285 Carey, John. *New Statesman* [London], LXX (December 31, 1965), 1032–1033.

C286 Carruth, Hayden. "Requiem for God's Gardener," *Nation*, CIC (September 1964), 168–169.

C287 Cookson, William. "Roethke's Last Poems," *Agenda* [London], III (September 1964), 21–27.

C288 Davis, Donald. "Two Ways Out of Whitman," *The Review*, XIV (December 1964), 18–19.

C289 Davison, Peter. "Madness in the New Poetry," *Atlantic*, CCXV (January 1965), 93.

C290 Dickey, William. "Poetic Language," *Hudson Review*, XVII (Winter 1964–1965), 596.

C291 Friedberg, Martha. "Sharing the Joy of Being Alive," *Books Today* (*Chicago Sunday Tribune*), September 6, 1964, pp. 64–69.

C292 Fuller, John G. "Trade Winds," *Saturday Review*, XLVIII (March 27, 1965), 10–11.

C293 Furbank, P. N. "New Poetry," *Listener* [London], LXXIV (October 21, 1965), 635.

C294 Garrigue, Jean. "A Mountain on the Landscape," *New Leader*, XLVII (December 7, 1964), 33–34.

C295 Harrison, Keith. "Solstice Time," *Spectator*, October 15, 1965, pp. 488–490.

C296 Hiscock, Barbara. "*The Far Field*: A Last Gift from a Great Poet," *University of Washington Daily* [Seattle], July 23, 1964, p. 2. (UW, UWSC)

C297 Johns, Godfrey. "Poetry with an Academic Accent," *Christian Science Monitor*, September 10, 1964, p. 5.

C298 Jones, Nard. "A View from Monday: 'The Far Field.' " *Seattle Post-Intelligencer*, June 15, 1964. (UW, UWSC)

C299 Kennedy, X. J. "Joys, Griefs and 'All Things Innocent, Hapless, Forsaken,' " *New York Times Book Review*, August 23, 1964, p. 5.

C300 Lieberman, Laurence. "Poetry Chronicle: Last Poems, Fragments, and Wholes," *Antioch Review*, XXIV (Winter 1964–1965), 537–539.

C301 Martz, Louis. "Recent Poetry: The Elegiac Mode," *Yale Review*, LIV (Winter 1965), 294–297.

C302 Meredith, William. "Cogitating with His Finger Tips," *Book Week* (*The Washington Post*), July 18, 1965, pp. 4, 15.

Includes a review of *On the Poet and His Craft*.

C303 Mills, Ralph J., Jr. "Roethke's Last Poems," *Poetry*, CV (November 1964), 122–124.

C304 Moss, Howard. "Renewed by Death," *The Times Literary Supplement* [London], LXV (January 27, 1966), 65.

Reprinted: "Poets Today: Theodore Roethke: *The Far Field*," in *T.L.S.: Essays and Reviews from the Times Literary Supplement*. New York and Toronto: Oxford University Press, 1967.

C305 Powers, Dennis. "Fine Final Lines of Theodore Roethke," *Focus (Oakland Tribune)*, July 16, 1964.

C306 Press, John. "Recent Poems," *Punch* [London], CCXLIX (November 3, 1965), 665.

C307 Pryce-Jones, Alan. "*The Far Field*," *New York Herald Tribune*, July 9, 1964, p. 19.

C308 ———. *Focus (Oakland Tribune)*, July 16, 1964. (UW)

C309 ———. "Roethke's Last Poems Show What World Lost," *Seattle Times*, July 27, 1964. (UW, UWSC)

C310 Ramsay, Paul. "A Weather of Heaven," *Shenandoah*, XVI (Autumn 1964), 72–73.

C311 Rosenthal, Macha Louis. "The Couch and Poetic Insight," *The Reporter*, XXXII (March 25, 1965), 52–53.

C312 Ross, Alan. "Selected Books," *The London Magazine*, January 1966, pp. 88, 91.

C313 Smith, John. "The Far Field," *Poetry Review* [London], n.s. LVI (Winter 1965), 248–249.

C314 Smith, William J. "Verse: Two Posthumous Volumes," *Harper's Magazine*, CCXXIX (October 1964), 133–134.

C315 Snodgrass, W. D. "The Last Poems of Theodore Roethke," *New York Review of Books*, III (October 8, 1964), 5–6.

Includes a review of *Sequence, Sometimes Metaphysical*.

C316 Southworth, James G. "Theodore Roethke: 'The Far Field,'" *College English*, XXVII (February 1966), 413–418.

C317 Stoneburner, Tony. "Ardent Quest," *Christian Century*, LXXXI (September 30, 1964), 1217–1218.

C318 Walsh, Chad. "A Cadence of Our Time," *Saturday Review*, XLVIII (January 2, 1965), 28.

C319 Willingham, John R. "Last Poems," *Time*, LXXXIV (July 10, 1964), 98.

C320 ————. "Poetry," *Library Journal*, LXXXIX (September 15, 1964), 3320.

C321 Zinnes, Harriet. "English: Poetics," *Books Abroad*, XXXIX (Summer 1965), 353–354.

On the Poet and His Craft: Selected Prose of Theodore Roethke (1965)

C322 Anon. "Notes, Etc. on Books, Etc.," *Carlton Miscellany*, VI (Fall 1965), 92.

C323 Anon. "*On the Poet and His Craft: Selected Prose of Theodore Roethke*," *Booklist*, LXII (November 1, 1965), 257.

C324 Anon. "*On the Poet and His Craft: Selected Prose of Theodore Roethke*," *Choice*, II (October 1965), 485.

C325 Bannon, Barbara. "Forecast of Paperbacks," *Publisher's Weekly*, CLXXXIX (February 14, 1966), 149.

C326 Booth, Phillip. "Nothing but What's Human," *Christian Science Monitor*, September 16, 1965, p. 11.

C327 Cambon, Glauco. "The Tangibles of Craftsmanship," *Kenyon Review*, XXVII (Autumn 1965), 758–762.

C328 Fields, Kenneth. "Strategies of Criticism," *Southern Review*, n.s. II (Autumn 1966), 974–975.

This is also a review of Denis Donoghue's *Connoisseurs of Chaos* (*see* II, C39).

C329 Geiger, Don. "New Books in Review," *Quarterly Journal of Speech*, LII (April 1966), 201.

C330 Goodheart, Eugene. "The Frailty of the 'I,' " *Sewanee Review*, LXXVI (Summer 1968), 516–519.

C331 Hicks, Granville. "Meeting the Genuine Mystery," *Saturday Review*, XLVIII (July 31, 1965), 15–16.

C332 Hoskins, Katherine. "Roethke in His Prose," *Poetry*, CVII (March 1966), 400–440.

C333 Jones, Nard. "A View from Sunday," *Northwest Today* (*Seattle Post-Intelligencer*), September 19, 1965, p. 2. (UW)

C334 Lazarus, A. L. "Book Reviews," *College English*, XXVII (May 1966), 647.

C335 Lupher, David A. "Lost Son: Theodore Roethke," *Yale Literary Magazine*, CXXXV (March 1967), 9–12.

C336 Malkoff, Karl. "Cleansing the Doors of Perception," *Minnesota Review*, V (October–December, 1965), 342–348.

C337 Meredith, William. "Cogitating with His Finger Tips," *Book Week* (*The Washington Post*), July 18, 1965, p. 2. Includes a review of *The Far Field*.

C338 Mueller, Lisel. "An Exacting Poet's Astute, Witty Essays on His Craft," *Panorama* (*Chicago Daily News*), August 7, 1965, p. 8.

C339 Muggeridge, Malcolm. "Books," *Esquire*, LXIV (August 1965), 46.

C340 Pinsker, Sanford. "Theodore Roethke, The Poet in Prose," *Tyee Magazine* [University of Washington, Seattle], I (Autumn 1965), 22–23. (UW)

C341 Rosenthal, Macha Louis. "Throes of Creation," *New York Times Book Review*, LXX (July 18, 1965), 4.

C342 Southworth, James G. "Books," *Western Humanities Review*, XX (Winter 1966), 79–80.

The Collected Poems of Theodore Roethke (1966 and 1968)

C343 Anon. "*The Collected Poems of Theodore Roethke*," *Virginia Kirkus Service*, XXXIII (September 15, 1965), 1021.

C344 Anon. "*The Collected Poems of Theodore Roethke*," *Booklist*, LXIII (September 15, 1966), 92.

C345 Anon. "*The Collected Poems of Theodore Roethke*," *Choice*, III (October 1966), 651.

C346 Anon. "*The Collected Poems of Theodore Roethke*," *Virginia Kirkus Service*, XXXIV (May 1, 1966), 502.

C347 Anon. "Pursued by Voices," *The Times Literary Supplement* [London], LXVII (July 4, 1968), 699.

C348 Benedict, Michael. "Completed Pattern," *Poetry*, CIX (January 1967), 262–266.

C349 Boyers, Robert. "A Very Separate Peace," *Kenyon Review*, XXVIII (November 1966), 683–691.

Reprinted: *The Young American Writers*. New York: Funk and Wagnalls, 1968, pp. 27–34.

C350 Carruth, Hayden. "In Spite of Artifice," *Hudson Review*, XIX (Winter 1966–1967), 689–692.

C351 Curley, Dorothy. *"The Collected Poems of Theodore Roethke,"* *Library Journal*, XCI (June 15, 1966), 3219.

C352 Davison, Peter. "Some Recent Poetry," *Atlantic*, CCXVIII (November 1966), 163.

C353 Dodsworth, Martin. "Towards the Baseball Poems," *Listener* [London], LXXIX (June 27, 1968), 842.

C354 Donoghue, Denis. "Aboriginal Poet," *New York Review of Books*, VII (September 22, 1966), 14–16.

C355 Ferry, David. "Roethke's Poetry," *Virginia Quarterly Review*, LXIII (Winter 1967), 169–173.
Reprinted: *see* II, C59.

C356 Fiedler, Leslie A. "Poet of Childhood," *Manchester Guardian*, XCVIII (June 6, 1968), 11.

C357 Freer, Colburn. *"The Collected Poems of Theodore Roethke,"* *Arizona Quarterly*, XXIII (Autumn 1967), 280–281.

C358 Fuller, Edmond. " 'A Poet of Love,' " *Wall Street Journal*, CLXVIII (August 5, 1966), 6.

C359 Gelpi, Albert J. "Roethke's Heritage," *Christian Science Monitor*, October 6, 1966, p. 31.

C360 Grant, D. *"The Collected Poems of Theodore Roethke,"* *Tablet* [London], July 6, 1968, p. 673.

C361 Hayman, R. *"The Collected Poems of Theodore Roethke,"* *Encounter* [London], XXI (February 1969), 74.

C362 Heaney, Seamus. "Canticles to the Earth," *Listener* [London], LXXX (August 22, 1968), 245–246.

C363 Ketching, Jessie. "Forecasts," *Publisher's Weekly,* CLXXXIX (June 27, 1966), 98.

C364 Lask, Thomas. "Celebrations and Defeats," *New York Times*, CXV (August 2, 1966), 31.

C365 Longley, M. "*The Collected Poems of Theodore Roethke*," *Dublin Magazine*, Spring/Summer, 1969, p. 86.

C366 Lupher, David A. "Lost Son: Theodore Roethke," *Yale Literary Magazine*, CXXXV (March 1967), 9–12.

C367 Malkoff, Karl. "Exploring the Boundaries of the Self," *Sewanee Review*, LXXV (Summer 1967), 540–542.

C368 Martz, Louis L. "Recent Poetry: Roethke, Warren and Others," *Yale Review*, LVI (December 1966), 275–277.

C369 Mills, Ralph J., Jr. "Recognition," *New York Times Book Review*, LXXI (July 17, 1966), 5, 30.

C370 Mueller, Lisel. "A Poetic Pilgrimage: The Life Work of Roethke," *Panorama* (*Chicago Daily News*), July 23, 1966, p. 7.

C371 Simpson, Louis. "New Books of Poems," *Harper's Magazine*, CCXXXV (August 1967), 90.

C372 Skelton, Robin. "The Poetry of Theodore Roethke," *Malahat* [Vancouver, B.C.], No. 1 (January 1967), pp. 141–144.

C373 Slater, Joseph. "Verse," *New Yorker*, XLII (September 24, 1966), 239–240.

C374 ———. "Immortal Bard and Others," *Saturday Review*, XLIX (December 31, 1966), 24.

C375 Spender, Stephen. "Roethke: 'The Lost Son,' " *New Republic*, CLV (August 27, 1966), 23–25.

C376 Stephens, Alan. *"The Collected Poems of Theodore Roethke,"* *Denver Quarterly*, I (Winter 1967), 101–112.

C377 Symons, Julian. "New Poetry," *Punch* [London], CCLIV (June 19, 1968), 902.

C378 Thwaite, Anthony. "Guts, Brain, Nerves," *New Statesman*, LXXV (May 17, 1968), 659.

C379 Tillinghast, Richard. *"The Collected Poems of Theodore Roethke,"* *Southern Review*, V (1969), 594–596.

C380 Toynbee, P. *"The Collected Poems of Theodore Roethke,"* *Observer* [London], May 5, 1968, p. 26.

C381 Vendler, Hellen. "Recent American Poetry," *Massachusetts Review*, VII (Summer 1966), 641ff.

C382 Walsh, Chad. "Plant and Phantom: The Odyssey of a Major American Poet through Deep Regions of the Self," *Book Week* (*The Washington Post*), XXXI (July 31, 1966), 1, 12.

C383 Woodcock, George. "Daring Greatness," *New Leader*, LXIX (September 12, 1966), 21–22.

Selected Letters of Theodore Roethke (1968 and 1970)

C384 Anon. "Lives and Letters," *Virginia Quarterly Review*, XLIV (Autumn 1968), 160.

C385 Anon. *"Selected Letters of Theodore Roethke,"* *Antiquarian Bookman*, XLI (June 3, 1968), 2198.

C386 Boyers, Robert. "The Roethke Letters," *Georgia Review*, XXII (Winter 1968), 437–445.

C387 Brown, A. *"Selected Letters of Theodore Roethke,"* *Spectator*, July 11, 1970, p. 16.

C388 Bullis, Jerald. *"Selected Letters of Theodore Roethke,"* *Massachusetts Review*, XI (Winter 1970), 209–212.

C389 Burke, Kenneth. "Cult of the Breakthrough," *New Republic*, CLIX (September 21, 1968), 25–26.

C390 DeVany, Julia C. "Reviews," *Spirit: A Magazine of Poetry*, XXVI (Spring 1969), 137–139.

C391 Dunlop, William. "Roethke's Letters Reveal a Man," *Northwest Today (Seattle Post-Intelligencer)*, May 3, 1968, p. 4.

C392 Fuller, Edmond. "Poets on Poetry," *Wall Street Journal*, CLXXI (August 15, 1968), 10.

C393 Fuson, Ben W. *"Selected Letters of Theodore Roethke,"* *American Literature*, XL (November 1968), 436.

C394 ———. *Library Journal*, XCIII (September 1, 1968), 3006.

C395 Heyen, William. "He Blusters, Sorrows and Laughs," *Saturday Review*, LI (June 22, 1968), 78.

C396 Howard, R. *"Selected Letters of Theodore Roethke,"* *Poetry*, CX (February 1969), 359.

C397 Kach, Stephen. "The Poet's Scene," *New York Times Book Review*, LXXIII (September 29, 1968), 34.

C398 Ketching, Jessie B. "Forecasts: Non-fiction," *Publisher's Weekly*, CXCII (April 8, 1968), 43.

C399 Krim, S. *"Selected Letters of Theodore Roethke,"* *London Magazine*, September 1971, pp. 70–91.

C400 Lask, Thomas. "Life Was as Difficult as the Art," *New York Times*, January 1, 1969, p. 19.
Includes a review of *The Glass House* (*see* II, B26).

C401 Leimbacher, Ed. "Epistolary Roethke," *Seattle Magazine*, July 1968, pp. 10–11.

C402 McClellan, Elwood. *"Selected Letters of Theodore Roethke,"* *Michigan History*, LIII (Winter 1969), 319–322.

C403 Malkoff, Karl. *"Selected Letters of Theodore Roethke,"* *Southwest Review*, LIV (1969), 329–332.

C404 Morgan, Murray. "The New Books," *The Argus* [Seattle], LXXV (May 24, 1968), 8.

C405 Rosenthal, M. L. *"Selected Letters of Theodore Roethke,"* *New Statesman*, LXXVIII (July 10, 1970), 25ff.

C406 Rumley, Larry. "Theodore Roethke's Letters Published by U. W. Press," *Seattle Times Magazine*, May 5, 1968, p. 1.

C407 Sherman, Paul. "Making it as a Poet," *Nation*, CCVIII (January 6, 1969), 27–28.

Straw for the Fire (1972)

C408 Heyen, William. *"Sorties* and *Straw for the Fire,"* *Saturday Review*, LV (March 11, 1972), 70.

C409 Leibowitz, Herbert. *"Straw for the Fire,"* New York *Times Book Review*, April 9, 1972, pp. 4, 10.

C410 Shapiro, Karl. "Scraping the Bottom of Roethke Barrel," *New Republic*, LXVI (March 4, 1972), 24.

D Foreign Biography and Criticism

This section cannot be considered complete; it merely suggests the range of biographical and critical interest in Roethke and his poetry in non-English-speaking nations (with the one exception of South Africa).

Biography

D1 Anon. "In Memoriam," *Ord Och Bild: Kulturtidskrift för de Nordiska Länderna* [Stockholm], *Häfte* 5, 1963, p. 408. (UW)

D2 Anon. "Le Prix Pulitzer, 1954 A Theodore Roethke," *Le Journal Des Poètes* [Paris], XXIV (June, 1954), 3. (UW)

D3 Bosquet, Alain. "Trois Poetes Contemporains des Estate-Unis," *Présence*, VII (Winter 1957–1958), 34. (UW)

D4 Fukuda, Rikutaro. "Theodore Roethke: Poets I Met in America," *The Study of English* [Japan], LI (October 1962), 24–26. (UW)

Reprinted in English in *The Glass House*, pp. 273–276 (*see* II, B26); a typescript in English is located at the University of Washington Manuscript Division.

Criticism

D5 Biogongiari, Piero. "Roethke: La Ricerea di Unidentita," *Letteratura*, XXXI–XXXV (Gen–Giu 1967), 259–264.

193

D6 Brown, John. *Panorama de La Litterature Contemporaine aux Etats-Unis*. Paris: Librarie Gallimard, 1954.

D7 Christie, Erling. "Navn Og Tendenser I Amerikansk Ettsrkrigspoesi," *Vinduet: Flydendals Tidsskvift: For Litterature* [Oslo], XI (1957), 70–71. (UW)

D8 Donoghue, Denis. "Theodore Roethke: Toward *The Far Field*," *Lugano Review* [Switzerland], I (1965), 50–72.

D9 Fauchereau, Serge. "Lecture de Theodore Roethke," *Critique*, CCXXXI–CCXXXII (August–September 1966), 730–735.

A review of *Words for the Wind, The Far Field, On The Poet and His Craft*, and *Theodore Roethke* by Ralph Mills, Jr.

D10 Hall, Donald. "Les Jeunes Poètes Americains," *United States Lines*: *Paris Review* [1954?], unpaginated. (UW)

D11 Lombardo, Agostino. "Poesia Americana," *Lo Spettatore Italinao*, VII (February 1954), 72–75.

A review of *The Waking*.

D12 ———. "La Poesia di Theodore Roethke," in *Theodore Roethke: Sequenza Nordamericano E Altri Poesie*. Milan: Mondadori, 1966.

See I, D1.

D13 Meier, Erika. "Translation of 'Orchids,' 'The Visitant,' 'Bring the Day!' by Alain Bosquet," January 1958 [unpublished?]. (UW)

D14 Meliadò, Mariolina. "Nota Della Traduttrico," in *Theodore Roethke: Sequenza Nordamericano E Altri Poesie*. Milan: Mondadori, 1966.

D15 ————. "Theodore Roethke," *Studi Americani* [Rome], IX (1964), 425–545. (UW, UWSC)

D16 Palm, Göran. "Noter Till Roethke," *Upptakt* [Stockholm], IV (1955), 18. (UW)

See II, F8.

D17 Riley, Peter. "New English Poetry," *Levende Talen* [Netherlands], CCXXXIV (1968), 226–231.

D18 Sahl, Hans. "Wiedergeburt der Elgie Der Lyriker Theodore Roethke," *Die Newe Zeitung*, July 18, 1954. (UW)

Reprinted: *Sueddeutsdve Zeitung*, Munich.

D19 Seidel, Frederick. "The Art of Poetry III," *Paris Review*, VII (Winter–Spring 1961), 57–95.

An interview of Robert Lowell, who makes random reference to Roethke.
Reprinted: *Writers at Work*, Second Series. New York: The Viking Press, 1963; *Modern Poetics*, ed. James Scully. New York: McGraw-Hill, 1965.

D20 Shapiro, Karl. "Recent American Poetry" [title in Russian], *Amerika*, n.s. No. 28 (Yeha 5, [1959]), pp. 8–11.

See I, D35.

D21 Stammler, Heinrich. "Dicter in Amerika: Richard Eberhardt, Richard Wilbur, Theodore Roethke," *Merkur* [Stuttgart], X (November 1956), 1070–1073. (UW)

D22 Toerien, Barend J. "Theodore Roethke, Met Opmerking oor Nuwere Amerikaanse Poësie," *Tydskrif vir Letterkinde* [Johannesburg], No. 2 (May 1963), pp. 34–43. (UW)

E Films and Recordings

This section lists recordings, films, and a video tape having biographical and critical significance. All of the items, with the exception of the films, are located at the University of Michigan or the University of Washington. Readings of Roethke's poetry by others are listed separately in I, E27–39.

Films

E1 Coleman, Alice C. *A Class Study of Theodore Roethke's 'The Waking.'* Commission on English of the College Entrance Eamination Board (16 mm, b&w, sound), New York, 1965.

A pamphlet of the script of this film is available through the Commission on English, 687 Boylston Street, Boston, Massachusetts (*see* II, C30).

E2 Kunitz, Stanley and Robert Lowell. *A Tribute to Ted*, WCBS-TV, #631027, New York, 1963.

This is a positive print of the Camera Three program broadcasted from New York City on October 27, 1963. Includes critical and biographical comments by Lowell and Kunitz on "Night Journey," "Elegy for Jane," and others, and scenes of Roethke reading from the film *In a Dark Time* (*see* I, E1). This print can be ordered from WCBS-TV Film Library, 524 West 57th Street, New York.
      Reviews: W. L. Werner, "Bookworm," *Centre Daily Times* [State College, Pa.], October 29, 1963, p. 9f (PSC); C. J. Screen. "C.B.S. Offers Warm Tribute to Roethke," *Seattle Times*, October 28, 1963. (UWE, UWSC)

E3 Warren, Robert Penn. *The Fifth Annual Theodore Roethke Memorial Reading*, May 25, 1968. University of Washington, Seattle, ‡A 92-3-68 (1 reel), 1968. (UWE)

This is a video tape of the reading in which Warren makes a critical assessment of Roethke. The reading is introduced by Arnold Stein, who makes brief biographical remarks about Roethke.

Recordings

E4 Bentley, Nelson, Donald Hall, Allan Seager, and A.J.M. Smith. "Tribute to Theodore Roethke." WUOM, University of Michigan, Ann Arbor, 1965. (UW)

Brief reminiscences by Bentley and Smith and lengthy reminiscences and critical assessments by Allan Seager and Donald Hall are included. Broadcasted over WUOM in May 1965.

E5 Ciardi, John, Stanley Kunitz, and Allan Seager. "An Evening with Ted Roethke." WUOM, University of Michigan, Ann Arbor, 1967. (UW)

Includes reminiscences and critical assessments of Roethke. Recorded in Saginaw at the Arthur Hill High School to inaugurate the Theodore Roethke Memorial Foundation on May 24, 1967. Includes a dedicatory poem by Ciardi (*see* II, F24).
Reference: "An Evening with Ted Roethke," *Michigan Quarterly Review*. VI (October 1967), 227–245 (*see* II, B10).

E6 Humphries, Rolfe. "The Early Theodore Roethke: Reminiscences and Reading." University of Washington, Seattle, (1 tape, speed 3¾), 1966.

Includes biographical remarks and the reading of several unpublished poems with an introduction by Solomon Katz. (UWE)

E7 ———. "Theodore Roethke Memorial Reading, May 25, 1966." University of Washington, Seattle, (1 tape, speed 3¾), 1966. (UWE)

Includes brief biographical comments on Roethke and a dedicatory poem to Roethke with an introduction by Nelson Bentley.

E8 Kizer, Carolyn, Howard Nemerov, and Beatrice Roethke. "First Roethke Poetry Award." WUOM, University of Michigan, Ann Arbor. (UW)

This is a recording of the ceremonies at which Howard Nemerov received the first award on May 21, 1968. The introduction and presentation of the award were by Burrows Morley. Carolyn Kizer spoke on her "Reminiscences of Roethke." Howard Nemerov spoke after receiving the award for his book *The Blue Swallows*. A second taped interview following the program included comments by Nemerov, Kizer, and Beatrice Roethke.

E9 Lowell, Robert. "Theodore Roethke Memorial Reading, May 25, 1965." University of Washington, Seattle, (2 tapes, speed 7½), 1965. (UWE)

Includes biographical and critical comments by Lowell on "Open House," "The Lost Son," "The Shape of the Fire," "The Far Field," "The Heron," "Meditations of an Old Woman," "Meadow Mouse," "Geranium," "The Lizard (He too has eaten Well)," and "In a Dark Time." Includes an introduction by William Matchett.

Review: "Pulitzer Prize Poet Lauds Roethke," *University of Washington Daily* [Seattle], May 26, 1965, pp. 1, 3. (UWE)

E10 MacLeish, Archibald. "Theodore Roethke Memorial Reading, May 25, 1967." University of Washington, Seattle (1 tape, speed 3¾), 1967.

Includes brief comments on Roethke and an introduction by Solomon Katz.

Review: Tom Hubert. "Fitting Tribute to Theodore Roethke," *University of Washington Daily* [Seattle], May 26, 1967, p. 12.

E11 Ransom, John Crowe. "Theodore Roethke Memorial Reading, May 24, 1964." University of Washington, Seattle, 1964. (UWE)

Includes critical comments and a reading of some poems. This recording was unavailable for examination. *See also* II, F67.

F Dedications

This section, while probably incomplete, reflects the esteem in which Roethke was held by his colleagues and by contemporary poets. Most of the material was written after Roethke's death; however, the *Portfolio* (II, F11) was dedicated to Roethke on the eve of his departure to Bennington College in 1943 (*see* II, B65). The issue was comprised of work his students had done at Pennsylvania State College under his guidance.

Miscellaneous

F1 "Autumn Comes," *Daily Collegian* [State College, Pa.], LXVII (October 19, 1966), 3.

> An excerpt from "The Waking" ("Great Nature has another thing to do / To you and me; so take the lively air, / And lovely, learn by going where to go") appears with nine photos of the Pennsylvania State University Campus.

F2 Byrd, B. "I Want a Row of Bright Clean Books," *Southern Poetry Review*, XI (Spring 1971), 15–16.

F3 Ciardi, John. "Theodore Roethke: A Passion and a Maker," *Saturday Review*, XLVI (August 31, 1963), 13.

F4 "A Garland for Theodore Roethke," *Michigan Quarterly Review*, VI (Fall 1967), 252–275.

> Poems in memory of Roethke by James Cole, Robert Huff, Richard Murphy, Lewis Turco, John Berryman, Winfield Townley Scott, John Montague, John Kolars, John Ridland, Myron Turner,

Robert Lowell, Robert Conquest, Paul Roche, Robert Sund, Alfred Ebelt, and James Lewiston appear in this issue (see individual entries below).

F5 Harmon, William. "From 'Van Diemen's Land' (Book v of 'Looms')," *Antioch Review*, xxx (Fall/Winter 1970–1971), 445.

F6 K[izer], C[arolyn]. "For Theodore Roethke May, 1908–August, 1963," *Poetry Northwest*, iv (Summer 1963), 3.

F7 Mills, Ralph J., Jr. "Theodore Roethke 1908–1963: A Tribute," *Northwestern University Quarterly Review*, vi (Winter 1964), 13–15.

F8 Palm, Göran. "In Memoriam," *Ord Och Bild: Kulturtid-Skrift för de Nordiska Länderna* [Stockholm], Häfte 5, 1963, p. 408. (UW)

F9 ———. "Till Theodore Roethke," in *Hudens besok Dikter Norsteldts*. Stockholm: P. A. Norstedt & Soners, 1961.

The autographed copy, located with Roethke's library in storage in Seattle, reads: "For the *tone* in *Praise to the End*!"

F10 Pflum, Richard. "Dark Festival (An appreciation after reading T. Roethke)," *Southern Poetry Review*, xi (Spring 1971), 26–27.

F11 "Poetry Issue Dedicated to Theodore Roethke," *Portfolio* [student publication of Pennsylvania State College], v (April 1943), 1, 10. (UW)

See the introduction for this section.

F12 "Roethke's Twilight Testament," *Seattle Magazine*, i (April 1964), 12–13. (UW)

This is a memorial printing of "The Far Field" with two sketches of Roethke by Laurie Olin.

F13 "The Rose," in *The Tyee 1964* [published by the associated
students of the University of Washington].
Seattle, 1964. (UWSC)

This memorial section includes a water color of Roethke (1962),
three ink sketches, and two photographs by Mary Randlett on
sepia paper. "The Rose" is printed on pages 118–120 and an
excerpt ("I sway outside myself / Into the darkening currents")
from section I of "The Rose" appears with watercolor on page 117.

F14 Skelton, Robin, ed. "To the Memory of Theodore
Roethke 1908–1963," in *Five Poets of the Pacific
Northwest*. Seattle and London: University of Washington
Press, 1964, p. vii.

Includes a drawing by Carl Monis below the dedication and a
reference to Roethke's influence on Northwest poetry on page xv.

F15 Styron, William. *Set this House on Fire*. New York:
Random House, 1959, p. 234.

The last stanza of "The Waking" ("I wake to sleep") serves as an
introduction to a section of the novel.

F16 Tate, Allen. "The Memoriam—Theodore Roethke,
1908–1963," *Encounter* [London], XXI (October 1963), 68.

Includes "The Moment" (*see* I, C198).

Music

F17 Smit, Leo. "Four Part Song from a Left Shoe and Three
Friends," A personal song for Theodore Roethke
["Happy Birthday"]. (UW)

Poetry

F18 Allman, John. "Theodore Roethke's Movie: The
Nightmare of Joy," *Southern Poetry Review*, XI
(Spring 1971), 13.

F19 Berryman, John. "Dream Song 153," in *The Dream Songs.* New York: Farrar, Straus, and Giroux, 1969, p. 172.

F20 ———. "A Strut for Roethke," in *77 Dream Songs.* New York: Farrar, Straus, and Giroux, 1964, pp. 20–21.

Reprinted: *The Times Literary Supplement* [London], August 23, 1963, p. 642; *New York Review of Books*, I (October 17, 1963), 22; *Michigan Quarterly Review*, VI (Fall 1967), 255–256.

F21 Billings, Robert. "Ted and Edith" [unpublished].

F22 Brinnin, John Malcolm. "Roethke Plain," *Atlantic*, CCXXV (March 1970), 58–60.

F23 Burke, Kenneth. "Post-Roethkian Translation," *The Hopkins Review*, VI (Winter 1953), 6–7.

F24 Ciardi, John. "Was a Man," *Saturday Review*, XLIX (April 9, 1966), 16.

Reprinted: *This Strangest Everything.* New Brunswick: Rutgers University Press, 1966; *Michigan Quarterly Review*, VI (Fall 1967), 240–241; *Cimarron Review*, No. 7 (March 1969), pp. 7–8.

F25 Cole, James. "Christmas Eve: For *Theodore Roethke*," *Virginia Quarterly Review*, XL (Winter 1964). (UW)

Reprinted: *Michigan Quarterly Review*, VI (Fall 1967), 252.

F26 Conquest, Robert. "A Seattle Parkland (In Memory of Theodore Roethke)," *Encounter* [London], XXIV (October 1966). (UW)

Reprinted: *Michigan Quarterly Review*, VI (Fall 1967), 267–278.

F27 Davis, William Virgil. "The Gypsy Moth" and "Roethke" [unpublished].

F28 Deutsch, Babette. "Lament for the Makers: 1964,"
Atlantic, CCXIV (December 1964), 72–73.

Reprinted: *The Collected Poems of Babette Deutsch*. New York:
Doubleday & Co., 1969, pp. 5–6.

F29 Dickson, Edgar H. "Late Note to Theodore Roethke,"
Sounds of Pacific Northwest Poetry. Washington State
Poetry Foundation, W4 RM - 8758 (12", 33 1/3 rpm,
side #2).

See I, E37.

F30 Ebelt, Alfred. "Roethke's Valley," *Michigan Quarterly
Review*, VI (October 1967), 272–274.

F31 Eberhart, Richard. "The Birth of the Spirit (for Theodore
Roethke, 1908–1963)," *Harvard Advocate*, April
1965, p. 10.

F32 Edwards, Thomas. "Roethke," *Alkahest*, No. 3
(Fall 1969), pp. 22–23.

F33 Enrico, Harold J. Untitled: "Many had come to hear you
read, and some . . ." [unpublished]. (UW)

This poem was written after Roethke's World's Fair reading in
1962. *See* II, A7, p. 216.

F34 Galvin, Brendan. "For Theodore Roethke," *Sage*, XI
(Fall 1967), 270.

F35 Gardner, Isabella. "This Room is Full of Clocks,"
Encounter [London], XXI (November 1963), 52.

Reprinted: *Michigan Quarterly Review*, VI (Fall 1967), 266–267.

F36 Hall, Donald. "Apples," in *The Alligator Bride: Poems
New and Selected*. New York: Harper and Row,
1969, p. 82.

F37 Hallock, P. R. "The Sidelong Pickerel Smile," *Alkahest*, No. 2 (Fall 1968), 20–21.

F38 Heyen, William. "In Memoriam: Theodore Roethke," *Southern Review*, VI (January 1970), 181–184.

F39 Hill, Jeanne. "The Blue Face of the Pool" [unpublished].

F40 Huff, Robert. "On the Death of Theodore Roethke," *Poetry*, CVII (March 1966), 360ff.

> Reprinted: *The Course*. Detroit: Wayne State University Press, 1966; *Michigan Quarterly Review*, VI (Fall 1967), 252–253.

F41 ———. "Spring Run (In a Way of His Manner for an Old Michigan Bear)," in *Colonel Johnson's Ride*. Detroit: Wayne State University Press, 1959.

> Reprinted: *Michigan Quarterly Review*, VI (Fall 1967), 262–264.

F42 Humphries, Rolfe. "Interval (for Theodore Roethke)," "Theodore Roethke Memorial Reading, III." (Tape Recording, 3¾ speed, 1 reel), 1966.

> *See* II, E6. Most of the words are from Roethke's unpublished poem of the same title (*see* II, A7, p. 77).

F43 Kimmelman, Burt. "Roethke's Pond" [unpublished].

F44 Kirby-Smith, Tom. "After Roethke," *Southern Review*, VII (Winter 1966), 110–111.

F45 Kolars, John. "Roethke," *Michigan Quarterly Review*, VI (Fall 1967), 257.

F46 Kunitz, Stanley. "Journal for My Daughter" (part 5), in *The Testing Tree*. Boston: Atlantic, Little, Brown, 1971, p. 5.

F47 Lewisohn, James. "Theodore Roethke (A Little
Memory)," *Beloit Poetry Journal*, XVII (Winter
1966/1967), 1.

Reprinted: *Michigan Quarterly Review*, VI (Fall 1967), 274.

F48 Locke, Edward. "Four Odes on the Death" [unpublished].
(UW)

A copy is located at the University of Washington Manuscript
Division.

F49 Long, Clayton, "Argumentum Ad Hominem, 1963,
for Theodore Roethke," *Prairie Schooner*, XXXIX
(Fall 1965), 243.

F50 Lowell, Robert. "For Theodore Roethke (1908–1963),"
The Observer Weekend Review [London],
February 23, 1964.

Reprinted: *Near the Ocean*. New York: Farrar, Straus, and Giroux,
1966; *The Minnesota Review*, VIII (1968), 358.

F51 Malanga, Gerard. "The Tearing Wind" [unpublished].

F52 Malkoff, Karl. "For Theodore Roethke," *Southwest
Review*, LIV (Summer 1969), 247.

F53 Manner, George. "The Bear: A Tribute to Theodore
Roethke," *Southern Review*, VI (January 1970), 170–171.

F54 Miranda, Gary. "The Pig," *The Minnesota Review*,
VIII (1968), 358.

F55 Montague, John. "Company (I.M. Theodore Roethke),"
Michigan Quarterly Review, VI (Fall 1967), 256–257.

F56 Murphy, Richard. "The Post on the Island, *To Theodore
Roethke*," in *Sailing to the Island*. New York: Chilmark
Press, 1963, p. 53; London: Faber and Faber, 1963.

Reprinted: *Michigan Quarterly Review*, VI (Fall 1967), 253–254.

F57 Ridland, John. "Two Imitations," *Michigan Quarterly Review*, VI (Fall 1967), 258.

F58 ———. "Whirlybird: Roethke Reading," *Poetry Northwest*, II (Winter 1961/1962), 26.
Reprinted: *Michigan Quarterly Review*, VI (Fall 1967), 257–258.

F59 Roche, Paul. "The Greenhouse Dionysus (An Incantory Celebration and Memento)," *Michigan Quarterly Review*, VI (Fall 1967), 270.

F60 Schevill, James. "For Theodore Roethke," *Southern Review*, II (October 1966), 911–912.

F61 Scott, Winfield Townley. "Roethke," *Poetry*, CVII (August 1966), 287ff.
Reprinted: *Michigan Quarterly Review*, VI (Fall 1967), 256.

F62 Stafford, William. "Meeting Roethke" [unpublished].

F63 ———. "Roethke," *Southern Review*, III (October 1967), 946–947.

F64 Stephens, Alan. "Thinking of Roethke's Death (by the McKenzie One Evening)," *Michigan Quarterly Review*, VI (Fall 1967), 266.

F65 Stone, John H. "A Note for Theodore Roethke," *Western Humanities Review*, XIV (Summer 1970), 260.

F66 Sund, Robert. "A Day in Summer, 1963," *Michigan Quarterly Review*, VI (Fall 1967), 271–272.

F67 Swift, Joan. "John Crowe Ransom Reads Theodore Roethke (May 24, 1964)," *Southern Review*, IV (April 1968), 339.
See II, E11.

F68 Turco, Lewis. "Aspects (In Memoriam: Theodore Roethke)," *December Magazine*, Fall 1966.

Reprinted: *Michigan Quarterly Review*, VI (Fall 1967), 254–255.

F69 Turner, Myron. "On the Death of Mr. Roethke (Cremated August 2, 1963)," *The Literary Review*, Fall 1967.

Reprinted: *Michigan Quarterly Review*, VI (Fall 1967), 259.

F70 ———. "Preludes for Roethke," *Michigan Quarterly Review*, VI (Fall 1967), 259–263.

F71 Watkins, Vernon. "At Cwmrhydyceriw Quarry," *Encounter* [London], XXII (February 1964), 66.

F72 Witherup, William. "On the Death of Theodore Roethke" [unpublished].

F73 Youle-White, Michael J. "Theodore Roethke: Or Lost in His Father's Great Greenhouse in the Floral Gardens," *The Citadel*, Fall 1966.

Reprinted: *Michigan Quarterly Review*, VI (Fall 1967), 265.

G Unpublished Materials

The bibliographic materials listed in this section were useful
references in the compilation of this bibliography; however,
the Roethke papers and the *Inventory* of those papers at
the University of Washington Manuscript Division were
indispensable. Information from the *Inventory* was reproduced
by permission of Richard C. Berner, University Archivist.

The University of Washington Manuscript Division also
has a number of minor essays on Roethke's poetry
done by students and friends which are not listed here.

Bibliography

G1 "Addenda to Bibliography of August 8, 1958, prepared
by John William Matheson of the School of Librarianship."
(UWR)

This is a mimeographed sheet of bibliographic materials from
August 1958 to January 1960 (*see* II, G4).

G2 "Annual Bibliography, University of Washington
Department of English." (UWE, UWR)

These bibliographies cover the period from 1952 to 1963.

G3 McLeod, James R. "Theodore Roethke: A Bibliography
and Manuscript Checklist, 1908–1968." M.A. thesis,
Eastern Washington State College, 1969. (UW)

G4 Matheson, John William. "Theodore Roethke: A Bibliography." M.A. thesis, University of Washington, 1958. (UWR)

See II, G1.

G5 "Theodore Roethke." (UW)

This is a list of books, honors and awards, pariodicals, forthcoming books, broadcasts, kinescopes, records, and a movie for the period 1941–1962.

G6 "Theodore Roethke: Bibliography." (UW)

A bibliography compiled by Katharine Stokes for the years 1937–1948.

G7 "Theodore Roethke: Prose Writings, Exclusive of Reviews, Since 1958." (UW)

G8 "Theodore Roethke: Prose Writings, Exclusive of Reviews, to 1958." (UW)

G9 *Theodore Roethke Inventory.* (UW)

An extensive list of Roethke materials comprising some 153 standard document cases located at the University of Washington Manuscript Division. This inventory includes the following sections: I. Biographical Materials; II. Correspondence: Incoming; III. Correspondence: Outgoing; IV. Literary Manuscripts: Poems; V. Literary Manuscripts: Prose; VI. Criticism; VII. Notebooks; VIII. Notes; IX. Theodore Roethke as Student; X. Other Poets in Theodore Roethke's Hand (Poems of Other Writers Handwritten by Theodore Roethke); XI. Teaching; XII. Clippings; XIII. Bibliographies of Theodore Roethke's Work; XIV. Financial Records; XV. Legal Miscellany; XVI. Medical Miscellany; XVII. Selective Service Miscellany; XVIII. Sketches by Theodore Roethke; XIX. Photographs; XX. Ephemera; XXI. Book Lists; XXII. Memorabilia; XXIII. Tape Recordings; XXIV. Miscellany; XXV. Covers; XXVI. *Subgroup*: Part One: Roethke's Family; Part Two: From the Richard Blackmur

Collection at Princeton University Library; Part Three: Letters to Dorothy Gordon from Theodore Roethke (1933–1945); Part Four: Copies of Poems from Mr. and Mrs. Theodore E. Norton; Part Five: Materials Donated by Rolfe Humphries; Part Six: Letters to Rolfe Humphries; Part Seven: Materials Added by Mrs. Beatrice Roethke, 9 September 1966, as Result of Her Formal Collecting Program.

Biography

G10 Bagster-Collins, Mary Kunkel. "Chronology of Roethke's Letters to Mary Kunkel Bagster-Collins, 1935–1958."

The list shows the proper sequence of the letters, where they were written from, and what Roethke was doing (for further information, *see* II, A7 pp. 144–146 and II, B61).

G11 Brown, Robert F. "A Letter from Ted Roethke." Term paper, Pennsylvania State University, November 30, 1967. (PSC)

The letter was to Ridge Riley and was written on February 1, 1950 (for further information, *see* II, A7, p. 167).

G12 Ehrenwerth, Susan. "Theodore Roethke at Penn State." Term paper (English 414), Pennsylvania State University, March 17, 1965. (PSC)

The paper includes interviews with the following: Lyne Hoffman (March 15, 1965), Margaret Spangler (March 9, 1965), William Werner (March 14, 1965), John Bowman (March 9, 1965), Joseph Rubin (March 12, 1965), Ridge Riley (March 15, 1965), Lynn Christy (March 9, 1965). The paper also includes an excerpt from a letter to Theodore Gates by Roethke dated July 20, 1936 (for further information, *see* I, A12, p. 39, and II, A7, p. 131).

G13 Kizer, Carolyn. "Reminiscences of Roethke," May 21, 1968.

Presented at the "First Roethke Poetry Award" in Saginaw (*see* II, E8).

G14 Seager, Allan. "Chronology of the Roethkes' Marriage, 1952–1963." (UW)

A list of the major events, trips, awards, compiled by Allan Seager after interviews with Beatrice Roethke as part of the preparation for *The Glass House* (*see* II, B26 and II, G31).

G15 ————. Interviews for *The Glass House* at The Bancroft Library at the University of California, Berkeley.

Those interviewed include: Dorothee Bowie, Robert Crouse, Peter and Catherine DeVries, Donald Hall, Judge Eugene Huff, Lyne Hoffman, John Haag, Rolfe Humphries, Donald McCluskey, Eric Rhodin, Ken McCormick, Burrows Morley, Violet Roethke Mortensen, Mary Kunkel Bagster-Collins, Judith Baily Jones, Stanley Kunitz, W. H. Auden, Mary Garrett, Dick Humphreys, Howard Moss, John Sargent, Ossio Pearl, June Roethke, Louise Roethke, Margaret Roethke, Solomon Katz, Max Nicolai, Beatrice Roethke, Arnold Stein, David Wagoner, Philip Shelley, A. J. M. Smith, John Clark, Katharine Stokes, Carlton Wells, Helen Ward, Jerry Willis, Tom Kinsella, John Montague, John Davenport, Eva Rosenfeld, William Hoffer, and Eric White.

G16 Smith, Amanda. "Theodore Roethke: The Penn State Years." Term paper (English 414), Pennsylvania State University, March 17, 1965. (PSC)

The paper includes interviews with the following: John Bowman (March 15, 1965), Stanley Weintraub (January 27, 1965), Lynn Christy (March 12, 1965), John Haag (March 11, 1965), Margaret Spangler (March 12, 1965), Joseph J. Rubin (March 12, 1965). The paper also includes excerpts from the following letters: Roethke to Theodore Gates, July 20, 1936; September 3, 1936; February 27, 1943; April 19, 1945 (*see* I, A12, p. 39, and II, A7, pp. 131–132).

Critical Studies

G17 Adams, Michael Charles. "Image Patterns in Theodore Roethke's 'Meditation of an Old Woman.'" M.A. thesis, University of Washington, 1971.

G18 Bullis, Jerald. "Theodore Roethke: A Study of His
Poetry." Ph.D. dissertation, Cornell University, 1970.
DA, 31: 6593A.

G19 Flint, Roland H. "Many Arrivals Make Us Live: A Study
of the Early Poetics of Theodore Roethke, 1941–1953."
Ph.D. dissertation, University of Minnesota, 1968.
DA, 30: 318A–319A.

G19a Galvin, Brendau James. "What the Grave Says, The
Nest Denies: Burkean Strategies in Theodore Roethke's
'Lost Son' Poems." Ph.D. dissertation, University of
Massachusetts, 1970. *DA*, 31: 2384A–2385A.

G20 Gloege, Randall George. "Suspension of Belief in the
Poetry of Theodore Roethke." Ph.D. dissertation,
Bowling Green State University, 1969. *DA*, 31: 1757A.

G21 Heyen, William Helmuth. "Essays on the Later Poetry
of Theodore Roethke." Ph.D. dissertation, Ohio
University, 1967.

G22 Kaiyala, Marguerite LaVoy. "The Poetic Development
of Theodore Roethke in Relation to the Emersonian-
Thoreauvian Tradition of Nature." Ph.D. dissertation,
University of Washington, 1970. (UW)

G23 LaBelle, Jenijoy. "Theodore Roethke and Tradition:
'The Pure Serene of Memory in One Man.' " Ph.D.
dissertation, University of California at San Diego, 1968.
DA, 30: 2029A.

G23a McDade, Gerard F. "The Primitive Vision of Theodore
Roethke: A Study of the Aboriginal Elements in His
Poetry." Ph.D. dissertation, Temple University,
1970. *DA*, 31: 1806A.

G24 McKenzie, James Joseph. "A New American Nature Poetry: Theodore Roethke, James Dickey, and James Wright." Ph.D. dissertation, Northwestern University, 1970. *DA*, 31: 5560A.

G25 Malkoff, Karl. "The Poetry of Theodore Roethke: A Critical Study." Ph.D. dissertation, Columbia University, 1966. *DA*, 30: 1969A.

This dissertation was published as *Theodore Roethke: An Introduction to the Poetry* (*see* II, C82). *See also American Literature*, XXXVII (May 1965), 236.

G26 Reichertz, Ronald Robert. " 'Once More, the Round': An Introduction to the Poetry of Theodore Roethke." Ph.D. dissertation, University of Wisconsin, 1967.

G27 Stevens, Phillip Boyd. "A Study of Kinesthetic Imagery in Selected Poetry of Theodore Roethke." Ph.D. dissertation, Northwestern University, 1970. *DA*, 31: 5560A.

G28 Wolff, George Andrew. "The Production of Time: Themes and Images in the Poetry of Theodore Roethke." Ph.D. dissertation, Michigan State University, 1966. *DA*, 27: 3023A–3024A.

Reviews

G29 Chapman, Ruth. Untitled. Radio station WRHP, n.p., March 16, 1948. (UW, typescript)

A review of *The Lost Son and Other Poems*.

G30 Hambleton, Ron. "Critically Speaking." CBC (4:30 P.M.–5:00 P.M.), March 15, 1959. (UW, typescript)

A review of *Words for the Wind*.

G31 Hope, Scott. "Books and Bookman." Radio station
KFAX, San Francisco, August 20, 1961. (UW, typescript)
A review of *Words for the Wind*.

Letters

G32 Letters about Roethke, 1954–1964, at The Lilly Library,
Indiana University, Bloomington, include: Henry Rago
to Judith Johnson (2); Dave Wagoner to Henry Rago (3);
Judith Johnson to Henry Rago; Harry Gaffney to per-
mission editor of *Poetry*; Charles B. Cox to *Poetry*;
Stella E. Bromirski to Henry Rago; Donald Ellegood
to Henry Rago; Henry Rago to Dave Wagoner (2);
Kathleen Malley to permission editor of *Poetry*;
Dorothy M. McKittrick to permission editor of *Poetry*;
James Schevill to Henry Rago (2); Henry Rago to John
Pym; Kathleen Malley to Henry Rago; Henry Rago
to "Stanley" [Kunitz] and "Richard"; "Stanley"
[Kunitz] to Henry Rago and "Richard"; "Richard" to
"Stanley" [Kunitz]; Henry Rago and C. A. Pollard to
Louis Untermeyer. (IU)

These letters were originally held by the University of Chicago.

G33 Letters to or about Roethke, 1930–1959 at The Bancroft
Library, University of California, Berkeley, include:
William W. Johnston, June Roethke, R. Gale Noyes,
James W. Tupper, Theophil Klingman, Louis A. Strauss,
Lloyd C. Emmon, Lewis Webster Jones, George Lundberg,
T. S. Eliot, W. Wilbur Hatfield, Judson Jerome, Marianne
Moore, Robert B. Heilman, Daniel Hoffman, L. S.
Woodburne, Patricia Coombs, Richard M. Ader, Mary
Bagster-Collins, Louise Bogan, Kenneth D. Burke,
René Char, Catherine DeVries, John Davenport, James
Dickey, Harold F. Graves, Veronica Gosling, Lillian

Hellman, James T. Jackson, Violetta Mortensen,
Edward Nichols, Mary Randlett, Beatrice Roethke,
Philip Shelley, Katharine Stokes, Eric White, Chad Walsh,
and Armitage Watkins. (UCB)

G34 Letters about Roethke, 1945–1965, at The Suzzalo Library,
University of Washington, Seattle, include: Marguerite
Caetani to Beatrice and June Roethke (8); Rolfe
Humphries; and the following to Beatrice Roethke:
George Abbe, Donald J. Adams, Léonie Adams, Elizabeth
Ames (3), Dore Ashton (2), John Aston, W. H. Auden,
(Mrs.) Leonard Bacon, Leroy Baumgartner, Ben Belitt,
John Betjeman, Elizabeth Bishop, George Bluestone,
Louise Bogan (7), Yves Bonnefoy, Alain Bosquet,
John Malcolm Brinnin (3), Van Wyck Brooks (2),
Kenneth Burke (16), H. S. Canby, George Carlson,
René Char (4), John Ciardi (4), William Cole, Alice C.
Coleman, Elliott Coleman (2), Patricia Coombs (3),
Thomas B. Costain, Mildred Cousins, Malcolm Cowley (4),
David Cornel DeJong, Babette Deutsch (5), Dennis
Devlin, Peter DeVries, James Dickey (2), Phyllis Flanders
Dorset (6) [reminiscence], Jacob Drachler (2),
Elizabeth Drew, K. D. Duval (2), Charles Edward Eaton,
Richard Eberhart (2), Edith Emmet, Paul Engle, Harold J.
Enrico, Bergan Evans, Charles E. Feinberg (5),
Catharine G. Foster, Lloyd Frankenberg (2), Evelyn
E. Gardner, Robert Gardner, Mary Garrett, Zulfikar
Ghose (3), Sol Gilbert, Carey Guidici, Dorothy Webster
Gordon (9), Otto G. Graf, (Mrs.) Horace Gregory (6),
John Gunther, John Haag (4), Mary Harlow (3),
Janet Hart, S. I. Hayakawa, J. Healy, Roger Hecht,
Lillian Hellman (2), Robert Hillyer (5), Verna Hobson,
(Mrs.) Stewart Holbrook, Doris Holmes (6), Eleanor
Holt, Irving Howe, Ted Hughes, Barbara Hull (3),

Rolfe Humphries (15), James Turner Jackson (3),
Randall Jarrell (2), Weldon Kees (2), Ernest Kroll (2),
Philip A. Larkin, James Laughlin, Florence Becker
Lennon, Harry Levin, Agostino Lombardo, Chester Clayton
Long, Elizabeth Lowell, Edward Locke, Ludmila
Marjańska (2), William Matchett, Jackson Mathews (3),
Louis L. Martz, W. S. Marvin, Betty Miller, Marianne
Moore, Burrows Morley (2), Theodore Morrison, Samuel
French Morse (2), Violet Roethke Mortensen, Howard
Nemerov, Eddie Nichols, John F. Nims (3), Daphne
Norton (2), Robert Gale Noyes, William O'Connor,
Anthony Ostroff (2), Richard Outram, Roy Harvey
Pearce (2), Katherine Anne Porter (5), Kenneth Porter
(4), Betty Powers (3), James F. Powers (2), John Ransom,
Kenneth Rexroth (4), William J. Rice, Selden Rodman
(2), Carl Roethke, William A. C. Roethke (3), Ned
Rorem (2), Diarmuid Russell (2), Hans Sahl (2),
Emile Schneider, Mark Schorer (3), Seymour C. Schuman,
Joy Schuyler, Allan Seager, Richard Selig (2), Roger
Senhouse, Evelyn Shapiro (2), Howard A. Shapiro,
Karl Shapiro (2), Phillip Shelley, Louis Simpson, Leo
Smit, Arthur J. M. Smith, William D. Snodgrass (2),
James G. Southworth, Robert W. Stallman, Hugh B.
Staples, Arnold Stein, Holly Stevens Stephenson, Katharine
M. Stokes (12), William Styron (2), Alan Swallow (3),
Josie Swift, Allen and Isabella Gardner Tate (5),
Harmon Tupper (2), Louis Untermeyer, Carmen Valls,
Peter Viereck (3), Chad Walsh, Robert Penn Warren (2),
John Warringer (2), Vernon Watkins (3), William
Werner (2), Dorothy Whiteside, Elgin Williams (3),
(Mrs.) William Carlos Williams, Leota Geraldine S.
Willis, Yvor Winters, Mary Woodburn, George Woodcock,
James Wright (11), Louis Zukofsky.

Index of Names

References to Biographical Notes and Awards, Memorials, Reminiscences, Tributes are abbreviated: BN and AMRT.

Index of Poems and Prose Pieces

References to Biographical Notes and Awards, Memorials, Reminiscenses, Tributes are abbreviated: BN and AMRT. Comments by Roethke on the works listed in this section are indicated by the abbreviation "TR" which follows the main entries.

"Heart, You Have No House," I, A14; C243.

"Her Becoming," see "Meditations of an Old Woman."

"Her Convalescence," I, C206.

"Her Dream," I, C152.

"Her Longing," I, A9, 10; C181; D2.

"Her Reticence," I, A9, 10; C191.

"Her Time," I, A9, 10; C199.

"Her Words," I, A9, 10; C168; D2.

"Her Wrath," I, A9, 10; C168; D2.

"The Heron," BN 1955; I, A1, 4–6, 10, 11; B1, 3; C24; D40; E5, 6, 9, 21, 33; II, C14; TR: I, A11, 12; E22; II, C14.

"Highway Michigan," I, A1, 10; B3; C53; TR: I, A12.

"The Hippo," I, A6, 10; E36; F22.

"His Foreboding," I, A9, 10, 13; C192; II, B20.

"His Words" (from "The Dying Man"), I, A12; C123.

"How to Write Like Somebody Else," I, A11; C217.

"Hurray for Weeds," see "Long Live the Weeds."

I Am! Says the Lamb, BN 1960, 1961; AMRT 1965; I, A6, 10; II, C261–273.

"I Cry Love! Love!" BN 1955; I, A3–5, 10; B25; C90; E6, 7; TR: I, A12.

"I Knew a Woman," BN 1961, 1962; AMRT 1963, 1964, 1966; I, A5, 10, 13; B11; C110; D36, 39; E10, 11, 16, 19, 21; II, C23, 56, 106; TR: I, A12; E10.

"I'm Here," see "Meditations of an Old Woman."

"I Need, I Need," BN 1954, 1955, 1961, 1962; I, A3–5, 10, 11; D15, 41; E6–10, 16; TR: I, A11; D46; E7, 10.

"I Sing Other Wonders," I, A14.

"I Sought a Measure," I, A12; C12.

"I Strolled Across an Open Field," see "The Waking."

"I Teach Out of Love," I, A14; C239.

"I Waited," I, A8–10; C133; E38.

"Ideas of Order by Wallace Stevens" [review], I, C245.

"Idyll," I, A1, 10; C43.

In a Dark Time [film], BN 1963; AMRT 1963, 1964, 1966; I, E1; II, C115; E2.

"In a Dark Time," BN 1959, 1960; I, A8–10, 13; B21; C149; D2; E10, 13, 21, 33; F13; II, C33, 61, 72, 103, 109; E9; TR: I, B19; E1, 13.

"In Evening Air," BN 1959; I, A8–10, 13; C150; E13, 21; TR: I, E13.

"In Praise of Prairie," I, A1, 10; C27; TR: I, A12.

"In the Bush of Bones," I, A14; C237.

"In the Lap of a Dream," I, A14; C229.

"In the Large Mind of Love," I, A14; C224.

"In the Time of Change," I, C19.

A2–5, 10, 13; C80; D11, 29,
39, 42; E2, 4, 7, 9, 10, 16–18,
31, 33, 39; II, C43, 83; E9;
G19a; TR: I, A11, 12; E7, 10.
The Lost Son and Other Poems,
BN 1948; I, A2, 4, 5, 10; II,
A6; B31; C131, 160–193; G28;
TR: I, A12.
"Love Has Me Haunted," I, A14.
"The Loveless Provinces," I,
A14; I, C236.
"Love's Progress," I, A5, 10;
C112; E16.
"Lull," I, A1, 10; C49; TR: I,
A11.

"The Manifestation," I, A9, 10;
B25; C146, 157, 205; D2; TR:
I, E13.
"Many Arrivals," *see* "The
Manifestation."
"Marguerite Caetani," I, C260.
"The Marrow," I, A8–10, 13;
C177.
"The Meadow Mouse," I, A9, 10;
C201; D2; E36, 37; II, E9.
"Meditation at Oyster River," BN
1961; I, A9, 10; C156; D2;
E14; II, C126; TR: I, A12.
"Meditation in Hydrotherapy," I,
A10; C21.
"Meditations of an Old Woman,"
BN 1956; I, A5, 10, 13; B25;
C120, 127, 132, 134, 135; D10,
31, 34, 39, 42; E30; F23;
G16; TR: I, A12.
"Meditations of a Sensitive Man"
[Review], I, A11; C256.
"Memory," BN 1960; I, A5, 10;
C125; E16; F14; II, C127.

"Method," BN 1930; I, B24; C1;
E10, 37; TR: I, E10.
"Mid-Country Blow," I, A1, 4, 5,
10, 12; E21; TR: I, A12.
"The Middle of a Roaring
World," I, A14.
"The Minimal," I, A2, 4, 5, 10;
C64; D24; TR: I, A12.
"The Mire's My Home," I, A14.
"The Mistake," I, A10; B11.
"The Moment," I, A9, 10, 12;
C198; D2; II, B27; F11; TR:
I, A12.
"The Monotony Song," I, A6, 10;
C88; F61, 22.
"Moss-Gathering," I, A2, 4–6, 10,
13; B25; C75; E10; TR: I,
E10.
"The Motion," I, A8–10, 13;
C153; E10, 13; TR: I, E13.
"My Dim-Wit Cousin," I, A1, 10.
"My Flesh Learned to Die," I,
A14.
"My Instant of Forever," I, A14.
"My Papa's Waltz," BN 1960,
1961, 1962; I, A2, 4–6, 10, 13;
C60; D35, 36, 39, 42; E1, 2,
5, 8–10, 16, 18–20; F10; II,
C25; TR: I, A12; E8, 10.
"Myrtle," I, A6, 10; B5; E36; F22.
"Myrtle's Cousin," I, A6, 10; B5.

"A Nest of Light," I, A14; C227.
"Night Crow," BN 1960; AMRT
1964; I, A2, 4, 5, 10; C71;
D53; E9, 10, 20; F16; TR: I,
E10.
"Night Journey," BN 1962; I, A1,
4, 5, 10; C54, 261; E2, 36; II,
E2; TR: I, A12.

240